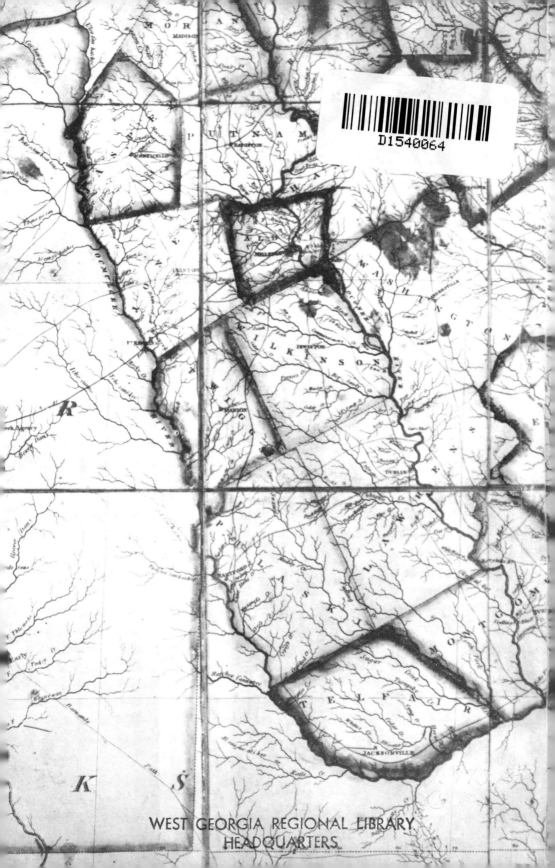

The modern traveler, speeding across a Georgia river, is little aware of the extent to which Georgia's early civilization followed its waterways. From a modest beginning on the Savannah in 1733, Georgia expanded outward from river to river. With the gradual acquisition of territory from the Indians, Georgia pushed westward from the Savannah to the Ogeechee; from the Ogeechee to the Oconee, and from the Oconee to the Ocmulgee. After a frontier civilization was firmly established along the Ocmulgee River, Georgia's boundary line moved on to embrace the Flint and, finally, to reach the Chattahoochee.

In these pages the writer has sought to tell the story of the Ocmulgee River interwoven with the mainstream of history. The book tells of the ancient red people who dwelt along the Ocmulgee and who fixed the Creek Confederacy upon its banks. It portrays the struggles of encroaching Europeans for possession of the territory, and pictures the withdrawal of the Creek Indians in a gradual retreat westward.

PIONEER DAYS ALONG THE OCMULGEE

PIONEER DAYS
ALONG THE OCMULGEE

By

Fussell M. Chalker

Published by F. M. Chalker
Carrollton, Georgia
1970

Printed by

THOMASSON PRINTING AND OFFICE EQUIPMENT COMPANY, INC.

Carrollton, Georgia

To L. P. C.

FOREWORD

The modern traveler, speeding across a Georgia river with hardly a glance at the water below, is little aware of the extent to which Georgia's early civilization followed its waterways. From a modest beginning on the Savannah in 1733, Georgia expanded outward from river to river. With the gradual acquisition of new territory from the Indians, Georgia pushed westward from the Savannah to the Ogeechee; from the Ogeechee to the Oconee, and from the Oconee to the Ocmulgee. After a frontier civilization was firmly established along the Ocmulgee River, Georgia's boundary moved on to embrace the Flint and, finally, to reach the Chattahoochee.

In these pages, the writer has sought to tell the story of the Ocmulgee River interwoven with the mainstream of history. The book tells of the ancient red people who dwelt along the Ocmulgee and who fixed the Creek Confederacy upon its banks. It portrays the struggles of encroaching Europeans for possession of the territory, and pictures the withdrawal of the Creek Indians in a gradual retreat westward.

The narrative tells of the restless pioneers who forged their way to the Ocmulgee and describes their struggles against the elements, the wilderness, and the uncertain foes which they encountered.

Finally, the book gives an account of a frontier order which has long since faded, but whose influence flows on in the mainstream of the modern world.

ACKNOWLEDGMENTS

In early life, I was closely associated with much of the territory encompassed within this work. I recall many fascinating tales told by old residents whose lives were centered around the river world and whose memories were steeped in its lore. Fireside circles provided the background for stirring accounts of pioneer customs, Indian troubles, timber rafting, steamboating, and other topics depicting early life along the Ocmulgee. The accounts of the old settlers have made it possible in some measure to portray the Ocmulgee domain of bygone days and to recapture its forgotten moods. In acknowledgment of the lingering influence of the departed narrators, I mention John Moses Barrentine of Fitzgerald, James L. Floyd of Cochran, Thomas Fuller of Sibbie, Israel Mannheim of Hawkinsville, John Land of Rochelle, Elizabeth Rhodes and John D. Wilcox of Browning, Thomas Stone of Bowen's Mill, and Judge Warren P. Ward of Douglas.

Numerous friends possessing strong ties with the Ocmulgee territory provided invaluable letters and memoirs. Foremost among these were Mrs. E. J. Dorminey of Fitzgerald, Guy Fuller of Sibbie; Mrs. H. A. Haskins, John Snell Lancaster, and Mrs. John Wesley Turner of Hawkinsville; James H. McCranie of Eastman; Dr. D. B. Nicholson of Athens; W. C. Reaves of Rhine; Dennis Taylor of Abbeville, and Mrs. James L. Wilcox of McRae.

If the inception of this work came from fireside tales, its fruition was the result of many hours of research in various archives, libraries, and county courthouses where age-dimmed records were available. In the course of the study, I had the pleasure of meeting numbers of people who gave generously of their time and energies in helping preserve the record of the Ocmulgee world of bygone days.

Cordial assistance was rendered by the staffs of the public and private institutions which I visited. Included in this category were the following: The National Archives, Washington, D. C.; Alabama Department of Archives and History, Montgomery; Georgia Department of Archives and History, Atlanta; North Carolina Department of Archives and History, Raleigh; South Carolina Archives Department, Columbia; Atlanta Public Library, Atlanta, Ga.; Birmingham Public Library, Birmingham,

ix

Ala.; Emory University Library, Atlanta, Ga.; Furman University Library, Greenville, S. C.; Georgia College at Milledgeville Library, Milledgeville, Ga.; Georgia State Library, Atlanta; Mercer University Library, Macon, Ga.; University of Georgia Library, Athens; Virginia State Library, Richmond; West Georgia College Library, Carrollton, Ga.; and West Georgia Regional Library, Carrollton, Ga.

Miss Carroll Hart, Director, and the staff of the Georgia Department of Archives and History were especially helpful in making early Georgia records available for the furtherance of the work.

The late John H. Goff of Emory University, an authority upon early Georgia pathways and settlements, gave generous assistance in the pursuit of a mutual interest.

Mrs. Philip Bryant of the Georgia Surveyor-General Department supported the project with words of encouragement mingled with the expenditure of time and energy in locating and making available documents which otherwise would never have come to view.

Marion Hemperly of the Georgia Surveyor-General Department shared a gratifying interest in the development of the work and produced many obscure papers and maps which greatly contributed to its completion.

James C. Bonner of Georgia College at Milledgeville graciously presented invaluable documents not otherwise available to the writer.

To all who have contributed any part, great or small, in the production of this work, I express my sincere appreciation.

Carrollton, Georgia   Fussell M. Chalker
December 14, 1969

CONTENTS

	Foreword	vii
	Acknowledgments	ix
I	The Ocmulgee River	1
II	Realm of the Red People	3
III	Wilderness Intrigue	8
IV	Shifting Scenes	15
V	The Frontier Moves Forward	21
VI	The Pioneers Reach the Ocmulgee	26
VII	New Ways Arise along the Ocmulgee	32
VIII	Pioneer Life	41
IX	Pioneer Pathways	49
X	Christianity Brought to the Ocmulgee	56
XI	Drifting Down to Darien	67
XII	Whites Face Redskins across the Ocmulgee	75
XIII	Distant Drums	87
XIV	Echoes along the Ocmulgee	92
XV	Holding the Frontier	102
XVI	Pushing into the Indian Country	108
XVII	Marching Down the River Road	116
XVIII	Smoldering Embers	121
XIX	Old Hickory to the Front	128
XX	Hostile Flames Reach the Frontier	131
XXI	A Bitter Feud Erupts	137
XXII	The Whites Cross the Ocmulgee	146
XXIII	New Ways beyond the Ocmulgee	153
XXIV	Open Roads beyond the Ocmulgee	161
XXV	Christianity Borne Onward	165
XXVI	Indian Troubles beyond the Ocmulgee	173
XXVII	Lingering Shadows	181
XXVIII	The Indians' Last Thrust	186
XXIX	Rolling Wheels and Wayside Stops	190
XXX	Steamboats on the Ocmulgee	196
	Notes	202
	Bibliography	219
	Index	231

CHAPTER I

THE OCMULGEE RIVER

As a giant winding artery, the Ocmulgee River flows through the heart of Georgia. Known to its ancient red inhabitants as the stream of bubbling or boiling water, the Ocmulgee rises from faintly bubbling springs and is sustained by torrents of water boiling from deep caverns as it follows its course toward the sea.

The Ocmulgee River is formed by the union of three smaller streams springing from the foothills of the Blue Ridge Mountains in northern Georgia, with waters coming from the west, the north, and the east. The westernmost branch trickles from the heart of Atlanta where the modern city covers its banks. Increasing in volume as it flows southeastward, the trickle swells into a stream of such proportions that it gains the name of South River. The northernmost headstream arises in the broken hills of Gwinnett County and follows a serpentine course southward as the Yellow River. The easternmost fork of the Ocmulgee springs from the uplands of Gwinnett and swings southwestward as the Alcovy or Ulcofauhatchee River.

Although arising at separate and widely-distant points, the headstreams, in their downward sweep, draw closer and closer until they finally form a union where the waters of Lake Jackson now ripple. Gathering at this common rendezvous, the headstream waters blend to form the Ocmulgee River.

Now flowing out of the lake created by the merging branches, the waters of the Ocmulgee move southward on their long, winding journey to a faraway destination. Down through the red hills of the Piedmont country they go rushing and splashing over the rocky river bed. Increasing in strength through the inflow of Towaliga and Falling creeks, the swiftly-moving current reaches the Fall Line at Macon in the very heart of Georgia. Here the turbulent waters gain momentum and go tumbling over the dropping way.

Now the rugged hills of the north give way to the gentle slopes of the south, and the troubled Ocmulgee waters settle down to the tranquil flow of a smoother river bed.

Meandering through the rolling country below the Fall Line, the Ocmulgee gradually grows in volume as it receives the waters of the generous streams flowing in from both sides. A short distance downstream and the creeks of Tobesofkee and Echeconnee draw in from the west, and a bit farther, Flat Creek and Savage Creek push in from Twiggs county to the east.

Continuing its downward course, the swelling Ocmulgee gains the western waters of Big Indian and Mossy creeks from Houston County on the right, and a few miles below, receives the liberal flow of Shellstone Creek emerging from Bleckley County on the left. As the Ocmulgee passes the town of Hawkinsville, the current murmurs over the Uchee Shoals, an ancient crossing place for the Uchee Indians. A few miles more, and the blue waters of Tucsawhatchee or Big Creek drift from the west to balance the flow of Limestone and Mosquito creeks drawing in from the east.

Downstream a bit, and the waters of Cedar Creek and Bluff Creek come in from Wilcox County on the right to vie with the flow of Crooked Creek and Cypress Creek drifting down from Dodge County on the left. Just below Abbeville, the Ocmulgee pushes over the rocky formation of Statham's Shoals, then gracefully turns its course around the lofty eminence of Jordan's Bluff.

By now the winding stream has begun to make a great sweeping curve toward the east, forming the Big Bend of the Ocmulgee. Along the bend, the river receives torrents of blue water boiling from deep, caldron-like springs and pouring into the run of the river from both sides.

Now from the right flows Big House Creek, known to the Indians as Al-ka-sac-ki-li-ki, appropriately signifying "a kettle boiling in a creek."[1] From its juncture with this unique waterway, the Ocmulgee swings on down the bend, passing under the heights of Red Bluff, Gilder's Bluff, and Mobley's Bluff, all towering above the right bank. Then, gently, the left bank sends into the mainstream of the Ocmulgee the waters of Griffin's Creek, Mizell's Creek, and Horse Creek, all winding in from the slopes of Telfair County.

Reaching the apex of the Big Bend near Jacksonville, the Ocmulgee turns and moves in a northeasterly direction toward Lumber City, standing upon the left bank. Here the run of the river receives a new infusion from the Little Ocmulgee or Auchenhatchee pushing in from the left. From this junction, the renewed waters continue in a northeasterly course to the fork where the Ocmulgee joins the Oconee to form the broad Altamaha River.[2] From the fork, the mingled waters move slowly southeastward along the gentle bed of the Altamaha until they finally merge into the vastness of the Atlantic Ocean.

CHAPTER II

REALM OF THE RED PEOPLE

In the misty ages of the far-distant past, the primitive realm of the Ocmulgee was occupied by men of a prehistoric order. The ancient mounds rising from the Ocmulgee Old Fields at present-day Macon reveal long periods of human occupation. But of the nature of the mysterious people who dwelt upon this site and who piled up the monumental mounds, little is known except what has been disclosed by probings of the mounds themselves.

In the long course of events after the mound builders faded from the scene, the Ocmulgee world became the dwelling place of the noted Indians who became incorporated within the Creek Confederacy.[1] Of these primitive red inhabitants more knowledge has sifted down through lingering tradition and through the written record of early observers.

At a very early time, a body of Indians known as the Hitchiti made their appearance along the waters of the Ocmulgee and spread their settlements well over the southern part of modern Georgia. Here the Hitchiti were likely the dominant tribe and their language the prevailing speech of the region extending from the Atlantic Ocean westward to the Chattahoochee River.[2]

The Ocmulgee territory was the apparent center of the Hitchiti domain. During the early years of their occupancy, the ancients dwelt within the forks of the Ocmulgee and Oconee rivers and on the land extending out from both streams. At a later period, the Hitchiti concentrated their settlements higher up the Ocmulgee where they became the occupants of the area embracing the Ocmulgee Old Fields.[3]

The reign of the Hitchiti Indians was terminated by the invasion of a body of fierce newcomers from the west. These were the Muscogees. Coming in great strength, the Muscogees overran the natives dwelling within their paths and gained dominion over the Ocmulgee world. In the course of time, Muscogee elements became firmly established along the waters of the Coosa, Tallapoosa, Chattahoochee, Flint, Ocmulgee, and Oconee; and pushed their settlements as far east as the Savannah River.[4] While becoming entrenched in their new realm, the Muscogee Indians took into their fold the tribes which they had won by

3

persuasion or subdued by force. Then, with these parties united, the Muscogees and their affiliated tribes emerged into the Creek Confederacy. From time to time other elements were taken into the union until the Creek Confederacy became one of the most powerful of the Indian confederations in America. Tradition has it that during the early period of their reign over the Ocmulgee world the Muscogees fixed their seat of government at Ocmulgee Old Fields, where other primitive powers had held sway in the past. [5]

The Indians composing the early elements of the Creek Confederacy were well distributed over the territory comprising present-day Georgia when strange newcomers from a faraway land ventured into the domain of the red people. Not long after the discovery of America by Christopher Columbus, inquisitive Spanish explorers began to push into the mysterious new world. From these early explorations glowing accounts were spread abroad of the charm and fabulous wealth of the newly-discovered country.

Enchanted by the reports reaching him, the Spaniard, Hernando de Soto, resolved to lead a large expedition to the new world to tap its reputed treasures of gold and silver. After making elaborate preparations for the venture, DeSoto's party set sail for the unexplored territory. Landing at Tampa Bay in 1539, the Spaniards proceeded cautiously northward through Florida and reached the approximate site of Tallahassee in time to go into winter encampment.

With the advent of spring in the year 1540, DeSoto led his party a short distance northward and crossed over into the bounds of present-day Georgia. Now ensued the scene of a spectacular procession pushing its way through the primitive land. The long column of foreign adventurers, advancing amid the din of clanging armor, neighing horses, and squealing pigs, presented sights and sounds standing out in startling contrast to the natural tranquillity of a simple wilderness world.

As the clamorous procession moved on, the Spaniards came upon the towns and villages of the red-skinned natives dwelling in their own ancient way. When the Indians beheld the awesome spectacle of the advancing horde, they responded in varying degrees of wonder and fear. In some cases the frightened natives fled precipitously, leaving their abodes and belongings to be despoiled by the intruders. At other times the wondering red people hospitably welcomed the strangers and lavished their possessions upon the wayfarers, only to be left with their storehouses bare, their food squandered, and their treasures stolen.

DeSoto's route through Georgia has long been the subject of interesting speculation and, although no certainty exists as to the precise path followed, many authorities are in agreement as to the general course. [6] It is conceded that the Spaniards entered Georgia in the southwest corner in today's Decatur County. Crossing the Flint River near Bainbridge, the party presumably proceeded up the Flint in an irregular course. By the time the wanderers reached the area where the old Chehaw Indian town of Au-muc-cul-le later stood on Muckalee Creek near Leesburg, they had strayed somewhat west of the mainstream of the Flint. Now moving generally eastward, the explorers apparently pushed on to the Flint which they could have conveniently crossed at a noted Indian crossing near the site of the later Indian village of Phillemmee, and opposite the long-dead white settlement of Pindertown in Worth County. [7]

Once over the Flint, the straggling column is believed to have moved in a northeasterly direction toward the Ocmulgee River. It is quite possible that the heavy feet of the Spaniards tramped over the route of the primitive pathway which, from its association with the Oswichee Indians, came to be known as the Oswichee Trail. It is not likely that the Oswichees as such had formed their association with the old trail at this early time, but the primitive pathway was doubtlessly already in existence for the accommodation of other unidentified natives, or as an avenue for wild animals following unerringly the most convenient course through the wilderness. At any rate, the same favorable terrain which led the Oswichee Indians to tramp out their pathway in later years could have provided the travel-weary Spaniards the most feasible route to follow. [8]

If the Spanish explorers did in fact follow the course of the Oswichee Trail, they would have proceeded generally northeastward from the Pindertown area toward the Big Bend of the Ocmulgee. Reaching a point just southwest of the site of Rochelle in Wilcox County, the wanderers would have found their pathway dividing into two branches. The left fork led northeastward directly to the Ocmulgee at today's Abbeville. The right branch turned southeastward, crossed Big House Creek above the later Barrentine Ford, and struck the Ocmulgee between Bowen's Mill and Jordan's Bluff. [9] Along this stretch of the river the Ocmulgee makes its turn toward the east: thus the observant explorers would have discovered the eastward-flowing stream as portrayed by a narrator in the party. [10]

Upon reaching the Ocmulgee, DeSoto's men, in all likelihood, explored the river bank for a considerable distance, probing its secrets and seeking the most favorable place to cross the stream.

It is generally agreed that the Spanish procession crossed the Ocmulgee in the vicinity of Abbeville. The nature of the river in the neighborhood gives plausibility to this conclusion. For long stretches the Ocmulgee flows through wide swamps affording but limited means for the crossing of such a large, cumbersome body as DeSoto's army. At intervals, however, the stream moves through channels at rising bluffs where the spreading waters are confined to narrow limits to provide good crossings.

In the vicinity of Abbeville may be found several such places. In the northern outskirts of the town stands Poor Robin Bluff where firm ground leads to the water's edge to give favorable access to the stream. Directly east of the town is the old crossing place of the Oswichee Indians on the well-beaten Oswichee Trail. [11] Then, a short distance below Abbeville, the channel of the river is conveniently narrowed as it sweeps around the rising heights of Jordan's Bluff. These places were commonly used in later years by the Indians for crossing the Ocmulgee, and the favorable conditions inducing the red people to employ such desirable crossing places would doubtlessly have invited the same consideration on the part of the Spanish explorers.

After crossing the Ocmulgee in the Abbeville region, the men would have found themselves in the neighborhood of the old Copeland settlement in present-day Dodge County. From this crossing place, the Spanish column is presumed to have turned northward and followed the edge of the river across Mosquito Creek and Limestone Creek to the important Indian town of Ocute, placed in the vicinity of the Uchee Shoals at old Hartford and opposite today's Hawkinsville. Still continuing upstream, the explorers could have crossed Jordan's Creek and Shellstone Creek to reach an important Indian landmark at Buzzard's Roost Bluff near Westlake in the southwest corner of Twiggs County. [12] In their movement upstream, the Spaniards found the countryside thickly settled with red-skinned natives.

It is suggested that the explorers turned away from the Ocmulgee in the vicinity of Buzzard's Roost Bluff, and rambled in an easterly direction toward the Oconee River, striking the latter stream at Carr's Shoals six miles above modern Dublin. The presence at a later time of Gallimore's Path or Smith's Trail, an avenue covering this route, would indicate the feasibility of such a pathway for the straggling column seeking the most favorable terrain. [13]

After crossing the Oconee, the inquisitive Spaniards pushed on generally eastward. A logical route would have been the Lower Uchee Trail, a pathway later traveled by the Uchee Indians when moving in an east-west direction. Striking the Lower Uchee

Path at Carr's Shoals, the men could have followed the trailway to cross the Ogeechee River at Galphin's Old Town near Louisville in Jefferson County. [14] From the Ogeechee crossing, the plodding explorers moved on to the important Indian town of Cofitachequi on the east bank of the Savannah River below the site of Augusta.

After spending some time in the hospitable town, DeSoto's army departed, proceeded irregularly westward, and rambled on to the Mississippi River, destined to become the western boundary of the Colony of Georgia. After the long, fruitless ordeal of his wandering journey, DeSoto died and was buried in the waters of the wide Mississippi.

CHAPTER III

WILDERNESS INTRIGUE

With the attention of European powers focused upon America, old world rivalries manifested themselves in a crucial struggle for possession of the new world. European explorations and discoveries in the little-known realm led to exaggerated territorial claims and to bitter conflicts. In the course of events, the nebulous domain which was destined to become Georgia formed a debatable land upon which rival European powers descended to engage in subtle intrigue and in savage warfare.

Now that Spain was successfully asserting her claims through the revealing expeditions of her exploration parties, France sought to acquire a foothold upon the new world. In 1564 the Protestant element in France established a small colony at the mouth of the St. John's River in Florida. This movement did not escape the attention of the resentful Spaniards. A Spanish expedition was promptly sent against the French; their feeble settlement was destroyed, and many of the occupants were slaughtered. [1]

Jealous of any intrusion by her rivals, Spain embarked upon a movement to strengthen her hold upon the new world by establishing permanent settlements and firmly planting the Spanish civilization within the territory. Founding St. Augustine in 1565, the Spaniards endeavored to weld the settlement into a stronghold from which they could consolidate their claims over the distant horizons of the debatable land. [2]

Deeming the support of the natives vital in the accomplishment of her goals, Spain dispatched missionaries among the Indians to win them to the Catholic faith and to the Spanish order. By a peculiar alliance between the missionary and soldier, the Spaniards established missions and military posts along the fringes of the Atlantic Coast through Georgia and into the lower part of Carolina. Still pressing outward from St. Augustine, the Spaniards forged a chain of forts and missions within the territory extending along the later Georgia-Florida boundary line as far west as Pensacola on the Gulf of Mexico. The Spaniards found the Apalachee Indians dwelling in the neighborhood of modern Tallahassee especially receptive to their overtures, and won many to Catholicism and to useful military loyalties. [3]

8

But the Spaniards were not destined to hold undisputed dominion over the new world. In 1670 a dynamic new element presented itself to the primitive realm in the form of English settlers who founded a colony in lower Carolina and aggressively pressed into the territory claimed by Spain. Like their Spanish rivals, the English sought to gain the support of the Indians in advancing their colonial expansion and in providing lucrative trade channels for themselves. [4]

Dr. Henry Woodward, the energetic first settler of lower Carolina, resolved to break the Spanish territorial claim and to open trade for the English with the vast Indian domain to the southwest. Not long after the founding of Charleston, Woodward boldly pushed into the Indian country to pierce the trade barriers. At this time the Muscogee Indians, known to the Spaniards as the Apalachicolas, were firmly established along the waters of the Chattahoochee River where they were in the process of consolidating neighboring tribes into their powerful confederacy. Dwelling beyond the fringes of the Spanish-dominated Apalachee country which embraced the territory near the confluence of the Chattahoochee with the Flint, the Muscogees were near, but not within the orbit of Spanish influence. But with the open waters of the Chattahoochee leading upward into the Muscogee domain, the Spaniards were pressing upstream to draw the Muscogees into their councils. It was during this period of Spanish expansion that Henry Woodward ventured into the Muscogee country to open trading posts for the Carolinians. The Spaniards, seeking to dominate the Indian world, were quick to resist the overtures of the upstart Carolinians now boldly pushing their packhorse trains into the territory claimed by Spain. [5]

But the audacious English made devastating inroads into the Indians' councils of trade and influence. With superior goods to tempt the redskins, the astute Carolinians easily led the red people into their trading circles and into intriguing alliances. By 1690 the inducement for English trade had become so enticing that the Muscogees migrated to the waters of the Ocmulgee where they would be nearer the Carolina trading centers, and more removed from punitive action by the jealous Spanish. [6]

Now the Cowetas established their principal settlement at Ocmulgee Old Fields, the traditional site upon which the Muscogees had formed their confederation in the dim ages of the past. The Ocmulgee River was known to the English traders as Ochese Creek, and it was during this new period of occupation that the Muscogees and related tribes became known as Creeks, and the bond holding them together as the Creek Confederacy. [7]

In their removal from the Chattahoochee to the Ocmulgee, the Creeks were guided by their venerable leader known to the Carolinians as Old Brim, or Emperor Brim. Having long directed the affairs of his people with unusual insight into the changing conditions within the Indian domain, Old Brim established on the Ocmulgee an order designed to enhance the Indian cause with the English, but kept a wary eye upon any foreign element attempting to undermine the strategic position of the Creek Confederacy. [8]

By 1700 an old European power had reappeared upon the unsettled scene to seek trade and military alliances with the Southern Indians. The French, having been repulsed on the Atlantic Coast by the Spaniards, had gained control of the Mississippi territory to the west, had established settlements on the Gulf of Mexico, and were pushing up the waterways directly into the Indian country.

Now began a three-way struggle for Indian trade, influence, and territory amid a wilderness intrigue interwoven with chicanery and brute force. The Indian domain occupied the center of the stage in the disputed territory. Pushing into the Indian country from the southwest were the French; from the south, the Spanish; and from the east, the English.

Each participant possessed certain advantages in the struggle. The French, controlling the mouth of the Mobile River and its tributaries, the Alabama, Coosa, and Tallapoosa, could follow the broad waterways into the heart of the Indian country. The Spaniards in Florida held the mouth of the Apalachicola and its branches, the Chattahoochee and the Flint, important water avenues leading directly into the land of the red people. In addition to their strategic waterways, the Spanish had the advantage of being the first upon the scene, of being firmly established, and of already enjoying strong support from neighboring Indian tribes. The English, operating out of Charleston and other lower Carolina trading centers, had no convenient means of reaching the realm of the red people by water. Instead, the ingenious Carolinians tramped out trading paths leading overland from their posts into the deepest recesses of the Indian country. [9]

In spite of the natural advantages of the Spanish and French, the English offered superior goods, and their talents for bargaining with the red people gave them the edge over their rivals. Welcomed by the trade-loving Indians, the Carolinians erected well-stocked houses operated by resident traders in each sizable Indian settlement. Here the red men could conveniently bring their skins and furs to be exchanged for the coveted wares of the English civilization. [10]

Savannah Town on the Savannah River in Carolina became the chief reservoir from which English supplies were conveyed by packhorse trains far out into the Indian nations. From Savannah Town a great trading path led westward toward the Ogeechee River. Crossing the stream at the Shoals of the Ogeechee, the trail divided into two important branches, the Upper Trading Path and the Lower Trading Path. The upper branch led directly to the Indian settlements clustered around the traditional Creek landmark of Indian Springs on the upper waters of the Ocmulgee. The Lower Trading Path led southwestward along the Fall Line, crossed the Oconee at Rock Landing, and proceeded to the principal Creek settlement of Coweta, nestled within the shadows of the ancient mounds at Ocmulgee Old Fields. From the Indian settlements on the Ocmulgee River, the trading lanes eventually continued through the Creek country and into the land of the Choctaws and Chickasaws, where the Carolina traders actively pushed their pack trains during the period from 1692 through 1696. [11]

With the English gaining the Indian trade of the Spaniards, the latter devised all manner of tactics aimed at obstructing their rivals. Using their Apalachee Indian allies as aids, the Florida Spaniards led incursions into the Creek country to harass the natives, to capture the Carolina traders, and to destroy the English trading posts.

The French, likewise, contributed to the harassment of the English and their red allies. Now in control of the vast area stretching along the Mississippi River from Canada to the Gulf of Mexico, the French had become a serious threat to the English. During these critical years, France and England were in a general state of warfare which was reflected in America as a struggle between English and French frontiersmen for the possession of an entire continent. [12]

With the English precariously perched on a long, thin line bordering the Atlantic Ocean, the French threatened to advance from the back country and drive their rivals into the sea. Taking advantage of the animosity existing between the Spanish and the English, France's forest diplomats now sought the aid of the Spaniards in their crusade against the English colonists. By uniting forces and inciting the vast bodies of Indians against their common foe, the hostile coalition hoped to launch a drive against the English which would break their hold upon the continent.

Now, with the principals enmeshed in wilderness intrigue, open hostilities erupted within the debatable land. Amid sparrings back and forth, in 1701 a party of Carolinians and Creek Indians made an incursion into the Spanish-dominated Apalachee country. The following year a similar coalition invaded the land of the Timucuan Indians and destroyed the mission of Sante Fe, situated near today's Statenville in Lowndes County. [13]

Spurred on by French instigators, the Florida Spaniards were determined to have revenge. In the summer of 1702 Governor Zuniga sent out a force of 900 Apalachee Indians commanded by Captain Uriza, and directed against the English outposts and Creek settlements within the Ocmulgee domain. By the subtle Indian system of communication, news of the intended invasion reached Anthony Dodsworth and other English traders at Coweta Town on the Ocmulgee. With the support of Emperor Brim, the traders collected a force of some 500 friendly Creek warriors and advanced to meet the foe.

Moving generally southward along the ridge separating the Ocmulgee River from the Flint, Dodsworth's party encountered the invaders on the east side of the Flint River eighty miles below Coweta Town. Finding themselves facing an overwhelming force, the astute English traders resolved to outwit the enemy. Knowing that it was customary for Indians to attack just before dawn, the traders instructed the Creek warriors to stir up their campfires, arrange their blankets around the fires in a manner resembling sleeping men, and then draw back into the shadows. Shortly afterward, the Spaniards and Apalachee Indians stealthily surrounded the camp, discharged their arms at the obscure figures, and moved in upon the empty blankets.

With their ruse working as planned, the Creek warriors swiftly charged upon the enemy, killed or captured most, and routed the rest. This seemingly insignificant clash at an obscure spot between the Ocmulgee and Flint rivers has been called the first active blow struck by the English for control of the vast Mississippi Valley. [14]

Now, Governor James Moore of South Carolina, anticipating a Spanish invasion attempt, resolved to attack the Spaniards within their own territory. Leading a force of whites and Indians, Moore assaulted St. Augustine. But the inhabitants fled to the safety of the fort, and all efforts to storm the impregnable stronghold met with failure. Foiled in his attempt to destroy the enemy, Governor Moore burned the town and returned to South Carolina. [15]

Undaunted, Moore resolved to strike again. He suspected that the French and Spaniards were conniving with the Apalachee Indians for a strangling assault upon the Creek frontier, to be followed by an invasion of South Carolina itself. With keen insight Moore laid his plans to break the enemy strategy of encirclement. Now he would strike at the Apalachee settlements forming the keystone of the hostile arc. [16]

In the waning days of 1703, Colonel Moore set out for the Ocmulgee with fifty Carolina volunteers. Tramping along the Lower Trading Path, the party reached Coweta Town, the Creek stronghold at Ocmulgee Old Fields. Here the Carolinians recruited some 1000 friendly warriors who were eager to go against their old foes. [17]

Marching generally southwestward along the ridge standing between the Ocmulgee and the Flint, the army reached Ayaville, a distant Apalachee town centered around a fort. Although they met with smart resistance, Moore's forces took the fort by storm. On the next day, the invaders were attacked by a strong force from Fort St. Louis. Again the fighting was brisk, but Moore's men killed 200 Indians and captured the Spanish captain along with eight of his troops.

Two days later, the apprehensive king of Attachooka, entrenched inside a strong fortress with 130 occupants, prudently dispatched provisions to Colonel Moore and made his peace. The invading party then marched through the rest of the Apalachee towns whose occupants deemed it discreet to surrender before such awesome forces. Moore's men captured 300 Indians, the entire population of three towns, and most of four others. The remainder of the Apalachee natives fled to the sanctuary of St. Augustine. By Moore's decisive conquest of Apalachee, Carolina was made free from immediate danger of enemy invasion.[18]

Colonel James Moore's victories enhanced English trade with the red people. Eventually, the Indian country became permeated with Carolina traders who made their abodes in sizable Indian towns. Now the English were enjoying the bulk of the Creek trade, and all appeared well.

But beneath the surface, the red people were becoming disenchanted with the Carolina traders and vulnerable to subtle Spanish overtures. Some of the traders were crafty in their dealings with the Indians and took advantage of the natives in matters of commerce and in their domestic affairs, as well. The Carolinians, moreover, had become addicted to the subtle art of ensnaring red people to sell into slavery and were prone to use their Creek allies as aides in capturing the victims. [19]

The resistance of the Creek Indians was centered in the person of Emperor Brim. From his influential seat at Coweta Town on the Ocmulgee, the astute leader slyly waited for the opportune moment to strike at the growing power of the English. Unknown to the complacent Carolinians, elements of discord, encouraged by Old Brim, were steadily mounting among the red people. [20]

Suddenly, rebellion flared. In 1715 the Yamassee Indians, dwelling within the very gates of South Carolina, turned upon their unsuspecting white neighbors and dealt them a devastating blow. This hostile action was reflected far out in the Creek Nation. Simultaneously, hostile Indians descended upon the English trading houses, slaughtered the traders, and looted the stores of their wares. This unexpected conflict was known as the Yamassee War, and before it was over, the natives left a trail of destruction along the Carolina frontier and deep within the Indian country. [21]

Although caught off guard by the sudden ferocity of the Yamassee War, the Carolinians rallied their fighting men for retaliation. By decisive action, the English drove the Yamassees from the Carolina frontier and into the receptive arms of the Spaniards in Florida.

In the course of the conflict, the torch was applied to the Creek stronghold of Coweta Town and the settlement was left in ashes. So desolate was the scene at Ocmulgee Old Fields that for many years afterward, the red people viewed the place with awe and warily avoided camping upon the site when passing that way. [22]

CHAPTER IV

SHIFTING SCENES

Hardly had the warwhoops of the Yamassee War faded away than events were set into motion within the debatable land pointing to a crescendo of things to come. Having engaged their English neighbors in conflict, the Creek Indians deemed it prudent to remove their dwellings from their advanced position on the Ocmulgee to the remote streams flowing through western Georgia and Alabama territory.

Now ensued a shifting of Indian population into the pattern of occupation existing at the time of the founding of Georgia and during the formative years of the colony. As the pattern unfolded, the Indian domain emerged into a land of well-defined settlements connected by a system of heavily-trodden pathways.

The Cherokee Indians occupied the fertile valleys hidden among the sweeping mountains of northern Georgia. In time, the southern boundary of the Cherokee country followed a line extending generally westward from the Savannah River in present Elbert County, through Suwanee Town in Gwinnett, across the Chattahoochee River at Standing Peachtree where the upper fringes of Atlanta now spread, and on by the way of Buchanan into Alabama territory.

Below the Cherokee country sprawled the domain of the Creek Indians. The Creek Nation extended westward from the Savannah River to the ridge east of the Tombigbee River in Alabama territory, and southward from the Cherokee country to the Gulf of Mexico.

Over the years, the Creek Indians drifted into two general divisions; the Upper Creeks, and the Lower Creeks. The Upper Creek bodies dwelt along the Alabama, Coosa, and Tallapoosa rivers in Alabama territory. The Lower Creeks occupied settlements spread along the waters of the Chattahoochee and Flint rivers, and at other favorable places between the Chattahoochee and the Savannah. Situated as they were within or adjacent to the territory destined to become Georgia, the Lower Creeks were in a position to play a greater role in the events relating to the colony than were the more remote Upper Creeks.

15

The dominant element within the loosely-united body of Lower Creeks continued to be the Muscogees. The chief towns of the Muscogees were Coweta, the red war town; and Cusseta, the white peace town. After their withdrawal from the Ocmulgee River, the Cowetas established their principal settlements along the west side of the Chattahoochee near modern Columbus. At the same time, the Cussetas formed a sprawling town on the east side of the Chattahoochee a short distance below Coweta. [1]

On a sharp bend in the lower Chattahoochee River known as Oswichee Bend, the ancient Oswichee Indians established their principal town, with an offshoot settlement on the Flint River six miles below the mouth of Kinchafoonee Creek. [2]

Closely associated with the Oswichees were the Chehaws who occupied a large town just below and adjoining Oswichee Town. At the same time, the Chehaws formed a group of villages which dotted the west side of the Flint River from the upper part of Lake Blackshear down to modern Albany. The chief Chehaw settlement on the waters of the Flint was Au-muc-cul-le, located on the east bank of Muckalee Creek near today's Leesburg. [3]

A very old element of the Lower Creek body was the Hitchiti people whose settlements had long been identified with the southern part of Georgia. In the shifting scene following the Yamassee War, the Hitchiti established their principal towns on the east bank of the Chattahoochee below Cusseta, and on the Flint River below Kinchafoonee Creek. [4]

A Hitchiti town whose name was reminiscent of its early connection with the Ocmulgee River was Ocmulgee Town. In the new alignment of Indian settlements, Ocmulgee Town was located on the west side of the Chattahoochee as a close neighbor to the towns of Oswichee and Chehaw. Since all three settlements were situated in a point-shaped bend in the river, they were known as "the point towns." In addition to those in the principal town, a small body of Ocmulgee Indians formed a village on the Flint River eight miles above the mouth of Kinchafoonee Creek. By this time the Ocmulgee people had dwindled to a mere remnant of the once-proud occupants of the historic Ocmulgee Old Fields on the Ocmulgee. [5]

A small but distinctive group of Indians included in the Lower Creek division was the tribe known as the Uchees. Drifting down from the north at an unknown time, the Uchees ultimately became loosely incorporated within the Creek Confederacy, while retaining their own language and racial identity. At one time or another, the Uchees occupied settlements on the Savannah River near Augusta and Ebenezer; on the Ogeechee River; and at the Uchee Shoals on the Ocmulgee opposite today's Hawkinsville. While retaining their old settlements on the Savannah, most of the Uchees retreated with other Lower Creeks and established a colorful town on the west bank of the Chattahoochee at the mouth of Uchee Creek. Eventually, smaller Uchee settlements arose on the Flint River in the vicinity of the future white town of Oglethorpe. [6]

In the lower part of Georgia and the upper part of Florida arose a body of red people known as Seminoles. The Seminoles were runaway Muscogees who isolated themselves from the parent tribes and intermingled with some of the Hitchiti and remnants of other tribes occupying Florida at the time of DeSoto's expedition. The Seminole country was centered around Lake Miccosukee near the site of modern Tallahassee. [7]

While the Creek Indian settlements were emerging into a new pattern following the Yamassee War, the European struggle for domination over the disputed Georgia territory continued unabated. During the dislocations of the Yamassee conflict, the emboldened French pushed up the waterways into the Upper Creek country and erected Fort Toulouse near the junction of the Coosa and Tallapoosa rivers. [8] From this advanced stronghold, the French engaged in active trade mingled with backcountry intrigue designed to wield control over the red people. Through a combination of military power, traffic in trade, and forest diplomacy, the French endeavored to separate the Indians from their former intercourse with the English.

At the same time, the Spaniards, from their bases in Florida, continued their tenacious struggle to hold their claims over the disputed land by conniving with the French and Indians to weaken the position of the English.

But the stubborn English were not to be outdone. After the fires of the Yamassee War had cooled, the Carolinians made an uneasy peace with the Creeks and pressed for trade and treaties to further their interests. Again the canny Carolinians gained the upper hand in their intercourse with the Creek Indians. Over the years the red people had become largely dependent upon the products of the Englishman's civilization, and their avid desires for trade dominated their latent spirit of animosity. Soon the avenues of commerce were open again, and the old trading paths leading from South Carolina into the Indian country teemed with pack trains.

Occupying the center of the stage in the three-way European struggle for control over the debatable land, the astute Creeks perceived the strategic importance of their situation and recognized the necessity of following a course aimed at self-preservation. Using all the wiles at their command, the red men endeavored to keep the white Europeans so divided that no single power could become strong enough to overwhelm the natives and seize their treasured domain. [9]

England, beset with threats from enemy forces upon the southern flank of her American colonies, now strove to strengthen the South Carolina frontier which comprised much of the disputed land. Coinciding with the wilderness struggle in America were economic, political, and religious conditions in Europe calling for relief. Pressed by troublesome conditions on both fronts, England explored measures to alleviate her critical problems at home and abroad.

Riding the wave of colonial expansion, England sought to ease her problems with a single stroke. By establishing a new colony on the precarious South Carolina boundary, she could form a buffer zone affording military protection to her American colonies. At the same time, by opening the colony to her own subjects seeking a better life in a new world, and to the oppressed people in other European countries, England could relieve her own internal troubles and create abroad promising new avenues of industry and trade.

At this opportune moment, the movement for expanding England's colonial horizons found expression in the person of General James Edward Oglethorpe. Possessing a philanthropic spirit combined with military acumen, Oglethorpe was admirably suited for the task of pressing for the type of colony which England so urgently needed. Portraying to English authorities the advantages of such an enterprise, Oglethorpe convinced his listeners and gained a personal commission to lead a select body of English colonists upon an unique venture into the new world.

When General Oglethorpe landed upon the site of the Georgia colony in 1733, he came with an official grant from the king of England. Designed to provide the land for the creation and expansion of the colony, the grant covered the territory lying between the Savannah and Altamaha rivers and extending westward from their headwaters to the South Seas. Under the terms of the royal grant, the Ocmulgee River thus became the theoretical western boundary of the Georgia colony. But the designated land was in the actual possession of the Creek Indians. The white people's course to the banks of the Ocmulgee would be long, and crowded with obstructions.

Oglethorpe acknowledged the Indians' ownership of the desired territory and proceeded by amicable means to gain their consent for the founding of the English colony upon Indian soil. While plans were being made to lay out the proposed town of Savannah, Oglethorpe sought an agreement with the Yamacraws for the establishment of the settlement within their neighborhood. The venerable chief, Tomochichi, was so impressed with Oglethorpe's friendly manner that he agreed to the location of the Georgia settlement upon Yamacraw Bluff, an eminence rising above the waters of the Savannah River. [10]

Having gained the good will of the Indians dwelling within the neighborhood of Savannah, Oglethorpe sought to win the support of other tribes holding claims to the territory upon which the Georgia colony would spread. From his friend Tomochichi, he learned the names and abodes of the leading Lower Creek chiefs; then, with the aid of the Micco, Oglethorpe made arrangements for the leaders to come to Savannah for a council. By fleet runners, Tomochichi conveyed Oglethorpe's invitation to the principal chiefs of the Lower Creeks. Receiving the greetings in a spirit of cordiality, the red men were soon on their way to Savannah to greet the white chief.

Upon their arrival, the Indians were received by Oglethorpe in one of the new houses in the rising settlement. The genial host was immensely pleased that such a distinguished group of chiefs and headmen had made the journey from their distant towns as representatives of the tribes known to him as "the Coweeta, Cussetas, Osweecheys, Cheehaws, Echetas, Pallachucolas, Oconas, and Eufaule." Through the eloquent overtures of their spokesman, Oueekachumpa of the Oconas, Oglethorpe was assured of the warm support of the red people. [11]

In this atmosphere of mutual cordiality, Oglethorpe and the chiefs reached an agreement which enhanced the prospects for the infant colony. Under the terms of the treaty, the Indians agreed to submit themselves to the general government of the English and to dwell in peace with the newcomers. At the same time, the Creeks ceded to the Georgia trustees most of the territory lying between the Savannah River and the Altamaha, extending inland to the head of tidewater. [12]

Under the leadership of General Oglethorpe, Georgia enjoyed peaceful relations with her Indian neighbors during the formative years of the colony. But by 1739, the astute general perceived that the French and Spaniards were attempting to incite the red people against the English colonists. Learning that the Indians were planning to hold a Great Council at Coweta Town on the Chattahoochee River, Oglethorpe resolved to attend the meeting in person, hoping to perpetuate the existing state of tranquillity.

Accompanied by a small escort party, the English leader set out upon his mission. Proceeding up the Savannah River by water, Oglethorpe landed at the Uchee town located twenty-five miles above Ebenezer. From this place, the party set out across the wilderness to Coweta Town over 300 miles away.[13] On his journey westward, Oglethorpe camped upon the bank of the Ocmulgee River within sight of three ancient mounds.[14]

After the long, wearisome journey, Oglethorpe and his party arrived at Coweta Town. Shortly afterward, the Indian chiefs entered into their Great Council with the English general in attendance. During the ensuing deliberations, the genial philanthropist again won the favor of the red people. Once more the Indian chiefs declared their friendship and pledged to continue the terms of the treaty agreed upon at Savannah.[15]

Throughout the years of Oglethorpe's management of the Georgia colony, the paths between the whites and Indians were generally peaceful. In 1754 the noted leader departed for England, never to return to the colony which he had founded. But Oglethorpe's benign influence over the red people would linger yet awhile.

In the period following the departure of its founder, the Georgia colony grew steadily. As the need for territory increased, English authorities treated successfully with the Indians for additional land cessions. By the end of the year 1773, Georgia had come to occupy a long, narrow strip of land clinging to the edge of the Atlantic Ocean as far down as the St. Mary's River, and extending upward between the Savannah and Ogeechee rivers to the headwaters of the streams.[16]

But English control over the Georgia colony was drawing to an end. Conflict was arising between the mother country and her Georgia subjects. The Revolutionary War was approaching, and independence was on its way. All future negotiations with the Indians would be conducted under a new government.

CHAPTER V

THE FRONTIER MOVES FORWARD

After the Revolutionary War was won by the American colonies, and the United States established, hordes of immigrants pushed into Georgia from the Carolinas and Virginia. Some had fought upon Georgia soil during the war, and were eager to return to the growing state to make their homes. Along with the Carolinians and Virginians were many Georgians dwelling within the narrow eastern limits of the state who also sought fresh lands upon new frontiers. Thus, from within Georgia and from without, came strong demands for more land. The new Georgia Government, under obligations to reward those who had fought for Independence, and facing the necessity of providing for the expansion of Georgia's own boundaries, moved promptly to meet the demands.

Lying between the Ogeechee and Oconee rivers in the path of Georgia's westward movement, a vast area of fertile land extended from the broad Altamaha northward to the headwaters of the two streams. Pressed with the need for expansion, the growing state was eager to secure this vital strip from its red-skinned owners. But the tranquil days of Oglethorpe were now a matter of the far-distant past. In the intervening years, the Indians had become adamant in their determination to arrest the progress of the advancing whites. During the Revolutionary War, the Creeks and Cherokees had turned upon their white neighbors and waged devastating warfare upon the Georgia frontiers. With the savage depredations still fresh in their memories, the Georgians were resolved to rid the frontiers of the redskins and to gain their coveted lands for white settlers. But the conflict had only deepened the red people's determination to cede no more of their territory to the whites.

The mounting opposition of the Creek Indians to Georgia's westward movement was symbolized in the person of Alexander McGillivray, a half-breed chieftain who was rising to a dominant position in the Creek Nation. From his dwelling place among the Upper Creeks near the confluence of the Coosa and Tallapoosa rivers, McGillivray succeeded in welding the red people into a formidable force aimed at obstructing the pushing Georgia pioneers. Taking advantage of the traditional enmity between the Americans and the Florida Spaniards, the astute chieftain actively connived with the Spanish to thwart the United States at every turn and to retain a position of dominance for himself and the Creek Indians. McGillivray bitterly opposed the cession of the land between the Ogeechee and Oconee, and ignored all efforts to lure him to the conference table.

At this time, the recently-formed United States was governed by the Articles of Confederation, a weak bond which held the states loosely together. In the absence of any constitutional provision to the contrary, Georgia resolved to initiate a treaty with the Indians solely upon her own authority. Convinced that the Creeks should pay for the damages inflicted upon the frontier during the Revolutionary War, Georgia officials summoned the chiefs to a council at Augusta for the purpose of prying from them a cession of land. But the McGillivray party warily ignored the communication. and only a few lesser chieftains appeared for the meeting. Not to be outdone, the aggressive commissioners induced the minor chiefs to cede to Georgia all Creek lands extending from the Ogeechee River westward to the Oconee. [1]

The McGillivray party vehemently denounced the Treaty of Augusta, and denied its validity on the grounds that the territory belonged to the entire Creek Nation, and could not be bargained away by a few chiefs acting without authority from the Nation. [2]

In spite of the Indians' protests, Georgia promptly took possession of the ceded land and, by act of the General Assembly in 1784, created from it two vast new counties. From the upper portion was formed Franklin County, and from the lower part was established Washington County. The eagerly-sought lands were then opened to new settlers, with generous portions granted as bounties to the soldiers who had rendered service to Georgia during the Revolutionary War. Promptly, large numbers of immigrants marched into the new territory and established themselves as far west as the Oconee River.

Viewing the coming of the white pioneers with bitter resentment, McGillivray and his party resolved to drive the intruders from the land which the Indians tenaciously claimed as their own. Now, with aggressive white settlers and defiant redskins claiming and occupying the same territory, a series of conflicts erupted along the river frontier which came to be known as the Oconee War. In his efforts to force the whites from the disputed land, McGillivray incited the Creeks to savage depredations upon the Georgia frontier. At the same time, callous whites were equally ruthless in their dealings with their red neighbors. [3]

With serious trouble mounting between Georgia and the Creek Nation, the central government decided it was time to take a hand in the matter. In an effort to relieve the explosive situation, the government dispatched General Andrew Pickens and Benjamin Hawkins to Georgia to seek from the Indians a treaty which would satisfy both parties. The commissioners promptly sent forth messengers to the Creek chiefs calling them to a council at Galphinton on the Ogeechee River. In response, a party of red men from two towns appeared for the talk, but the dominant McGillivray faction remained conspicuously absent. Unwilling to treat with such a small number, the United States commissioners called off the meeting and forthwith departed from Galphinton. [4]

After the withdrawal of Hawkins and Pickens from the scene, two commissioners sent by Georgia to assist in the negotiations took matters into their own hands. The dogged warriors, Elijah Clarke and John Twiggs, pressed the Indians for a treaty. The red men responded affirmatively—though reluctantly—to the Georgians' overtures, and on November 12, 1785, entered into an agreement confirming the previous cession of lands lying between the Ogeechee and Oconee rivers. In addition, the Creeks ceded to Georgia the territory lying east of a line running from the forks of the Oconee and Ocmulgee rivers, down to the head of the St. Mary's on the Florida border. The latter area was a part of the domain beloved by the red people and known to them as the Tallassee County. Undaunted, McGillivray denounced the Treaty of Galphinton, and refused to acknowledge the validity of the cession. [5]

As relations grew worse between the Georgians and the Indians, the trouble-weary pioneers clamored for a settlement of the boundary dispute. Again, Georgia authorities sought another council with the Indians to be held at the junction of the Oconee River and Shoulderbone Creek. To impress the reluctant redskins with her military might, Georgia sent along a strong force under the command of General John Twiggs. At this advanced position on the Georgia frontier, on November 3, 1786, the Treaty of Shoulderbone Creek was made. This treaty confirmed the Treaty of Galphinton which, in turn was based largely upon the Treaty of Augusta, so the Georgians hoped the dispute was settled. But, having evaded the dubious warmth of Georgia's latest council fires, McGillivray quickly spurned the treaty and continued with renewed effort to harass the white settlers on the frontier. [6]

The Constitution of the United States was ratified in 1788, and subsequently replaced the impotent Articles of Confederation. Through the power provided by the Constitution, the federal government now proceeded to perform more forcefully the functions relating to the general welfare of the nation.

Viewing the troubled Oconee frontier as a serious source of danger, President George Washington invited McGillivray to the nation's capital at New York to discuss a possible treaty to settle the boundary dispute and to allay the Oconee conflict. The elusive chieftain who had evaded all previous efforts to lure him to the council chamber, now acceded to the request of the President of the United States and, with a large party of followers, made the long journey to New York. Here, after much deliberation flavored with flattery and liberal gifts, McGillivray finally agreed to a treaty by which the original lines set at the Treaty of Augusta were accepted, and the Indians surrendered all claim to the territory lying between the Ogeechee and Oconee rivers. In turn, the United States restored to the Indians the portion of the Tallassee County which the Creeks had previously ceded to Georgia at Shoulderbone. Moreover, the federal government guaranteed to the Creeks the right to retain all lands west of the Oconee, and declared as outlaws any white persons venturing into the restricted domain. [7]

The Treaty of New York brought no peace to the troubled scene. The Indians bitterly resented the loss of their old hunting grounds and refused to abide by the terms of the treaty. For their part, the Georgians were dumbfounded over the restraints placed upon them by the central government. With the daily menace of hostile redskins upon their frontiers, it was inconceivable to them that their own government should give such aid and comfort to their enemies. The Georgians especially deplored the action of the government in guaranteeing to the Indians the land west of the Oconee, for Georgia must expand westward. All treaties to the contrary, the Oconee War continued unabated. [8]

To further aggravate the situation, America's traditional enemies, the Florida Spaniards, were agitating the Creeks to gain a monopoly in trade and influence with the red people. It was becoming increasingly apparent to American authorities that, in spite of his professions of friendship, McGillivray was actually in alliance with the Spanish, and was using his influence over the Indians to strengthen the position of the Spanish against the United States. The Spaniards were holding McGillivray's support by means of bribery, and through the liberal distribution of arms and ammunition from the powerful trading establishment of Panton-Leslie & Co., based at Spanish Pensacola. [9]

The President of the United States became increasingly concerned over the explosive situation along the boundary between the State of Georgia and the Creek Nation of Indians. Washington viewed the Oconee War, with its overtone of foreign intrigue, as a vital phase of the entire American Indian problem, and feared that the conflict would develop into a general frontier conflagration.

In an effort to forestall the extension of the Oconee conflict and to protect the interests of Georgia's white citizens and their red neighbors, the President appointed James Seagrove as Agent for Indian Affairs. The Agent established posts for dealing with the Indians at Colerain on the St. Mary's River, and at Rock Landing on the Oconee frontier, but Seagrove was extremely reluctant to move out into the Indian country where his mission could be more effectively performed.

In 1796 Benjamin Hawkins was appointed to succeed Seagrove as Indian Agent. Hawkins had recently served as a commissioner for the United States in bringing about a favorable treaty with the Creek Indians at Colerain on the St. Mary's River near a point at which the State of Georgia, Spanish Florida, and the Creek Nation formed a common meeting place. By the Treaty of Colerain the terms of existing treaties were clarified and confirmed. At the same time, the federal government gained the right to maintain certain reserves of land inside the Creek Nation whereon forts and trading houses could be established.[10] The trading posts, duly set up and operated by the federal government, were known as factories, and through their formation the factory system of Indian trade was effected. The following year, Fort James was erected on the south side of the Altamaha River where Barnard's old trading path crossed the stream opposite Beard's Bluff, and Fort Wilkinson was established on the west side of the Oconee River near an important Indian gathering place at Rock Landing.[11]

Shortly after Benjamin Hawkins became Indian Agent, he proceeded directly into the heart of the Creek Country to make his home among the red people. By 1804 he had established a permanent Agency on the east side of the Flint River at the crossing of the Lower Trading Path. For the remainder of his eventful life, Hawkins tirelessly devoted his energies to the task of protecting the interests of the whites and the Indians, and to keeping peace among the troubled people in their many conflicts.

CHAPTER VI

THE PIONEERS REACH THE OCMULGEE

Long before the Oconee boundary dispute was settled, eager Georgians were casting wishful eyes upon the alluring country beyond the Oconee. Between the Oconee River and the Ocmulgee, they viewed a vast area of fertile land which was the dream of the westward-moving pioneers. Beginning at the juncture of the two rivers, the territory extended northward within the forks of the streams all the way up to their headwaters. Because of the nature of its situation, the entire area was known as the Ocmulgee Fork. The pushing pioneers were determined to gain the coveted domain for themselves.

In their efforts to secure the desired territory, the Georgians now faced formidable obstacles. The Creeks, still smarting over the loss of large areas already occupied by the Americans, were determined to arrest the westward movement of the land-grabbing whites. Moreover, the power to make treaties now rested exclusively in the hands of federal authorities far removed from the firebrand and scalping knife. To the consternation of the harassed Georgians, the federal government had even guaranteed to the Indians continued ownership of the needed territory.

With feelings on both sides at a high pitch, federal officials relented and authorized the Indian Agent, Benjamin Hawkins, to feel out the Creeks for any inclination toward another treaty whereby Georgia's western boundary might be extended to the Ocmulgee River. Reporting to the Secretary of War from Cusseta Town, on November 19, 1797, Hawkins stated that the Indians were not disposed to sell. On the contrary, it required "that a man be high in the confidence of the Indians to be able to mention the subject in the public square without being insulted." [1]

In the meantime, Hawkins was faithfully placing into effect a plan whereby additional territory could be given up by the Indians without undue hardship to themselves. The plan was simply to transform the economy of the red people from a system based upon hunting and fishing, requiring great areas of land, to a system of agriculture whereby an ample living could be derived from smaller areas through intensive use of the soil. To accomplish this aim, Hawkins was providing the red people with supplies, equipment, and training for farming, livestock raising, spinning, weaving, and other arts of the white man's civilization. As the Indians gradually took on the newcomers' way of life, their need for supplies increased. Since these goods were available at the trading posts, the red people became more dependent upon the whites for the maintenance of their new mode of living. With their needs increasing, their game decreasing, and their debts mounting, Hawkins could predict that the Creeks would soon be willing to part with more of their hunting grounds. [2]

In 1802 Thomas Jefferson, then President of the United States, concluded that the time was ripe for proposing a new treaty to the Creek Nation. To this end, he appointed as commissioners Benjamin Hawkins, General Andrew Pickens, and General James Wilkinson, with authority to negotiate with the Indians for a further cession of land. Accordingly, the commissioners summoned the chiefs and headmen to an assembly at Fort Wilkinson on the west bank of the Oconee River. The commissioners arrived at the fort ahead of time and settled down to await the coming of the red people whose paths led from distant parts of the Creek Nation. Gradually, a substantial number of Indians reached the frontier rendezvous and went into camp a short distance from the fort. [3]

As the commissioners opened the council, they were aiming at a cession which would include the entire area between the Oconee and Ocmulgee, but it soon became apparent that the red people were not ready to part with such a large portion of their treasured hunting grounds. The commissioners then modified their proposals in the likely belief that if they could only gain part of the Ocmulgee Fork, they would soon be able to persuade the Indians to give up the entire area. [4]

After extensive "talks," both parties settled upon an agreement whereby the Creeks ceded a long, narrow strip on the west side of the Oconee, stretching from the High Shoals of the Apalachee southward in a thin bulge to the mouth of Palmetto Creek below present-day Dublin. [5]

The Treaty of Fort Wilkinson pleased neither the Georgians nor the Indians. The white people were bitterly disappointed because they already had their hopes set upon gaining the entire Ocmulgee Fork, and the Indians were resentful over the loss of another slice of their diminishing domain. Knowing the whites as they did, the Creeks suspected that with a foothold on the coveted territory, the Americans would simply press their demands for the entire fork.

The Indians were correct in their calculations, for no sooner were the terms of the Treaty of Fort Wilkinson known than the whites burst into a storm of protest. Early in 1802 Georgia had ceded to the United States her western territory, the area extending generally from the Chattahoochee River to the Mississippi. The federal government, in turn, had specifically agreed to extinguish the Indian title to the land within the forks of the Oconee and Ocmulgee as early as this could be done peacefully. Now that the United States had settled with the Indians for only a portion of the promised territory, the Georgians felt betrayed by their own government, and vociferously expressed their sentiments. Again, federal officials sought to set into motion negotiations aimed at the acquisition of the entire territory contained within the Ocmulgee Fork.

In endeavoring to treat with the Indians, the Government was encountering a vexatious situation. This difficulty was centered around the person and power of William Augustus Bowles, an American-born British agent who had gone into Spanish Florida on a clandestine mission. Seeking out the red people, Bowles soon entrenched himself among the Seminoles and lower towns of Creek Indians within whose councils he exerted a peculiar influence. So strong was the hold of the adventurer upon the dissident Indian elements that they were lured into bestowing upon Bowles the high-sounding title, "Director General of Muscogee." In his self-gained office, Bowles endeavored to weld the red people into a force designed to assure their support for England, and to oppose the United States at every turn. Setting up a trading post at St. Marks to compete with the Spanish-sponsored firm of Panton-Leslie & Co., the intruder gained a substantial following among the hostile Indian elements. The United States, in turn, endeavored to offset the machinations of the crafty Bowles with the influence of the esteemed Indian Agent, Benjamin Hawkins. [6]

Throughout their efforts to induce the Indians to treat with them at Fort Wilkinson, the United States commissioners had found Bowles an obstructing force. Deeply involved in his Florida intrigues, Bowles had succeeded in diverting a substantial number of Indian leaders from Fort Wilkinson in opposition to the overtures of the commissioners. Now, with only a portion of the Ocmulgee Fork in their possession, the Americans were encountering effective opposition from the Bowles party as they sought to secure the remainder of the desired territory.

With discord erupting between the factions favorable to the United States as opposed to those supporting Bowles, Benjamin Hawkins faced the necessity of nullifying the influence of the agitator. By uniting his efforts with those of Spanish officials who were also feeling the impact of Bowles's disruptive maneuvers, Hawkins participated in a plan whereby Bowles was captured and turned over to Spanish authorities. This act removed the adventurer bodily from the scene, but it intensified the resistance of his followers against any proposed treaty. [7]

Still hoping to negotiate with the Creek Nation for the remainder of the Ocmulgee Fork, three United States commissioners, in May, 1803, convened a council at Oswichee, a Lower Creek town favorable to the Bowles party. The Oswichees were firmly resisting all efforts to impose upon them the white man's civilization, and openly declared their determination to adhere to the old times. They displayed their disdain for the white man's way by openly asserting their preference for the bow and arrow as opposed to the gun. [8]

In such a setting of hostility as Oswichee Town provided, the meeting was doomed to failure. Although Bowles was absent from the scene, his followers skilfully organized themselves into such an effective force that they were able to disrupt the negotiations. Feelings were running high, and the commissioners were openly insulted in the public square. Even President Jefferson was accused of "cunning and duplicity." The meeting at Oswichee finally broke up on a tone of discord and division among the red people. [9]

In spite of such discouragements, the Indian Agent continued to strive for the desired treaty. During the summer of 1804, Hawkins and David Meriwether as representatives of the United States, met with the Creeks in their General Council at Tuckabatchee. Here, for two months, the commissioners worked patiently with the frustrated red men to erase the strain of discord, with the ultimate hope of securing a cession for the remainder of the Ocmulgee Fork. [10] Little by little, the commissioners gained ground; and after two months, Hawkins was encouraged to write Governor Milledge of Georgia that, before the end of the year, the Ocmulgee would be set as the boundary line as high up as the three forks, at least, and probably at its source. [11]

In the fall of 1804, with negotiations still pressing, a delegation of Creek chiefs made its way to the Agency on the Flint to treat further with the Agent. The delegation was led by the influential Speaker, Hopoie Micco, although the chieftain was suffering intensely from an outbreaking of sores covering his body. At the Agency, on November 3, 1804, a treaty was finally agreed upon by the chiefs and Benjamin Hawkins acting as sole commissioner for the United States. Under the terms of the treaty, the remainder of the Ocmulgee Fork would be ceded to the United States for the use of Georgia. [12]

The territory now offered by the Creek Indians promised to Georgia the realization of a long-sought goal. The boundaries would begin at the High Shoals of the Apalachee, run a direct line to the Ulcofauhatchee (the first fork of the Ocmulgee above the Seven Islands), thence down the Ocmulgee to its confluence with the Oconee, up the Oconee to the line of the Treaty of Fort Wilkinson, and from thence to the beginning point, but saving and reserving all islands in the Ocmulgee for the Indians. At the same time, a tract lying on the east side of the Ocmulgee, four miles long and two miles wide, including the Ocmulgee Old Fields, would be reserved as a place for the red people to meet and trade with their white neighbors. Here would be erected a fort and a trading post or factory. The establishment would be under the direction of the Agent for Indian Affairs as long as the President deemed necessary.

As compensation for this treasured portion of their relinquished land, the Indians would be furnished two sets of blacksmith's tools and two strikers, for ten years. In addition, the Indians would receive from the United States the sum of $200,000.00 in stock, bearing interest at six percent, payable half-yearly at the factory on the Georgia frontier. [13]

In reporting his success to the Secretary of War, Hawkins stated that, under the provisions of the treaty, the United States would acquire more than a million acres, half of which was appraised as "unquestionably the best in the country." While immensely pleased at attaining his long-sought goal, Hawkins was painfully aware that some greedy whites would still be dissatisfied. On November 12, the Agent wrote Governor Milledge that in treating with the Indians, he had even sought a liberal portion of territory *beyond* the Ocmulgee. He had been "desirous of going from Kettle (Big House) Creek to its source, and from thence to the Okefenokee, so Georgia would be satisfied for ten years." But this had proved impossible. Hawkins blamed certain lawless Georgia frontiersmen for the resentment of the Indians. [14]

Although agreement had been reached upon the scene of negotiations, it now became necessary for the treaty to be submitted to the United States Senate for approval. Being far removed from the problems of the advancing Georgia frontier, the Senate rejected the hard-won treaty in objection to certain minor points. Secretary Dearborn then instructed the Indian Agent to bring a deputation of Indians to Washington to negotiate in person.

In the summer of 1805, Benjamin Hawkins led a delegation of six Creek chiefs on the long journey to the recently-established Capital of the United States in Washington. Among the chiefs was William McIntosh who was now rising to a position of prominence among the Creek Indians. Accompanying the party as interpreter was Timothy Barnard, the respected keeper of Barnard's Trading Post on the Flint River below the Creek Agency.

Amid the strange surroundings of the capital city of the white man's world, the representatives of the Creek Nation entered into negotiations with the Secretary of War for the official cession of the lands previously agreed upon with the Indian Agent. From the negotiations finally came a treaty generally confirming the terms of Hawkins' agreement back at the Agency. Under the terms of the Treaty of Washington, the Indians agreed that the Ocmulgee would be the dividing line between the white man's country and the Creek Nation. The waters of the Ocmulgee would be used by both white and red people for navigation and for fishing. The whites were denied the right to construct fish traps in the stream, but could use nets, provided the nets were drawn to the east bank. At the same time, the Indians granted the United States the right to open a pathway across the Creek Nation from the Ocmulgee to the Mobile River in Alabama territory. [15]

After completing the Treaty of Washington, the red men set out on the long journey back to the Creek Nation. To reach their homes they would skirt the hallowed soil of the Ocmulgee Fork, once the scene of their principal habitations and the site of their ancient capital. No doubt their hearts were heavy as they passed the range of the domain of their forefathers, to confine their abodes to the diminishing lands beyond the Ocmulgee River. Behind them lay vast areas of their once-proud nation, surrendered bit by bit to the ever-advancing Georgians.

In sharp contrast to the dejection of the departing red men was the jubilation of the whites as their long-hoped-for treaty became a reality. Long had the Georgians dwelt before the barriers of the Indian boundary under ever-mounting pressures from their own land needs augmented by a steady stream of new settlers pushing into the frontiers. In their land-hunger, the whites had often cast wishful glances upon the alluring territory extending westward to the Ocmulgee River. With the flood of immigrants at its crest, the final obstruction was at last removed. Now a stream of eager settlers would move onward until they reached the river of bubbling water. The pioneers had gained the Ocmulgee.

CHAPTER VII

NEW WAYS ARISE ALONG THE OCMULGEE

With the beginning of the nineteenth century, the land along the Ocmulgee River lay within the domain of the red people and comprised a vital part of the Creek Nation. Here the Indians had established their primitive civilization and followed their simple ways. Along the waters of the Ocmulgee, the natives had erected their towns and villages, or their hunting camps. Well-worn trails, winding through the woods and crossing streams at shallow fords or rising bluffs, bore the print of countless moccasins as generations of red people had pursued their course along the Ocmulgee. The presence of the Indians so permeated the countryside that the very streams bore the euphonious names which the natives had given them from an intimate knowledge of each stream.

But soon the simple world of the natives would be changed, and the primitive mode would vanish before a new way of life. As the red people retreated westward, hordes of whites from the east would press into the country, bringing with them their own civilization. To the Ocmulgee and its generous streams, American pioneers were coming to clear land, to erect dwellings, and to establish an order which had come down to them through a long and cherished heritage.

With the acquisition of the first portion of land between the Oconee and Ocmulgee by the Treaty of Fort Wilkinson, two counties were created from the ceded lands. When the remaining territory within the forks was acquired by the Treaty of Washington, the additional land was included in these counties so that the entire Ocmulgee Fork comprised two mammoth counties. [1] The dividing line ran from Fort Wilkinson on the Oconee to the Ocmulgee Old Fields on the Ocmulgee. Baldwin County embraced all territory extending from the line to the headwaters of the Oconee and Ocmulgee. Wilkinson County encompassed the vast area extending within the forks from the dividing line down to the juncture of the two rivers.

With the rapid settlement of the lands within the Ocmulgee Fork, Georgia's population shifted sharply westward. The old Capital at Louisville was no longer in the center of the populous areas. As a result of this westward movement, a demand arose

32

for the seat of government to be moved to a place more in keeping with the trends of migration. Accordingly, in 1804, the Georgia General Assembly passed an act relocating the state capital in the town of Milledgeville now arising on the west bank of the Oconee just above Fort Wilkinson. [2] The establishment of the Georgia capital within the Ocmulgee Fork brought increased importance and prestige to the new world.

Soon after the creation of the counties of Baldwin and Wilkinson, it became apparent that the counties were entirely too large to serve a sprawling population spread out on a far-flung frontier. With severe limitations to travel in the unfamiliar country, it was impossible for the people to make the long journey to the centers of government without undue hardship. As a result, a movement was begun among the inhabitants to have the unwieldly counties divided into smaller units. In response, on December 10, 1807, the General Assembly passed an act whereby the mammoth counties were divided into a number of smaller counties.

From the domain of Baldwin came Putnam, Morgan, Jones, and Randolph. At the same time, Wilkinson was divided into three counties. The upper portion retained the name of Wilkinson; the middle part was formed into Laurens; and the lower section was organized into the county of Telfair. [3]

Upon the creation of a new county in the undeveloped Ocmulgee country, it was necessary for the county to be organized and for its government to be set into operation. This required that county officials be selected, courts be established, and public buildings be erected. At the same time, it was imperative that a military system be provided to protect the exposed settlers from attack by hostile Indians roaming beyond the Ocmulgee. Officers were to be chosen, and all able-bodied men of military age recruited, drilled, and instructed in the basic principles of warfare.

A county reflecting the frontier way was Telfair, formed from the southernmost portion of Wilkinson County. As originally laid out, Telfair County embraced the area lying immediately within the fork of the Oconee and Ocmulgee rivers. The upper boundary was defined by a line leaving the Ocmulgee at the northwestern corner of the Fourteenth Land District near the Oswichee Trail, and running northeastward directly to the Oconee, touching the latter stream in the vicinity of Berryhill Bluff. From these two points, one on the Oconee and the other on the Ocmulgee, the boundary lines extended down both rivers to the place at which they flowed together to form the Altamaha. [4] On its Ocmulgee boundary, Telfair County lay within a great loop in the river where the stream, in its downward course, made a sweeping curve around the western and southern extremities of the county. This giant curve was known as the Big Bend of the Ocmulgee.

Upon the creation of Telfair County, steps were taken to set all county functions into operation. At the same time the act creating the county was passed, the General Assembly provided for the appointment of Justices of the Inferior Court with authority to fix a site for public buildings, and to arrange for the election of necessary officials. Chosen for this service were James Alston, William Carroll, William Lott, Jr., Jesse Byrd, and Thomas Raines. On September 17, 1808, an election for public officials was held in the infant county with the following chosen: Clerk of Superior and Inferior Courts, Duncan Curry; Sheriff, Cullen Edwards; Coroner, Benjamin Mitchell Griffin. Thomas Watts was chosen as Representative to the General Assembly, and William Lott as Senator, both to serve for the year 1809.[5]

With Indians prowling on the Telfair frontier, early steps were taken to protect the inhabitants through the formation of a military system. The county was divided into four militia districts, with officers chosen to organize and train the men residing within each district. To be chosen for the responsible task of leading his companions during these years of danger was a token of the high esteem in which an officer was held by his neighbors. In addition to the military officials in each district, two Justices of the Peace were selected to perform local civil functions.

Receiving commissions on September 14, 1809, from Militia District Number 340, were Thomas Willcox, Captain; Daniel McCranie, Lieutenant; William Carroll, Ensign. Justices for the same district were Lemuel Mobley and Frederick Jackson. Receiving commissions on February 12, 1810, from District 337, were Cullen Edwards, Captain; James Carver, Lieutenant; Jesse Carver, Ensign. Justices for the district were Joseph Bell and Joel Wooten.[6]

The first military officials for Militia District Number 339 were granted commissions by Governor David B. Mitchell on June 18, 1810. Recipients of these honored commissions were William Griffin, Captain; Jehu McCall, Lieutenant; and Nathaniel Hudson, Ensign. Justices for the district were Norman McLeod and Murdock McDuffie.[7]

The earliest officials for District 338, which embraced the county seat, have not been determined, but Justices for the district were John Smith and Abraham Powell, both commissioned on April 29, 1809.[8]

Josiah D. Cawthon, an early settler in the Copeland area, was commissioned on August 25, 1811, as Major of the 82nd Battalion, and placed in command of all Telfair military forces. [9]

During its formative years, the infant county encountered considerable difficulty in getting its courts established. The county was large and sparsely settled, and those attending the court sessions were forced to travel great distances over Indian trails or crude roadways. Travel under these conditions was slow and dangerous. Coinciding with the early years were the Indian troubles which plagued the county. Throughout these perilous times, with war clouds hanging over the frontier, the inhabitants were devoting their energies to the tasks of carving homes from the wilderness, and protecting themselves from hostile forces. The danger of redskins lurking along the lonely paths doubtlessly deterred many from attending the court sessions. It was more prudent to remain within the comparative safety of home, or settlement blockhouse, than to risk ambush along an uncertain way.

Nevertheless, the growing county moved forward as rapidly as circumstances permitted. The first term of Superior Court was held on April 16, 1810, at the house of John Peterson, with Judge Thomas Carnes presiding. Grand Jurors and Petit Jurors had been drawn on the first Monday in January, but only the Grand Jurors were called and sworn. [10] The only other action taken at this first term of Telfair Superior Court was to select the jurors for the next term. The men selected in the new county represented many veterans from the old centers of civilization back east, along with a liberal sprinkling of young men just beginning their public service in a rising new county. [11]

Another effort was made to set the court into operation on April 15, 1811, at the house of Mark Pridgen, with Judge Peter Early presiding. Again the effort was doomed to failure when only five Grand Jurors made their appearance, and *none* of the indicted persons. In the face of such odds, no Petit Jury was called, and after hopefully selecting jurors for the next scheduled term, the court adjourned. [12]

The Telfair Superior Court finally got under way in October of 1811, and continued with regularity through the April term of 1813. Then, for an entire year no court was held. This was during the peak of Indian troubles on the Ocmulgee frontier when the energies of the inhabitants were grimly directed at self-survival, and courts were relegated to a position of secondary importance. [13]

Throughout the formative years before a permanent site was selected for public buildings, the Telfair courts were held in the homes of individuals dwelling at convenient locations. When the county was first created, provisions were made for the courts to be held at the house of Jesse Byrd. [14] The following year, the house of John Peterson was set as the seat of government, and it was here that the first term was held. [15] On December 8, 1810, the General Assembly authorized the Telfair Inferior Court to select an appropriate site on the Ocmulgee River in the Eighth Land District. Until such site could be determined and the public buildings erected, all public functions would be transacted at the house of Mark Pridgen near present-day Jacksonville. [16]

In the meantime, steps were taken to secure a permanent seat of government. On December 13, 1811, commissioners were authorized by the General Assembly to fix the site upon Lot 79 in the Eighth District, purchased from Jesse Wiggins, Jr. [17] The proposed site was located on the west bank of Horse Creek two miles from the Ocmulgee River. The following year, however, the eastern part of Telfair County was cut off and annexed to Montgomery County. The chosen site was no longer in the center of population, being ten or twelve miles too far to the east. [18] At this time the most thickly settled portion of Telfair County lay along the river in the shape of a crescent conforming to the Big Bend of the Ocmulgee. Since the house of Mark Pridgen was near the center of the crescent, it was continued as the temporary center for public county affairs.

In order to fix the seat of government at the most convenient place, the Inferior Court was authorized by the General Assembly to contract for not less than fifty, or more than 202 1/2 acres situated within two miles of the center of population, on or near the Ocmulgee River. [19] The spot finally chosen comprised part of Lot 340 in the Eighth Land District, belonging to John Parramore. In June of 1814, Parramore deeded the desired land to the Telfair Inferior Court composed of Charles McKinnon, Ziba Fletcher, Thomas S. Swain, and Abb L. Hatten [20] In time, the public buildings were erected at this point overlooking the Ocmulgee River and the Creek Nation beyond. The seat of government was named Jacksonville in honor of General Andrew Jackson whose achievements so vitally shaped the course of events on the Ocmulgee frontier.

At the same time that Telfair County was created from the lower part of Wilkinson, Laurens County was taken from the middle section. As originally laid out, Laurens stretched from the Oconee southwestward along the upper Telfair boundary to the Ocmulgee River. The area of the new county was soon found to be too extensive to provide effective government for a widely-scattered population. The citizens then sought successfully to have the large county divided into two counties. The General Assembly passed an act on December 13, 1808, whereby the western half of Laurens was set apart as a new county and given the name Pulaski. [21]

The steps required to launch a new county upon its course were promptly taken, and on May 4, 1809, public officials for Pulaski County were commissioned as follows: Richard H. Thomas, Clerk of Superior Court; John Rainey, Clerk of Inferior Court; Lewis Holland, Sheriff; and William Bracken, Coroner. [22] Edmund Hogan was named Senator, and Sanders Coalson Representative to the General Assembly.

Little delay was encountered in securing a permanent site for public buildings, and on December 13, 1809, the General Assembly fixed the seat of government upon Lot 394 in the Twenty-first Land District. [23] The place selected was situated on the east side of the Ocmulgee beside the old Uchee Shoals. At this accessible spot, a number of important Indian trails converged to make use of the shallow shoals in the Ocmulgee, which formed an excellent place for fording the stream. The chosen site was laid out into a town, and given the name Hartford. Management of the affairs of the frontier capital was placed in the hands of a body of commissioners chosen for that purpose on December 13, 1810. The original Hartford Commissioners were George Walker, Jacob Snell, Allen Tooke, William S. Lancaster, and Josiah Everett. [24]

Pulaski experienced the usual troubles of a new county in setting its courts into operation. On June 5, 1809, the Justices of the Inferior Court produced the first "list of fit and proper persons eligible to serve as jurors according to the best information that could be collected, there being no tax returns for the county." [25] The earliest effort to hold a full term of Superior Court was made on April 23, 1810. The court convened with Judge Thomas Carnes presiding, and Richard H. Thomas serving as clerk; but a jury list not having been properly prepared, the court adjourned until the following July. [26]

The July term opened according to plan, but the only apparent business transacted was the drawing of jurors to serve at the *next* term. The citizens now sufficiently established in the new county to be called as jurors formed a cosmopolitan body of immigrants from Virginia, the Carolinas, and eastern Georgia. [27]

With jurors properly selected, court again convened on October 22, 1810, but travel difficulties prevented the jurors from appearing on the first day, so court was adjourned until the following day. On the next day, another effort was made, but this time the *judge* failed to attend, so all attempts to get the embryonic court organized were abandoned until the following term. [28]

The Pulaski Superior Court was finally launched in April, 1811, with all necessary parties on hand. Presiding at this term was Judge Peter Early who, soon to become governor, would play a vital role in the unfolding drama of the Ocmulgee scene. [29]

Situated as it was across the Ocmulgee River from the Creek Nation, Pulaski County was ever in danger of attack from hostile Indians. From the beginning, it was necessary that steps be taken to establish military forces for the protection of the exposed inhabitants. Very early, the county was laid out into militia districts, with all eligible men in each district subject to call for periods of training, and for combat in case of need. The men in each militia district comprised a company commanded by a captain chosen by his companions in arms and commissioned by the Governor.

During the years of the Creek and Seminole Indian troubles, with hostiles threatening from the Indian country beyond the Ocmulgee, protection was provided by these military leaders and their men. Among those serving as captains during these perilous times were John Rosser, Archibald Lassiter, Lewis Lee, Gideon Kellam, Edward Bryant, John A. Williams, Benjamin Lanier, William Mayo, James Gouldwire Davis, Henry Senterfeit, and William Pace. The command of all Pulaski military forces was placed in the hands of Lieutenant Colonel Allen Tooke, with headquarters maintained at the military center of Hartford. [30]

Although engrossed in the task of establishing homes in a land beset with dangers from the elements, wild animals, and roaming savages, the early settlers in Pulaski County were ambitious for the education of their young ones. On November 22, 1810, commissioners were appointed to establish the Pulaski County Academy. The men who sought to light the lamp of learning in the wilderness were William A. Harper, Henry Fulghum, George G. Gaines, William S. Lancaster, and George Walker. [31]

Other counties were arising along the Ocmulgee. When, in 1807, Old Wilkinson was divided into three separate counties, the entire upper portion remained as the parent county and continued to bear the name of Wilkinson. Even after generously giving up vast areas of its original territory, Old Wilkinson remained a very large county, extending all the way from the Oconee River westward to the Ocmulgee. The remoteness of many inhabitants from the proposed seat of government led to a movement to again divide the parent county. Once more the carving knife was applied to Old Wilkinson, and the area lying along the Ocmulgee was cut off and organized into a new county. This latest offspring, born on December 14, 1809, was given the name Twiggs. [32]

Under the terms of the act creating Twiggs County, provisions were made for the Inferior Court to select a seat of government in the center of the county, or within two miles thereof. Accordingly, on December 8, 1810, the site was fixed upon a portion of Lot 73 in the Twenty-fifth Land District near Joyner's Spring and above Savage Creek. Appointed as commissioners to erect the courthouse and jail were John Harden, Jacob Ricks, William Davis, Lovett B. Smith, and James McCormick. Until the public buildings could be completed, all county affairs would be transacted at the house of John Harden. [33]

The public buildings were erected upon the designated spot, and a town was laid out named Marion, in honor of the South Carolina "Swamp Fox" of the Revolutionary War. Marion was located in the center of the county on a ridge rising above Savage and Flat creeks, two large streams flowing into the Ocmulgee River eight miles to the southwest. As finally laid out, the new county seat adjoined the southern boundary of the plantation of John Barton who had come from Warren County as a pioneer settler upon the Ocmulgee frontier. [34] Early Twiggs commissioners displayed a bit of ingenuity when they constructed a novel system for piping an endless flow of water from Barton's Springs to the courthouse yard. The water was conveyed through a hollow-log water pipe for a distance of 700 yards from source to outlet. [35] Marion soon became a thriving town and the center of commercial, political, and social life for a large area surrounding the county seat.

Twiggs County grew rapidly, with many substantial planters from Virginia, the Carolinas, and eastern Georgia coming in quest of fertile new lands. These prosperous settlers brought with them a strong element of culture which soon permeated the diminishing frontier wilderness. Progress toward education was evidenced by the creation of several academies. Marion Academy was incorporated in 1816 with Moses Fort, Archibald McIntyre, Samuel Dicks, Dr. Robert Cumming, and William Crocker serving as trustees. [36] The Ocmulgee Academy, located near the Ocmulgee River at Tarver's, was chartered in 1819, with Benjamin DuPree, Edmund DuPree, William W. Williamson, Henry Bunn, and Robert Glenn as trustees. [37] The Stone Creek Academy was incorporated in 1831, with William A. Tharpe, Elisha Davis,

Jeremiah Tharpe, William Davis, and Thomas Chapple named as trustees. [38] This early institution was located in the upper part of the county near Stone Creek Church. The school and the church were closely associated with the family of Vincent Allen Tharpe, a pioneer minister who came from Warren County to serve on the Ocmulgee frontier.

While Old Wilkinson was being divided into smaller counties, its northern neighbor, Baldwin, was undergoing a similar division. On December 10, 1807, several new counties were formed from the parent county, two of which fell within the Ocmulgee domain. These frontier counties were Jones and Randolph. [39]

Jones County lay along the upper boundary of Twiggs, with its southwest corner resting at the Ocmulgee Old Fields, where the new frontier stronghold of Fort Hawkins was arising from the ancient red people's sacred ground. On December 22, 1808, the seat of government for newborn Jones County was established at Clinton, conveniently situated near the center of the county, but somewhat remote from the affairs of the Ocmulgee mainstream. [40]

Jones County attracted from the older areas of the east many substantial planters who rapidly cleared land and established large plantations devoted to the extensive production of cotton during the period when cotton was becoming king.

Randolph County was located on the headwaters of the Ocmulgee River along the upper boundary of Jones. The frontier county was named for the prominent Virginian, John Randolph. Shortly afterward, Randolph came into disfavor with the inhabitants who demonstrated their sentiments by having the name of the county changed to Jasper, in honor of Sergeant Jasper, the flag-rescuing hero of the Revolutionary War.

The county seat of Jasper County, on December 10, 1808, was fixed at Monticello in the center of the county. [41] The fertile lands of Jasper drew large numbers of immigrants, and the frontier wilderness rapidly gave way to an extensive plantation system based upon the production of huge quantities of cotton.

By 1809, the last Georgia county had been established along the Ocmulgee frontier on lands ceded by the Indians at the Treaty of Washington. Little by little, the counties were populated by white newcomers from the east, and organized into the developing pattern of American civilization. With the formation of the last county, the order of the white people was firmly established in the former domain of the Creek Indians. All along the east bank of the Ocmulgee, from its headwaters down to its confluence with the Oconec, the world of the white American stood triumphant. A new way had arisen along the Ocmulgee.

CHAPTER VIII

PIONEER LIFE

The early settlers along the Ocmulgee were fitting their mode of living into the common pattern of a new frontier. Many of the newcomers had come from commodious homes and positions of honor in the realms left behind. Now, as pioneers in a strange land, they were energetically extending their familiar civilization to the primitive wilderness of the Ocmulgee world.

It has been related that, as soon as the coveted territory lying upon the Ocmulgee River was first acquired from the Creek Indians, steps were taken to make the land available for settlement by the pioneers pushing against the frontier. The Ocmulgee Fork was surveyed into land districts and divided into lots containing 202 1/2 acres, or fractions thereof. The land lots were then granted to Georgia citizens through a gigantic lottery system. All eligible Georgians were registered in the county of their residence; then draws corresponding to the registered names were made at the state capital and lots awarded to the holders of the fortunate draws.[1] Amid an air of hopeful suspense, the winners were announced, along with the identity of the lot as drawn.

With the Ocmulgee domain thus opened for settlement, waves of American immigrants surged into the territory. Many of the newcomers were holders of winning lottery draws, while others, eager for fresh lands on a virgin frontier, acquired tracts through purchase from the winners. For a period of time, brisk trading took place in frontier lands as prospective settlers sought the most desirable home sites.[2]

The lure of the promising Ocmulgee country reached far beyond the boundaries of Georgia. Away off in Virginia and the Carolinas, the opening of new territory to land-hungry Americans was greeted with excitement and hope. Stricken with "land fever," many Virginians and Carolinians decided to leave their old abodes and strike out for the beckoning Ocmulgee country.[3]

During the earliest days of immigration, there were no roads leading to the primitive domain, so it was necessary for first comers to proceed along narrow Indian trails. From constant usage and improvement, these busy avenues soon assumed the proportions of crude roadways over which immigrant carts and covered wagons were able to roll heavily along toward their destinations.

Since transportation presented such limitations, the early settlers were able to bring along only such articles of furniture, clothing, tools, and other supplies as were deemed necessary. These items were placed upon the backs of packhorses, or loaded into carts or covered wagons, to be conveyed laboriously along the rough pathways. Commodious houses were left behind, and most of their furnishings were disposed of, but occasionally, articles of a sentimental nature would be crammed into some available space. In this manner, a favorite book, a cherished dish, or a set of spoons handed down from an ancient ancestor, found its way to the frontier to brighten a simple log cabin devoid of many luxuries.

As the migratory stream swelled, the immigrants from Virginia, the Carolinas, and eastern Georgia converged upon the narrow lanes leading to Georgia's western frontier. Moving with a common purpose, the wayfarers traveled in caravans for protection against wild animals or savage Indians, and to provide companionship in the lonely, perilous venture.

Wending their tortuous way along the wilderness trails, the caravans would be halted for camp at the approach of darkness. The men would cut firewood and care for the livestock while the women prepared simple meals from dwindling supplies of food brought along, or wild game killed along the way, supplemented by wild fruits gathered from the forests. After the meal, the men sat around the campfires and talked about their dreams for a new life on the frontier; the women engaged in small talk, and the restless children played among the carts and wagons. During the night, many kept their senses alerted for any indication of danger from the enshrouding darkness. The silence was frequently broken by the eerie howls of wild animals echoing through the forests. As the flames of the campfires flickered low, many dreamed of familiar scenes left behind, but with the dawn of a new day, the pioneers turned their faces toward the beckoning land which lay ahead.

When the caravans drew near the Ocmulgee, they gradually diminished in size as each vehicle reached its destination, until the entire caravan finally dissipated itself within the vastness of the enveloping wilderness.

Upon reaching their long-sought goal, the pioneers set to work vigorously to prepare a permanent shelter against the rigorous elements. Trees were cut down, shaped into logs, and converted into a simple one-room cabin. The open spaces between the logs were chinked with clay, to keep out the bitter winter winds and the soaking rains. A huge fireplace, covering almost an entire end of the cabin, was designed to provide warmth and a means of cooking. The massive fireplace, tapering into a short chimney, was made in the form of a wooden frame with open spaces between the pieces of wood. These large cracks were chinked with clay to hold in the heat. Although the most primitive log cabins might have no floor except bare ground, many were floored with wide boards smoothed down by hand tools.

The furnishings of the early cabins were sparse and crudely made, with little provided but the barest necessities. Beds, tables, and chairs were essential articles found in the simplest of pioneer homes. A typical chair consisted of a frame made of tough hickory wood, with a seat fashioned from cowhide or deerskin. The dishes, bowls, and bread trays were frequently carved from available native woods.

The daily meals of the pioneers were cooked in the huge fireplace with the simplest of utensils. Meats were fried in thick iron skillets or spiders placed over glowing coals; vegetables were boiled in black iron pots suspended over the fire by means of pot hooks, or from metal cranes swinging from specially adapted frames; bread was baked in ovens resting in the fireplace and heated evenly on all sides by hot coals skilfully arranged by the housewife, or an occasional black slave.

To provide shelter for their milk cows, oxen, and horses, the pioneers erected small log barns with shelters extending outward and slanting slightly downward to provide for the run off of rains. The main part of the barn was used for the storage of corn, fodder, hay, and other foods needed by man and beast during the long winters when little else was available.

Dwelling upon an isolated frontier, far removed from a source of supplies, the pioneers were forced to clear land with all possible speed in order that their life-giving crops could be planted and gathered. Felling the huge trees which covered the land was a slow and laborious task. To expedite matters, the men girdled the trees with axes to cut off the flow of sap. The trees then died, leaving their skeletons standing ghost-like against the winter skies. In time, the trees would become weakened with decay, and with the blowing of seasonal winds, the giant trees would come crashing to earth. When weather permitted, the men rolled the logs into massive piles and burned them. In this manner new ground was gradually cleared and prepared for planting. While many trees were thus removed from the clearings, the stumps remained for years as silent reminders of the back-breaking struggles of the pioneers to carve a new life from the stubborn wilderness.

Faced with a common struggle for existence against the elements, the wilderness, and the dangers from wild animals or savage Indians, the early settlers often worked together in the performance of their most difficult tasks. When clearing new ground by the custom of log rolling, neighbors and kinsmen gathered to provide the necessary brawn in removing the heavy logs from the fields. The log rollings were occasions for social gatherings, with the women preparing lavish quantities of food in a festive atmosphere. Another utilitarian and social activity was the quilting party. On this traditional occasion, the women assembled at the home of a neighbor where quilting frames were arranged in the center of a room. The women then entered into the pleasurable occupation of sewing new quilts and engaged in the stimulating pursuit of small talk or gossip, thus relieving the monotony of everyday drudgery.

Corn shuckings provided another occasion for useful work combined with social activities. After the corn had been gathered in the fall, neighbors took turns in assembling at each other's houses to lend a hand in shucking the corn and making it ready for use. Corn shuckings were usually accompanied by entertaining dances, with the stirring tones of the fiddle piercing the stillness, accompanied by the rhythmic tramping of lively feet.

In their remoteness from a ready source of supplies, the early settlers were largely dependent upon their own efforts and resources in meeting their needs. Most of the implements used in tilling the soil, along with the necessities for everyday living, were made at home, or by a skilled neighbor, or a trained slave. The pioneers produced their own cotton and wool for clothing. The women employed the spinning wheel and the loom to fashion fabrics for the clothing worn by members of the family. Cowhides were tanned and converted into boots and shoes.

Much of the food for pioneer living came from the surrounding forests and streams. Wild game was abundant in the form of deer, turkeys, squirrels, and rabbits. The Ocmulgee teemed with fish, and when the shad were running, the whites and Indians gathered on their respective sides of the stream to lay in a liberal supply.

The products of the frontier clearings and forests were drifted down to Darien by rafts or pole boats. Necessary supplies, which could not be produced at home, were conveyed back upstream by pole boats and landed at convenient points for delivery.

In time, an overland system of communication with markets in eastern Georgia was developed through the use of ox carts or covered wagons. Gathering the products to be marketed, the men loaded them on their primitive vehicles; then, accompanied by neighbors driving similar vehicles, they formed small caravans bound for Darien, Savannah, or Augusta. The newly-carved roads were crude and rough, but little by little, the caravans crawled along amid the shouts of the drivers and the cracking of the bull whip. At the end of each day's journey, the caravans halted, and the men pitched camp for the night. Eventually, regular camp-sites became established along the routes from the frontier to the eastern market centers. After reaching their destination, the men bartered their produce for needed supplies and a bit of finery for the women and children back home. Then, back toward their familiar firesides the pioneer wayfarers went, to be greeted eagerly by waiting families.

A common source of income was derived from cattle raising. Along the waters of the Ocmulgee, wild grass and cane grew abundantly, providing a generous supply of food for livestock. Each cattle raiser marked his animals with his own distinctive brand, then turned them loose to range freely. Once a year, the cattle were rounded up by cow hunters and drivers who rode wildly over the range, locating the cattle, and driving them in, with cracking bull whips. The animals were herded into a common cowpen where each owner could pick out his own by means of the identifying brand. After the roundup, great herds were driven to market at Darien, Savannah, Augusta, or even as far away as Charleston.

To the people dwelling along the paths over which the cattle were driven, the event was an unforgettable experience. While the drove was yet far-off in the distance, great rumblings could be heard, drawing nearer and nearer. As the indefinable rumble approached, the sounds exploded into the thunder of hoof beats mingled with a continuous chorus of lowings interspersed with cracking whips and the whooping of the drovers.

Wild beasts presented a constant menace to the domestic animals raised by the early settlers. Wolves, wildly roving the countryside, were especially destructive. To eliminate the vicious beasts, the ingenious pioneers improvised wolf pits to snare the wolves. Large holes, eight to ten feet in diameter, and six to eight feet deep, were dug in the ground, with a slender pinnacle left standing in the center of the pit. Upon the pinnacle, a generous piece of fresh meat was placed. The pit was then loosely covered with brush and surrounded by a low fence. Drawn by the enticing odor of the meat, the ravenous wolves would seek the spot; then, leaping for the bait, they would fall into the bottom of the pit. Thus outwitted, the snarling beasts could be shot with ease by their captors. [4]

Vital to the early settlers was the grist mill. This useful facility was usually erected beside a stream affording sufficient water power to produce the rotating motion of the millstones needed to grind the corn into a fine meal much prized for food. The stream was frequently dammed up to create a pond, assuring a steady flow of water at all seasons. The grist mill was a favorite gathering place for the pioneer men. Collecting a supply of corn, they would set out on horseback or by ox cart for the neighborhood mill. Here, the men would find congenial companions and, while waiting for their corn to be ground, they would engage in lively discussions of daily happenings. The local grist mills frequently became the centers around which populous settlements arose.

Throughout the early years on the Ocmulgee, the pioneers lived in constant fear of the Indians who roamed the countryside. Occasionally, marauding parties invaded the frontier and molested the whites. The redskins' usual depredations were prowling, pilfering, and stealing livestock; but, if aroused from some sense of injury, they would go on the warpath and leave a trail of destruction behind them. When Indian troubles threatened their thinly-inhabited settlements, the whites erected stockades as places of refuge against possible attack. If an alarm was sounded that hostile redskins were approaching, horsemen were hastened from house to house, warning the occupants to flee to the safety of the stockade. Here, the refugees would remain forted in until the danger subsided.

An important phase of frontier life was centered around the military organization of the time. Being largely dependent upon her own resources for defense against hostile Indians or other potential enemies, Georgia maintained a civilian military force. The state militia was organized into divisions, brigades, regiments, battalions, and companies, with each unit commanded by appropriate officers. The counties were divided into militia districts, bearing identifying numbers. All able-bodied men between the ages of eighteen and forty-five were required to enroll for service. The eligible men in each district then formed a company commanded by a captain, a lieutenant, an ensign, and a designated number of noncommissioned officers. The officers were chosen by ballot on the part of the men enrolled in the company. [5]

Musters of the militia were required at regular intervals, and on the designated day, all eligible men were expected to rendezvous at the muster ground, dressed in uniform and fully equipped with firearms and other appurtenances. Muster days provided an element of excitement for participants and spectators, as relatives and neighbors assembled to view the impressive spectacle of their own men marching amid an aura of pomp and pride. In times of peace, the entire ceremony tended to be taken lightly, with even a touch of the farcical pervading the ranks and spreading to the gaping spectators; but when actual warfare found its way to the frontier, military affairs became deadly serious. While most activities of the local militia were routine, wars sometimes resulted in the calling of the Ocmulgee men to actual combat. In these early struggles, the pioneers faithfully performed their assigned duties — sometimes, with solemn results.

The early settlers in the Ocmulgee country were subject to the ailments common to the times and localities in which they lived. An illness vaguely diagonsed as "bilious fever" was oftentimes prevalent and fatal. Little or no professional medical aid was to be had, and such as was available was of dubious value. In cases of common complaints, home remedies — some learned from the Indians — were used. These usually consisted of herbs found in the woods, warm tallow applied to the chest for respiratory congestion, a few drops of turpentine on a spoonful of sugar for coughs, a poultice of corn meal mixed with hot water for pain or inflammation, and other simple remedies. When physicians were available, they were poorly trained and were prone to follow the traditional practice of "bleeding" the patient, a treatment which could prove fatal in otherwise curable conditions. The diseases of the wilderness frontier brought premature death to many children and adults, but numbers of hardy individuals were able to withstand the onslaughts of the elements, disease, and time, and lived to an advanced age.

A death was an occasion for deep mourning for the family of the deceased and a matter of widespread concern for neighbors. The bathed and freshly-dressed body was placed in a coffin, consisting of a simple wooden box fashioned by a neighbor who was handy with tools. During the period between death and burial, neighbors and kinsmen would bring the choicest cooked foods to the home of the bereaved family, and pay their respects by sitting up all night with the coffined remains. Throughout the long hours of the wake, an awesome silence hovered over the stricken abode, broken only by the sound of subdued conversation hushed by the solemn presence of death.

Churches were usually located at a considerable distance from the dwelling, so the early settlers frequently buried their dead in an appropriate place near the familiar scenes of their own homes, a custom which led to the appearance of many family burying grounds on sites overlooking the waters of the Ocmulgee. When churches were situated at convenient places, some of the pioneers were buried in the churchyard ground. Whether held in a church building or at the home of the departed, the funeral was a solemn occasion, consisting of an appropriate sermon by a pioneer preacher, accompanied by the melancholy tones of sadly-consoling music rising softly above the muffled sound of weeping.

The manner of marking the graves of the early settlers varied with the locality. Tombstones were rare on the frontier since it was necessary that they be shipped from distant places by pole boats or wobbly carts or wagons. In the absence of elaborate marble or granite monuments, the people used such materials as were at hand. On the upper waters of the Ocmulgee where rock was common, a new grave was easily marked with two rocks — one at the head, and the other at the foot. On the lower waters of the river where rock was rare, grave markers were carved out of heart-pine wood. A large headboard was placed upright at the west end of the grave to mark the head of the interred one, and a smaller marker was set at the east to identify the foot. These old pine markers were extremely durable and, weathering to a mellow gray shade, marked the last resting place of many pioneers long after their identity was forgotten.

CHAPTER IX

PIONEER PATHWAYS

The first white settlers to come to the Ocmulgee territory had two possible ways of reaching their destination. A few near-by residents could push along the waters of the river itself by means of pole-propelled rafts or flatboats, while immigrants from more distant places found it necessary to follow well-defined Indian trails leading overland from the settled parts of the east to the river frontier.

Although Indian trails were numerous, they were too narrow to provide amply for the passage of the many ox carts and covered wagons which wended their way to the new land, bearing the possessions of the pioneers. To provide full access to the Ocmulgee country, it was necessary to carve out broader avenues leading through the wilderness from the eastern settlements. At first, this consisted of clearing and widening the old Indian trails, but in time it became necessary to lay out entirely new roadways where no paths had previously existed.

During the formative years of the Ocmulgee counties, the construction and maintenance of roads came within the jurisdiction of the Inferior Court in each county. The court appointed commissions consisting of three responsible residents, to view the ground in order to determine the feasibility of cutting new roads, and to ascertain the nearest and best way for the roads to follow. After the commissioners decided upon the proposed roadways, the court appointed overseers to supervise the clearing and constructing operations. All able-bodied men between the ages of eighteen and forty-five residing within three miles of the proposed route were then called to perform the task of carving the desired pathway from the wilderness.

Among the first pioneer roadways to be established along the Ocmulgee was the River Road. [1] This avenue was gradually developed by widening the primitive Indian trail following the east bank of the stream from its headwaters down to the seacoast. The need for such a thoroughfare arose from the fact that the earliest settlers established their homes near the river, and a river road provided a means of connecting their clearings and settlements. The need was increased by threatening Indian troubles which could prove disastrous in the absence of an open avenue of communication.

Before many years had passed, the River Road lay as a narrow ribbon winding through the wilderness from Fort Hawkins, down the left bank of the Ocmulgee and Altamaha rivers, to Darien on the Atlantic Coast.[2] In its downward course along the Ocmulgee, the pioneer way extended the entire length of the Ocmulgee counties of Twiggs, Pulaski, Telfair, and part of Montgomery.

In Twiggs County the River Road led southward from Fort Hawkins, and clung to the high ground bordering the east bank of the river.[3] The road passed such noted landmarks as an Indian trading post at Durham's Bluff, and the large frontier establishment of Richard Smith at Buzzard's Roost Bluff in the lower part of the county.[4]

Entering Pulaski County from the lower Twiggs line, the River Road skirted the east bank of the Ocmulgee, crossed Shellstone Creek, and led on to Beaverdam Creek.[5] Along the route from the Twiggs County line to Beaverdam, the earliest settlers were Laban Kent, William Burnham, Chesley Davis, John Dees, Shadrack Atkinson, Joab Horne, William Isler, Ezekiel Taylor, Gideon Kellam, Simon Barden, William DeShazo, and Robert DeShazo.[6]

After crossing Beaverdam Creek near the site of Mount Horeb Church, the River Road proceeded on southward to Jordan's Creek. Living within this area were James Roach, Lewis Holland, Joel Dawson, Robert Montfort, Barnabas Hart, Sanders Colson, Daniel Cole, Allen Tooke, James T. Thomas, Dixon Jelks, William Jelks, Archibald Lassiter, Elisha Higgs, Orandates Watson, Turner Everett, Needham Stephens, John Isler, Stephen Gatlin, Furney Gatlin, Henry Senterfeit, Thomas Howell, Josiah Everett, Hinchey Warren, John B. Packer, and Jesse Powell.[7]

From Jordan's Creek, the River Road led directly to the frontier settlement of Hartford on the Ocmulgee River. Within this short stretch the early settlers were Samuel Jones, John Snelling, Robert Dewert, and Bartholomew Longino.[8]

The portion of the River Road extending from the Twiggs County line down to Hartford was generally known as the Upper River Road, and the section leading from Hartford down to the Telfair County line was called the Lower River Road.[9]

Now, issuing from the town of Hartford, the Lower River Road meandered southward to Limestone Creek, passing closely by the pioneer homes of Neil McAlpin, Charles Daniel, William S. Lancaster, and William Hilliard.[10]

From its fording place on Limestone Creek, the river thoroughfare made its way to the main run of Mosquito Creek. Dwelling within this section were William Taylor, Labon Watson, John Lester, Sands Stanley, Hardy Vickers, Thomas Baggett, Nicholas Baggett, Barton Baggett, John Baggett, Benjamin Smith, William Goodson, William Hall, and Colson Adams. [11] In the neighborhood of Mosquito Creek, the River Road crossed Baggett's Creek, a stream named for the pioneer Baggett family living near-by. [12]

After passing Mosquito Creek, the frontier roadway led directly to the Telfair County line, skirting the dwellings of such early settlers as Sutton Truluck, Benjamin Brown, Elisha Evans, John Sylvester, Lawrence Folsom, Stephen Mitchell, Sr., John Daniel, and John Willcox. [13]

Striking the Telfair County line near the site of Old Daniels Church, the thoroughfare led on toward the Copeland settlement. [14] Along this lower part of its course the River Road formed a narrow lane winding among giant oak trees with moss-draped branches forming a canopy over the passageway. Along the picturesque avenue meandering through the Copeland settlement stood the houses of William Cawthon, Josiah D. Cawthon, Philip Brown, Drury Reaves, David Sutton, Jesse Mixon, Moses Rountree, William Rountree, William Henley, Nehemiah Posey, William Posey, Jesse Butler, Murdock McDuffie, Abb. L. Hatten, James Graham, Caswell Ball, and Jehu Everett. [15]

Proceeding from the Copeland settlement, the tree-lined roadway led on down through the Temperance settlement. Along this rolling way dwelt the pioneer settlers, David McCall, Jehu McCall, John McAnnally, William Fletcher, Sr., John Fletcher, Griffin Mizell, William Griffin, Benjamin Mitchell Griffin, Norman McLeod, William Studstill, Daniel McDaniel, Edward Burke, Archibald McInnis, Alexander Carswell, David Callaway, Charles Burch, and David Hunter. [16]

From the Temperance settlement, the River Road curved eastward along the Big Bend of the Ocmulgee to the site of Blockhouse Church, and on to Jacksonville two miles beyond. The pioneers dwelling along this stretch were Charles McKinnon, Thomas Fain, Matthew Fain, James Parramore, Noah Parramore, John Parramore, Robert H. Dixon, James Wallace, Gibson Clarke, Samuel Lampkin, and Thomas S. Swain. [17]

Issuing from the county seat of Jacksonville, the narrow ribbon unfolded along the Ocmulgee to the run of the Little Ocmulgee, covering a section inhabited by William Harris, Mark Pridgen, Thomas Watts, William Ashley, James Rouse, Jesse Byrd, Abraham Powell, Thomas Fullwood, William Hatten, Lawrence Manning, and John Coffee. [18]

After crossing the Little Ocmulgee, the River Road proceeded in an easterly direction to the Oconee River, striking the stream at the site of Bell's Ferry a mile above the juncture of the Oconee with the Ocmulgee to form the Altamaha. [19] Living between the Little Ocmulgee and the Oconee were Thomas Mitchell, Batt Wyche, Benjamin G. Cray, Simon Whitehurst, Jacob Clements, and Lewis Griffin. [20]

Crossing the Oconee at Bell's Ferry, the River Road continued down the left bank of the Altamaha to the road's end at Darien on the seacoast. [21]

While the River Road was being opened to connect the clearings and settlements arising along the Ocmulgee, other avenues were being developed to connect the Ocmulgee frontier with the eastern settlements of Augusta and Savannah on the Savannah River, and the newly-established state capital of Milledgeville on the Oconee River. The routes of the east-west thoroughfares were determined by the location of good crossing places on the Oconee River which lay as a watery barrier between the east and the west. Crossing places on the formidable Oconee were provided by shallow, sandy fords, rocky shoals, and by bluffs confining the waters within narrow limits to make ferriage possible. The Indian trails had converged upon such places of passage, thereby setting a pattern which the white pioneers' roadways generally followed. Such crossing places were to be found at Rock Landing just below today's Milledgeville; at Carr's Shoals six miles above the site of Dublin; at the sand bar where Dublin now stands; and at a point just above the juncture of the Oconee with the Ocmulgee where Bell's Ferry was established.

The earliest known east-west roadway to reach the Ocmulgee was the Garrison Road. Upon completion of the Treaty of Washington in 1806, the United States erected Fort Hawkins at the Ocmulgee Old Fields on Georgia's outer frontier. With the boundary between the State of Georgia and the Creek Nation thus pushed westward from the Oconee to the Ocmulgee, the garrison at old Fort Wilkinson on the Oconee was moved to newly-built Fort Hawkins. In order to provide an avenue for moving troops and supplies to the outpost, a road was cut from the old Oconee base to Fort Hawkins. Packed hard by the feet of marching soldiers, the military path came to be known as the Garrison Road. [22]

Another early thoroughfare of military value to the Ocmulgee country was the road connecting Milledgeville and Hartford. With the Georgia frontier now resting upon the Ocmulgee River, it was imperative that close communications be maintained between the frontier and the state capital at Milledgeville. Ever uneasy about the Indians beyond the dividing stream, the inhabitants of Pulaski County sought an early avenue of protection by opening a road leading from Hartford toward Milledgeville. By 1810 this vital lifeline had been cleared as far up as the Twiggs County line. In an effort to forge the connecting link, the General Assembly, on December 15, 1810, passed an act authorizing certain commissioners to complete the Milledgeville Road. [23]

The designated route led southwestward from the capital city to Durham's Ford on Big Sandy Creek; from thence to Pasmore's on the old Upper Uchee Path; from thence to intersect the Hartford Road at the Twiggs County line. [24]

From the Twiggs-Pulaski boundary, the Milledgeville Road proceeded generally southward through the section later known as Longstreet, and crossed Evergreen Creek where Evergreen Church now stands. From this place, the thoroughfare turned slightly southwestward and continued on across the upper run of Jordan's Creek. A few miles below the Jordan's Creek crossing, the Milledgeville Road merged with the Uchee Road, and proceeded directly to its destination at Hartford. [25] By 1812 the new highway had reached a position of such importance that it was designated as a post road.

The pioneers who settled along the path of the Milledgeville Road leading from the Twiggs County line down to Hartford were Gideon Mayo, Charles Mayo, Bolen Swearingen, William H. Gross, Thomas McGriff, Christopher Rhodes, Jacob Snell, George Walker, Ezekiel Taylor, Jesse Powell, Henry Fulghum, Jacob Snelling, John Bennett, John Bradshaw, John Grinsted, and George G. Gaines. [26]

An early roadway fitting into the pattern established by Indian trails was the Uchee Road. Gaining its name from the Lower Uchee Path, the road followed closely the route of the Indian trail leading from Hartford on the Ocmulgee to Carr's Shoals on the Oconee. Leaving the Ocmulgee at the Uchee Shoals, the roadway led in a northeasterly direction through today's Cochran, skirted Trail Branch Church, and crossed into Laurens County on Lot 170 in the Twenty-second District. From the county line, the Uchee Road continued on through Laurens, crossed Turkey Creek, and reached Carr's Shoals on the Oconee six miles above Dublin. [27]

Pulaski County officials took steps as early as 1811 to develop the Uchee Road from the well-trodden Indian trail. In the course of the next few years, the pioneer way was completed through the efforts of the citizens dwelling along its route. These early road builders were James Jones, Asa Pipkin, Murdock McLeod, Ebenezer Ellis, William Bracken, Drury May, Daniel Dykes, William Little, Benjamin Harrison, Lewis Holland, Kinchen Dawson, and Robert Thompson. [28]

A pioneer pathway connecting Hartford with Dublin bore the unusual name of the Chicken Road. Following a route south of, but generally parallel to the Uchee Road, the Chicken Road led out of Hartford in an easterly direction toward the Empire settlement. From this place, the pathway continued generally along the line dividing present-day Dodge and Bleckley counties. Leaving the northeast corner of Dodge County, the Chicken Road passed through the Buckhorn settlement in Laurens County, then proceeded directly to Dublin on the Oconee River. [29]

While the Chicken Road was probably derived from an old Indian trail, its origin as a white man's way apparently dates from the year 1816 when the Pulaski Inferior Court appointed commissioners to view the ground for a proposed route from Hartford to Dublin. The commissioners appointed for the project were John Stewart, Daniel Dykes, John McGriff, Zion Davis, and Daniel McLenan. [30]

The unfolding Ocmulgee frontier was in need of direct lines of communication with Savannah, Georgia's oldest settlement and a vital trade center for the river inhabitants. At least two lanes connecting the Ocmulgee with the coastal city were established during the early frontier years. One such avenue followed the River Road down the left bank of the Ocmulgee and crossed the Oconee at Bell's Ferry. Just beyond the Bell's Ferry crossing, the Savannah Road veered away from the River Road to the left, and proceeded directly eastward along an established roadway to Savannah. [31]

An early thoroughfare leading from Hartford to Savannah by the way of Berryhill Bluff on the Oconee was created in 1811. Issuing from Hartford, the pathway led southeastward across the headwaters of Sugar Creek just above modern Eastman. Crossing Gum Swamp Creek at the site of Parkerson's Church, the road continued generally eastward to the Oconee River, striking the stream at Berryhill Bluff.[32] From the Oconee crossing, the highway proceeded eastward to its terminus at the coastal metropolis of Savannah.

Within a few years after the opening of the Ocmulgee territory to eager white settlers, an extensive system of roadways spread far out across the new world. During the first wave of immigration, the paths were designed to provide the means by which newcomers could make the journey from their old eastern abodes to the promising new land. Then, as the clearings and settlements developed, the roads were used as lanes of communication from place to place within the Ocmulgee country itself. After the pioneers had become firmly established on the frontier, the roadways served as avenues of trade with the old commercial centers of Augusta, Savannah, Darien, and Trader's Hill.

CHAPTER X

CHRISTIANITY BROUGHT TO THE OCMULGEE

The white pioneers who settled the new country along the Ocmulgee brought with them their traditional religious order. Being mostly of English, Welsh, and Scottish extraction, these venturesome pioneers were grounded in the Christian faith. With a vigorous record of independent religious observance behind them, they manifested their beliefs through the nonconformist movements.

During the reign of King Henry VIII, the English Church had separated itself from the dominant Roman Catholic Church, thereby becoming the Anglican, or officially recognized and supported Church of England. Even after the break with the Roman Church, zealous groups arose in England who believed that the Anglican Church had departed from the teachings of early Christianity, and replaced a fervent spirit with cold formality. Boldly taking their stand against the domination of the Church of England, these zealots became known as Nonconformists, Dissenters, or Separatists. In asserting their convictions, the Dissenters incurred the wrath of the Church of England, and became the objects of severe persecution. This harassment was a strong factor leading many Dissenters to leave the British Isles to seek religious freedom in the American colonies. Among these seekers were the Baptists of England and Wales, and the Presbyterians of Scotland and Northern Ireland.

During the Colonial Period in America, large numbers of Baptists and Presbyterians immigrated to Virginia, the Carolinas, and Georgia. But, since these Royal Colonies were dominated by the Established Church of England, the Dissenters again encountered harassments reminiscent of those from which they had sought escape. During the Revolutionary War Period, however, in the wave of independence which swept the new world, the Church of England declined in power while the nonconformist groups grew in numbers and in prestige. Many Anglicans were won over to the Baptist and Presbyterian churches through the efforts of the indomitable Dissenters. Then, coinciding with this native surge of religious fervor, the new Methodist movement spread from England to the frontiers of America where it became a dynamic force in shaping the rising pattern of American civilization. It was mostly from these zealous religious elements that the early settlers emerged who populated the new world of the Ocmulgee.

The Presbyterian influence manifested itself very early along the Ocmulgee. During the late 1700's, large numbers of Highland Scots immigrated from their native mountains to the eastern part of North Carolina. Being avid livestock raisers, many of the Scots were attracted to the vast wiregrass section of Georgia where they settled in Old Montgomery County. As staunch Presbyterians the Highlanders brought with them their own kirks and Gaelic-speaking ministers, so that they established a bit of old Scotland in the gently-rolling wiregrass country contrasting so sharply with the craggy mountains from whence they had come. [1]

When the new territory along the Ocmulgee was opened for white settlers, clans of transplanted Scots moved in, bringing with them their old religious faith. [2] The Scots coming from Montgomery County were augmented by others still immigrating from Scotland by the way of North Carolina. Although the Highland spirit lingered long among the clannish Scots, their Presbyterian order was largely absorbed by the large numbers of Baptists and Methodists surging into the new land. [3]

The most numerous early churches to arise along the Ocmulgee were of the Baptist persuasion. Coming from the older settlements where their religious order was especially strong, the Baptists brought with them the influence of the parent churches left behind. Among the venerable churches casting their seed across the Ocmulgee soil were Welsh Neck and Cashua on the PeeDee River in South Carolina, Little Brier Creek in Warren County, and Powelton in Hancock County.

Upon reaching the Ocmulgee, the early settlers lost little time in planting their own order of worship upon the soil so recently occupied by the red people. At first, simple worship services were held in the homes of the adherents of the faith, or under brush arbors set up at convenient places. These arrangements, though, were only temporary, and soon rustic log meetinghouses began to arise along the entire course of the Ocmulgee.

Although Baptist congregations were independent bodies within themselves, the churches, having a common faith and heritage, sought to maintain close ties of fellowship with each other through the formation of loose unions known as Associations. Most of the early Ocmulgee churches united with the Hephzibah Association, whose membership was made up of the

old established institutions back in the eastern part of Georgia. [4]
Very soon, however, the need for an Association closer by became apparent. The annual meetings of the Association were
rotated in such a manner that each member church eventually
served as host. But the Ocmulgee meetinghouses were on the
outer fringes of the Hephzibah Association and, with severe
limitations to travel, they encountered difficulty in maintaining
close relations with their distant sister churches. In response to
the need for a union to serve the frontier churches, the Ebenezer
Association was founded in 1814 at Cool Springs in Wilkinson
County. Most of the churches forming the new Association were
located within the recently-settled forks of the Oconee and Ocmulgee rivers. [5]

Early Baptist meetinghouses were usually located near creeks
or other sizable bodies of water affording facilities for the traditional mode of baptism by immersion. For this reason, the pioneer
churches oftentimes bore the names of the streams upon which
they were erected.

One of the first churches established along the Ocmulgee
River was Stone Creek Baptist Church. This old institution was
constituted on Setpember 3, 1808, and the first building was
erected upon a hill overlooking Stone Creek in Twiggs County,
not far from Fort Hawkins. [6] An early minister of the pioneer
church was Vincent Allen Tharpe who migrated from Warren
County to the Ocmulgee where he and his descendents played
an important part in the subsequent history of Stone Creek Church
and the surrounding territory. [7]

Among the earliest of the Christian shrines to arise above
the waters of the Ocmulgec was Mount Horeb Baptist Church.
This venerable institution was constituted on October 15, 1809,
by a group of early settlers dwelling in the upper part of Old
Pulaski, but present Bleckley County. [8]

Upon their arrival in the new land along the Ocmulgee with
the misty realm of the red people rising from the opposite bank,
these zealous Baptists were eager to form a church of their own
faith. Coming from differing backgrounds, but with a common
religious heritage, the newcomers convened and consulted together, and became constituted into the Baptist Church of Christ
at Mount Horeb. The founding Presbytery was composed of two
pioneer ministers, Levi Bush and Joseph Cutts. Leading in the
formation of the church were Chesley Davis and wife Lydia,
Mark Mason and wife Sara, Drury Dees and wife Sarah, William
Burnham, and possibly others. [9] At Mount Horeb's first official
conference, two items of importance were approved: Chesley

Davis was chosen as the first deacon, and Mark Mason was elected church clerk. [10] These men selected to guide the course of an infant church born upon a new frontier may be considered representative leaders of the early Christian order arising along the Ocmulgee.

Chesley Davis, the son of Absalom and Anne (Hackney) Davis, was born in Albemarle Parish, Sussex County, Virginia, where he was christened in the parish church on January 17, 1755. [11] Early in life Chesley moved with his father's family to Granville County, North Carolina, where his grandfather, Richard Davis, had preceded them. [12]

In 1778 the Absalom Davis family migrated to Abbeville District, South Carolina, where Absalom and sons, Chesley, Gidion, Lewis, and Wiley served the Patriot cause in the Revolutionary War. [13] Chesley alone participated in twenty-seven battles during the long conflict. [14] In the Battle of Cowpens, Chesley Davis served under his brother-in-law, Major (later Colonel) John Cunningham, who was in command of Elijah Clarke's Georgia and South Carolina troops. During the heat of the battle, Chesley narrowly escaped death from a deep sabre cut across the shoulders inflicted by a British horseman. But the Revolutionary Soldier survived his wounds and lived to fight again in the later conflict with the Cherokee Indians. [15] In the waning years of the Revolutionary War, the Davis family moved across the Savannah River and settled on Beaverdam Creek in Old Wilkes, but present Elbert County, Georgia. [16]

After the war was over, Chesley Davis received a bounty land grant for his services and migrated to Washington County where he settled in the portion of the county which, in 1793, was formed into Montgomery County. [17] At the turn of the century, he was serving as a Justice of the Peace in Montgomery County. [18]

In 1809 Chesley Davis moved his family to newly-created Pulaski County where he settled in the Twenty-fourth Land District on Lot 302 which his father, Absalom Davis, Sr., had drawn in the Land Lottery of 1807. [19] The new Davis abode stood upon an eminence overlooking the Ocmulgee River and the Creek Nation on one side, and Shellstone Creek on the other. Taking an active part in the founding of Mount Horeb Church, the battle-scarred veteran spent the remaining years of his life advancing the Christian cause on the Ocmulgee frontier. A son, Captain James Gouldwire Davis, early in life exchanged the sword for the cross, became a Baptist minister, and served the church of his father as its pastor. [20]

Mark Mason was a North Carolinian who migrated to Georgia and settled in Jefferson County. [21] Upon the opening of the lands on the Ocmulgee for settlement, Mason moved his family to Pulaski County and established his home on the River Road at Shellstone Creek just below the dwelling of Chesley Davis. [22] Mark Mason took an active part in the creation of Mount Horeb Church and served as clerk of the church from the time of its origin until his death in 1815. [23]

Mount Horeb grew rapidly in numbers and in strength. Within three years, the following newcomers had united with the church: Lucretia Brown, Benjamin Harrison, Elizabeth Harrison, James Bush, Sarah Lee, Fatha Dykes, Abigail Dykes, Susannah Dykes, Needham Bryant, Jemima Bryant, Mary Dykes, Joshua Lee, Jesse Lee, Simon Barden and wife Celie, Elizabeth Dickson, Solomon Brewer, Elijah Cathledge, Jemima Ford, Winifred Davidson, Ezekiel Waldrop, Jemima Loveless, William Loveless, Isaac Burkhalter, Sarah Burkhalter, Mary Warren, Samuel Hart, Barnabas Hart, Richard H. Davis, Ezekiel Taylor, Keziah Hart, Barbara Senterfeit, and _____ Howell. [24]

Upon its creation, Mount Horeb united with the Hephzibah Association, but in 1814 the church became one of the original founders of the Ebenezer Association. [25] At this time, Ezekiel Taylor, a newcomer to Mount Horeb from Washington County, was elected clerk of the Association, a position which he faithfully filled for the remaining years of his life. [26] The earliest representatives from Mount Horeb to the meetings of the Associations were Mark Mason, Simon Barden, James Roach, Ezekiel Taylor, and Isaac Burkhalter. [27]

Mount Horeb had no permanent house of worship for its first two years, but on November 16, 1811, a committee was appointed to superintend the construction of a meetinghouse for the use of the church. Serving on this building committee were Simon Barden, Henry Fulghum, George G. Gaines, James Roach, and Mark Mason. [28] The committee proceeded to select a site upon a bit of land deeded by John Isler to "the Church of Christ at Mount Horeb" on July 24, 1812. The site covered over an acre, situated in the northeast corner of Lot 331 in the Twenty-fourth Land District, adjoining Holland's and Roach's corner. [29] At this chosen place, a simple meetinghouse was erected upon an eminence rising above the south bank of Beaverdam Creek, overlooking the Ocmulgee River and the blue haze of the Creek Nation beyond.

Although no description of this early structure has been found, assuredly it followed the pattern of other frontier meetinghouses of the period. In this case, it was constructed of durable logs, with shuttered openings for windows. The furnishings were of the simplest nature, consisting of a rustic pulpit at one end of the sanctuary, facing two rows of seats—one for men, and one for women. The building faced west toward the Upper River Road, and had separate doors for men and women, as was the custom of the times. The pews were plain benches made of split logs, with the tops smoothed by hand tools, and held in an upright position by wooden legs driven into holes bored in the bottoms of the benches.

Negro slaves were admitted to membership in Mount Horeb along with their masters, so a section reserved for them would have been in keeping with custom. [30]

Mount Horeb's membership was distributed over a wide area, making it necessary for many to come long distances to the worship services and conferences. The usual means of transportation was by horseback, ox carts, wagons, and carriages. With the ever-present fear of Indians lurking along the way, the men went to church armed against surprise attack, in accordance with a long custom among the inhabitants of Georgia's frontiers.

An infant church springing from Mount Horeb was Trail Branch Baptist Church. As Mount Horeb gradually expanded, with the coming of new settlers, its membership extended well over the upper part of Pulaski County from the Ocmulgee eastward to the Laurens County line. The members dwelling in the eastern part of the county were compelled to travel as far as twenty miles through hazardous conditions to reach the meeting house. Since this group comprised a large portion of the membership, they soon started a movement to establish a place of worship nearer their own houses.

On February 23, 1811, Benjamin Harrison presented a petition on the part of himself and sundry members on Gum Swamp Creek for dismission from Mount Horeb to constitute a new church at Trail Branch, in the northeastern corner of Pulaski County. The petition was laid over, but at the next conference it was granted. The members named in the petition were Benjamin Harrison, Elizabeth Harrison, Joshua Lee, Jesse Lee, Sarah Lee, Solomon Brewer, James Bush, Fatha Dykes, and Susannah Dykes. Along with these were Will, Betty, and Barbara, persons of color. [31]

The newborn church encountered some difficulty in getting established, and on July 18, 1812, the mother church received a petition from the Church at Trail Branch requesting assistance in "a matter of difficulty," whereupon Simon Barden, Mark Mason, Drury Dees, Chesley Davis, and Samuel Hart were appointed as a committee "to attend them." [32] Evidently the difficulty was resolved, and two years later Trail Branch united with the Ebenezer Association as a growing church. Needham Bryant and Benjamin Harrison represented Trail Branch at its initial session with the Association. Other delegates to the Association during the formative years of the church were Henry Dykes, William Hawthorne, Ralph Kirkland, William Bryant, William Norwood, Phillip Dillard, William Loveless, and James Allen. [33]

Some distance down Gum Swamp Creek, on a neighboring stream known as Sugar Creek, was established an early Baptist Church which took its name from the stream upon which it was located. Sugar Creek Baptist Church was constituted about 1810 and united shortly thereafter with the Hephzibah Association. [34] The church withdrew from the Hephzibah Association in 1814 to join in the formation of the Ebenezer Association. [35] Representing Sugar Creek at this organizing session were Zion Davis and Hardy Vickers. Delegates to other early meetings of the Associations were John Kelly, Ozias Davis, Colson Adams, William Kinchen, and Ethelredge Harrell. [36]

A frontier church which rose to a position of considerable prestige was Richland Creek Baptist Church, located on Richland Creek in Twiggs County. This early place of worship was constituted in 1811, with these original members: John Denson, Jacob Ricks, Edward Nix, William Coates, Sarah Denson, Susannah Ricks, Elizabeth Lipham, Elizabeth Truluck, Sally Parrott, Anna Hammock, Sarah Glenn, Nancy Powell, and Chloe Hodges, a woman of color. [37]

Upon its creation, Richland Creek was admitted to the Ocmulgee Association, but shortly afterward, joined its neighboring churches in forming the Ebenezer Association. Representing Richland Creek at its first meeting with the Ocmulgee Association were John Denson and Jacob Ricks. Early delegates to the new Ebenezer Association were Micajah Fulghum, John Pitman, John Asbell, and Edward Hart. [38]

Richland Creek Church soon became the religious center for a large number of prominent planters dwelling in the vicinity of Marion, the thriving county seat of Twiggs County. Through the support afforded by its prosperous members, the church progressed from the original log meetinghouse to an impressive building featuring the classic lines of Greek Revival Architecture. Now was presented the unique situation whereby a body of Anglo-American Christians occupied an impressive edifice fashioned after a Greek temple, standing upon ground impregnated with reminders of its recent habitation by the ancient Creek Indians. Thus did the Ocmulgee domain provide the crossroads for old, and new, and varied ways of life.

A frontier church born of the Indian troubles haunting the early settlers, was Ocmulgee Baptist Church. At the height of the Indian conflicts along the frontier, a fort was erected on the River Road, two miles above the site of Jacksonville in Telfair County. The outpost consisted of a picket stockade, reinforced by two blockhouses situated in opposite corners of the stockade. In times of Indian alarms, the exposed inhabitants took shelter within the protecting walls of the modest stronghold. Drawn into close fellowship in the face of common danger, the refugees began holding worship services in one of the blockhouses. 39

This group of devout refugees formed a cluster around which, in 1814, was formed the Ocmulgee Baptist Church. During the year of its birth, despite the dangers of travel along uncertain pathways, the newborn church sent two delegates to the first session of the Ebenezer Association held at Mount Moriah Meetinghouse in Twiggs County. 40 The representatives for this occasion were two neighboring residents, Thomas Fain and William Harris. Members of the Ocmulgee Baptist Church who attended other early meetings of the Association were John Marshall, David Callaway, Charles Burch, Solomon Sikes, and Drury Reaves. 41

Old Ocmulgee Baptist Church was short-lived and soon faded away, but, eventually, upon the site of the old fort would arise another Christian shrine which would appropriately be known as Blockhouse Baptist Church.

Hopewell Baptist Church was created in 1829 to serve the people residing in the upper part of Telfair County. 42 The meetinghouse was located on the east side of the River Road in a grove of moss-draped oak trees. Some of the members of Hopewell came from the old Ocmulgee Church, and the creation of the new church probably contributed to the decline of the old.

Hopewell was admitted to the Ebenezer Association during the first year of the church's existence, with Frederick Brown and James Stephens serving as delegates. 43 Hopewell's representatives to other early sessions of the Association were David Ryals, John Davis, James Williamson, John Polm, Drury Reaves, Enoch Bowen, Berry Hobbs, Archibald Ball, Edward B. Mixon, Michael Conley, Ashley Cawthon, and John Reaves. 44 Due to the loss of the early records, it is impossible to determine all of the earliest members of Hopewell, but according to a local authority, other pioneer members were William Henley and wife Millie, Abner Burnham, and William Ryals, a Revolutionary Soldier. [45] A likely member was Philip Brown, a very early settler and the father of Frederick Brown, an original delegate from Hopewell to the Ebenezer Association.

According to the same authority, Hopewell was constituted by Wilson Conner, a well-known frontier missionary. One of the earliest ministers to serve the church was Drury Reaves, a pioneer settler in the Hopewell settlement. [46]

Next to the Baptists, the Methodists were most numerous along the Ocmulgee.

Georgia's association with the movement which grew into the Methodist Church was unique. In 1735, John and Charles Wesley, two ministers in the Church of England, came to the infant colony of Georgia to minister to the colonists and to convert the Indians to the Christian faith. John Wesley settled in Savannah, and Charles went with Oglethorpe to Frederica on St. Simon's Island. Both ministers were young and inexperienced in the ways of raw, new colonies. Encountering many difficulties in their mission, the men remained in Georgia but a short time, then returned to England, thoroughly disenchanted with the new world.

In spite of the brevity of John Wesley's stay in Georgia, the experience he gained from the venture left such a profound impression upon him that his Georgia mission may be called the seed from which the Methodist movement grew. On the voyage from England to Georgia, Wesley encountered violent storms at sea, which left him with the awesome realization that his own spiritual state was one of uncertainty and fear.

On board the ship was a band of devout Moravians who remained reverently composed during the most tempestuous periods of the storms. Through the insight gained from the Moravians, Wesley was led to go in search of a satisfying spiritual experience, a search which was to continue for an agonizing period of time. Finally, at Aldersgate in London, John Wesley gained the heart-warming inward assurance which he had so earnestly sought. Then, fired with the zeal of his own spiritual awakening, Wesley embarked upon a vigorous crusade to lead others into a similar experience. Wesley's religious movement spread over England with vigor, and from it the Methodist Church emerged.

The fervor of the Methodist movement reached the shores of America about 1766 and gradually spread to the shifting frontiers of the country. Shortly after the Revolutionary War, the infant Methodist crusade reached Georgia where it was carefully nurtured through the tireless efforts of the horseback-riding Bishop Francis Asbury.

In Wilkes County at this time lived Daniel Grant, a pioneer who had migrated to Georgia from Hanover County, Virginia, by the way of Granville County, North Carolina. Out of the abundance of the new land, Daniel Grant and a son, Thomas, amassed a considerable amount of wealth. The Grants generously devoted much of their means to philanthropic causes. Being early converts to Methodism, the devout laymen erected the first Methodist Church building to stand upon Georgia soil. This glimmering spiritual lighthouse was known as Grant's Meeting-house. [47]

As the changing Georgia boundaries moved ever westward, Methodist converts followed the migrant trails into the opening frontiers, and the impact of their faith was felt in the rising settlements. In the course of time, the Methodist movement was brought to the Ocmulgee by newcomers who had embraced the faith. The struggles of these early Methodists to establish societies of their order were supported by traveling ministers known as circuit riders. The first meetings were held at the homes of the adherents of the faith. Then came the erection of brush arbors where worshippers could be accommodated in an outdoor setting. From brush arbors, the Methodists progressed to the establishment of camp grounds and permanent stations.

The Methodist camp meeting was a singular frontier institution reflecting the conditions from which it emerged. The early Methodist Societies were too small and scattered to maintain full-time ministers for all congregations. Instead, they were served by mounted circuit riders who made the rounds of their isolated charges to provide the services of the church as often as possible. But, scarce in numbers and hampered by severe weather, swollen streams, sickness, and other hardships, the circuit riders were unable to make more than occasional visits to local societies. To meet the need for more abundant worship services and social fellowship, the isolated Methodists established at convenient places their own camp grounds.

The central feature of the camp ground was a large wooden structure covered by a massive roof but with the sides left open to admit cooling breezes in the hottest of seasons. Around the main structure or tabernacle was a cluster of tents or small cabins which provided temporary housekeeping facilities. Late every summer after crops had been "laid by" until harvest time, the inhabitants would come from varied points to assemble, to camp, and to hold "protracted meetings," or religious services continuing over a lengthy period of time. Outstanding Methodist ministers would come from distant places to preach to the assembled congregations. The preachers were fervent in their appeals and gained many converts among their listeners. The annual camp meeting was an event eagerly awaited by the people, and its influence in shaping the pattern of American civilization was inestimable. In the course of time, many camp grounds grew into permanent church stations served by circuit riders or full-time ministers of the Methodist order.

CHAPTER XI

DRIFTING DOWN TO DARIEN

The winding Ocmulgee River served the early white settlers as a vital artery of communication and transportation. At first, there were no roads connecting the river frontier with the settled regions to the east. Then, such roads as were gradually carved from the wilderness were crude and difficult to travel by creeping ox cart or lumbering wagon. During these early days, the Ocmulgee was an important avenue for supplying the river dwellers with their needs from the outside world and for shipping the products of their fields and forests down to the coastal markets.

One of the earliest means of navigation on the waters of the Ocmulgee was the log raft. In preparation for the long journey down to the seacoast, the pioneer men went into the forests and cut down giant timber trees which they processed into logs. Hauling the logs by ox-drawn timber carts to a calm place in the water, the men placed the logs side by side and bound them firmly together to form a floating raft. Then, loading their produce upon the structure, the rivermen started the cumbersome raft upon its journey down the flowing waters of the Ocmulgee.

As the raft moved with the current, its course was maintained through the skilful use of long poles in the hands of the raftsmen. By pushing along the river bottom and against the river banks, the men endeavored to keep the raft safely within the main channel of the stream and to prevent it from being dashed to pieces against the many obstructions threatening at every turn.

Late each day as darkness approached, the primitive navigators pulled up to a convenient landing, fastened the raft securely to stout trees standing on the river bank, and settled down for an overnight stay. But, with the coming of the dawn, the raftsmen were up and ready for another day of drifting toward their coastal destination.

After a long, perilous journey down the treacherous Ocmulgee—barring mishap, the men reached the seacoast trading center of Darien. The log raft, having served its purpose, was sold to a Darien saw mill, dismantled, and converted into lumber. Then the rivermen proceeded to bargain with canny merchants, offering their produce for the supplies needed back home.

Having accomplished their mission, the uplanders placed their wares upon their backs and set out for home, trudging along the River Trail, the well-worn moccasin path of the Indian traders. After the long, toilsome journey back up the river, the heavily-laden pioneers reached their home clearings, to be greeted joyously by their own folk so eagerly awaiting their return from the outer world. To those remaining, the homecoming of the wayfarers gave promise of enchanting tales of strange realms down the alluring river and of treasures brought from the seaport markets.

Not long after the settlement of the white pioneers along the Ocmulgee, a serviceable type of river craft known as the pole boat came into widespread use and continued for many years as the chief means of water transportation. The pole boat was a broad, flat-bottomed vessel designed to convey the largest possible cargo over the shallowest of waters. The craft was forced along the stream by means of poles skilfully wielded by brawny boatmen. By pushing in unison along the bottom of the river, the men could provide sufficient power to keep the boat moving slowly forward. [1] A common-sized pole boat was designed to employ a crew of twelve men, using ten-foot poles cut from ash saplings noted for their strength and durability. Each boat was operated under the direct command of a captain known on the river as a patroon.

The era of the pole boat on the Ocmulgee led to the rise of a picturesque figure in the person of the boatman or riverman. The life of a boat hand was one of mingled hardship and adventure. The navigation of the perilous stream required the utmost in strength and skill. The veteran boatmen learned all the tricks of the trade and how to apply them to the hazardous conditions encountered along the treacherous Ocmulgee.

The voyage down the river, although effected by drifting with the moving current, was so dangerous that it required constant vigilance and swiftness of action on the part of the crew. The current was usually sufficient to carry the craft along with little effort by the boatmen, but the task of guiding its course along the serpentine waterway posed its own problems. It was most necessary that the boat be kept within the safety of the main run of the river. As the vessel drifted down the changing stream, the chief operation was to avoid the many obstructions which lay in the water and to keep the craft from crashing into the river banks or becoming lodged upon shifting sand bars.

Charged with the task of steering the vessel along its precarious course was the boat's pilot. From his commanding position in the stern of the river craft, the pilot kept up a barrage of shouted commands to the pole men to turn the course from one direction to the other. With the east side of the Ocmulgee occupied by white people and the west side by Indians, the pilot roared out his orders in terms of this accepted fact. If the trumpet-voiced pilot wanted the boatmen to turn the bow to the east side, he would bawl, "Bow to the White!" If he wished a turn to the west side, he would shout, "Bow to the Indian!" In time, these vociferous river commands were shortened to, "Bow White!" or "Bow Indian!" Some energy-saving pilots even reduced the shouted orders to a simple but emphatic, "White!" or "Injun!" [2]

To the Ocmulgee boatmen, these terms signified more than a pilot's raucous command, for during these early years of river travel, the west bank of the Ocmulgee was still the domain of the Creek Indians. The woods and streams on the Indian side formed a hunting and fishing paradise freely roamed by the red-skinned natives.[3] The red people gathered at the riverside to fish in the teeming waters and presented a familiar sight to the boatmen, as they pursued their voyages along the Ocmulgee. Indian hunting parties, too, could be glimpsed within the sheltering woods bordering the dividing stream. Although most of the red people went their way peaceably, occasional marauders appeared upon the scene bent upon mischief. During periods of acute Indian troubles, hostile redskins presented a serious threat to the rivermen. As the men poled their way slowly along the secluded stream, they were always in danger of ambush from the river banks.

The voyage upstream against the strong current was a laborious and oftentimes dangerous undertaking. The operation of the pole boat under hazardous conditions required great strength and skill on the part of the seasoned crew. In the deeper parts of the stream where poles could not touch bottom, it was necessary to use iron hooks which could be caught within the overhanging branches of giant trees standing by the wayside. Then, by forcefully pulling against the hooks, the crew could inch the vessel slowly forward. In places where the channel was very narrow, or the current especially swift, it was necessary to use windlasses and ropes to advance the boat through the most impassable points. At best, the progress upstream was painfully slow. A boat with a crew of fifteen or twenty rugged men could cover little more than ten miles per day, and the entire voyage from Darien on the coast to Fort Hawkins at the upper terminus could take three or four weeks.

The rivermen had their own realistic terms for the variety of conditions encountered along the way. A long, gradual curve was a *round*, but a short, quick turn was a *point*. A sharp bend in the river was an *elbow*, while an extremely vicious bend gained the stronger term of *Devil's Elbow*. A light sheet of trash floating on a stagnant stretch of water was simply a *trash pile*, but a massive accumulation of deadly debris was magnified into *The Devil's Trash Pile*. A whirlpool in the troubled waters which threatened to draw the clumsy pole boat into its grasp was appropriately known as a *suck*. The process of pulling the vessel forward by means of hooks fastened to overhanging boughs was called *hooking*. When the craft swept dangerously close to the river bank, the boatmen used their long poles to push against the bank to avoid crashing. This intricate maneuver was known as *jamming*.[4]

The main route followed by the pole boats led from Fort Hawkins, at the Fall Line, down to the port of Darien on the seacoast. In between these terminal points were many landings of importance to the river inhabitants. Hartford and Jacksonville were major landing places, and other landings dotted the river banks along the entire route. In addition to the public landings frequented by all, many planters established their own private landings for the benefit of their growing plantations.[5]

The Ocmulgee pioneers depended largely upon the pole boat for obtaining needed wares from the storehouses in Darien, and for shipping the products of their frontier economy to market at the noted seaport. When the river dwellers accumulated a quantity of salt pork, beeswax, tallow, hides, turpentine, corn, cotton, and other commodities, they would prepare to send the produce to market. Carting their supplies to a convenient river landing, the men would hopefully place them on board a pole boat lying in waiting. Then, laden with its cargo, the river craft would cast off downstream. Upon reaching the confluence of the Ocmulgee with the Oconee to form the Altamaha, the vessel would continue down the broadened waters of the Altamaha to the journey's end.[6]

Darien was the traditional port for the Ocmulgee country, and the frequency with which well-laden river boats were sent down to the seaport gave rise to the euphonious old river expression, "Drifting down to Da-ri-an."[7]

After the pole boat reached the thriving port, its cargo was unloaded at a proper wharf, to be shipped to other ports along the Atlantic Coast or even to foreign countries. A cargo of supplies for the river people would then be placed on board the craft. These wares were brought to Darien from Savannah, Charleston, New York, or other faraway places.

While the river vessel was tied up at the wharf, the boat hands became a part of the life of the busy seaport town, mingling with merchants, other rivermen, and with deep-water sailors from distant lands. During their stirring stay, the boatmen picked up spicy items of news or entertaining yarns which they kept in store for the eager ears of the inhabitants back up the rivers.

Darien was not unmindful of the value of its commerce with the residents of the river country. Their trade was eagerly sought by the port's merchants and shippers. As early as 1809 the firm of Vinion-Dunham & Co. was operating a factorage and commission line at Darien and actively seeking business with the "Back Country" through advertisements in a newspaper published at Milledgeville—itself a part of the Back Country. The enterprising Darien business concern proclaimed its readiness to receive and forward goods to any port in the United States, on reasonable terms. Having a large and convenient warehouse, they would accept as storage all kinds of produce at reduced rates. They would keep a generous supply of groceries and other merchandise "suitable for the back country." [8]

The following year, Henry Hartford's Counting House on the Bay in Savannah advertised through the same medium that the people consigning cotton and other produce coming to them down the Oconee and Ocmulgee rivers could have free use of their Darien wharf, known as Hartford's Wharf, for landing, wharfage, and re-shipping. Here "fireproof stores" were provided for the reception of produce. The wharf was under the management of Scott Cray, who "stood ready to attend to all patrons." [9]

After all port transactions had been cleared, the pole boat was ready for the long, toilsome voyage back up the Altamaha, into the Ocmulgee, and on to its destination at Fort Hawkins or some other place along the way. Some pole boats made frequent stops at the many landings along the river to put off supplies eagerly awaited by the river dwellers. Here the merchandise was unloaded for distribution to planters within the neighborhood, or to stock frontier trading posts patronized by both white people and Indians. From the landings, the supplies were carted along the River Road and into lanes leading to the homes of persons receiving the desired goods.

The arrival of a river boat at a landing was a stirring event to the Ocmulgee people. In poling the vessel along, the boatmen moved in unison, singing or chanting in such a way that the movement of their brawny figures kept time with the rhythmic beats of the music. Oftentimes, on the sharply-bending river, the first sign of the approaching pole boat was the faint rhythmic singing, echoing over the water and along the wooded banks. The sound of the haunting refrain was like magic to the listeners, lending enchantment to the scene as the rustic harmony drew nearer and nearer.

The spectators eagerly awaited the landing of the rivermen. Dwelling in the isolation of a new country, they were always hungry for news from the old world. Many of these pioneers had come from honored positions of society and public life back in eastern Georgia, the Carolinas, and Virginia; and the arrival of each boat brought hopes of tidings of friends or relatives and of the state of affairs in the world which they had left behind.

The river landings were scenes of activity and excitement. To the men, the coming of a river boat meant sorely-needed supplies for the new life on the frontier; to the women it promised some bit of feminine finery from the fashion centers of the outer world; to the children, the event suggested hoped-for sweets and trinkets. To all the arrival of the river craft brought a glimpse of the enchanting world down the waters of the beckoning stream.

One of the best known public landings on the Ocmulgee during the pole boat era was Parramore's Landing situated just above Jacksonville in Telfair County. At this place, John Parramore, an early settler from Scriven County, operated a public house. Parramore's was the scene of numerous incidents affording an insight into the mode of river life common to the times. Near the landing lived Gibson Clarke, a son of the noted Revolutionary War leader, General Elijah Clarke. As an example of the commotions sometimes arising at the landing, Clarke was presented by the Telfair Grand Jury in 1814 for "committing assault" upon James Rogers at the house of John Parramore "by pointing a pistol at him." [10] Also, in April of 1818, James Pridgen and Stephen Vinton were presented for playing cards "at or near John Parramore's Landing on board of a boat lying in the Ocmulgee the last of March on sundry evenings." Gathered at the landing at the opportune time to witness the affair were four Telfair citizens, John Martin, Redding Hunter, Amos Hunter, and Elijah Hunter. [11] Again, charged the court in October of 1818, John Sikes and Christopher Edwards "did fight at Parramore's Public House to the terror of the citizens." [12]

Putting in at a river landing brought welcome respite to the weary boatmen. All along the journey they were kept perpetually on the alert against the hazards of the river, but putting into port brought a brief change in their arduous labors. Not the least of the boatmen's pleasures was the manner in which they were viewed by the people frequenting the landings and public houses. It was here, amid an appreciative audience, that the rustic characters could relate the many yarns picked up along the rivers and among the sailors in port at Darien. The public houses offered sly refreshments which so easily loosened the tongues of the garrulous rivermen and doubtlessly brought exaggerations to their salty tales.

The pole boat crews were not averse to taking advantage of any situation designed to lighten their labors. A common practice devised by their ingenious minds was to entice slaves on board and, by offering dubious rewards, induce the Blacks to pole the boats for a spell. Increasing with usage, this practice reached such proportions that the Grand Jury of Telfair County issued presentments calling upon the Georgia General Assembly to enact legislation to correct "the practice indulged in by the patroons of boats and others navigating the Ocmulgee River of having slaves of persons residing in the neighborhood of the river to pole the boats without authority of the owners . . . exposing the slaves to danger, and encouraging them to commit crimes, and neglect their duty." [13]

Since the hazards of navigating the Ocmulgee were greatly intensified by the many obstructions encountered along the route, steps were taken at an early date to clear the stream. In 1816, while Indians still roamed the west bank of the river, a commission was created for the purpose of improving navigation on the Ocmulgee. The aim of the commissioners was to clear the channel of menacing impediments from the mouth of the river up to the head of navigation. The commissioners chosen for this worthy project were John Willcox, James M. Taylor, William H. Gross, Lewis Calfrey, and Phillip Cook.[14] The following year, the commission met with an altered membership composed of: James Pearre, Tattnall County; Benjamin Cray, Montgomery County; John Willcox and Major James M. Taylor, Pulaski County; Lewis Calfrey and Phillip Cook, Twiggs County; Major Myrick, Abner Wimberly and Stokely Morgan of Jones County. During the same year, the General Assembly appropriated the sum of $10,000 for the purpose of improving navigation on the Ocmulgee from its mouth up to Fort Hawkins. Under the plan of improvement, numbers of slaves were purchased who, under the direction of an overseer, would cut logs and snags and remove them from the main channel of the stream.[15]

As the plantation system developed along the Ocmulgee, the demand for pole boats grew to such proportions that the production of the useful cargo vessels became an important river industry. One of the earliest boat builders was John Willcox who operated a boat yard near his residence in the lower part of Pulaski County. As the demand for boats increased, Willcox moved down the Ocmulgee to a new location near the Temperance settlement in Telfair County. Here, upon an island on the east side of the river, John Willcox established a boat yard where he produced large numbers of pole boats and other common river craft. [16]

With the rapid increase in the production of cotton on the Ocmulgee plantations, huge river boats came into use designed to convey great quantities of cotton to seacoast markets. As the number of Negro slaves increased, commodious cotton boats were poled by the Blacks from plantation landings to the seaport destinations. River shipment was given impetus in 1818 when Roger McCall and Harrison Smith set up shop near Fort Hawkins and commenced constructing vessels for the river trade with an eventual capacity of from 300 to 700 bags of cotton gathered from the upper Ocmulgee plantations and sent downstream to market. [17]

The river boats bore colorful names bestowed upon them by their imaginative owners. Some vessels displayed a feminine touch with such names as the *Jane, Rebecca, Nancy, Polly Green,* and the *Willing Maid.* Another, the *Macon,* indicated a preference for the river metropolis located at the head of navigation. Bearing the names of birds, mythological characters, and patriotic emblems were the *Blackbird,* the *Bluebird,* the *Summer Duck,* the *Apollo,* and the *American Eagle.* Honoring popular heroes of the day were the *General Jackson, Governor Early, Governor Shelby,* and the *Commodore Hull.* Some of the most colorful names depicted products, occupations, or people common to the Ocmulgee world such as the *Cotton Plant,* the *Ploughboy,* and the *Four Friends of Horse Creek.* One lone vessel proclaimed its independence by boldly displaying the name, the *Little Yankee.* [18]

Even at the height of the pole boat era, the days of the cumbersome river craft were numbered, for the tides of change were flowing up the Ocmulgee. Soon the time would come when the sturdy symbol of olden days on the Ocmulgee would pass and be forgotten.

CHAPTER XII

WHITES FACE REDSKINS ACROSS THE OCMULGEE

Now that the realm of the advancing Americans had been boldly extended to the east bank of the Ocmulgee River, with the ancient domain of the Creek Nation lying upon the opposite side, two separate worlds faced each other across the waters of the dividing stream.

At the time the first white settlers arrived, the Indians had little more than semi-permanent settlements directly on the Ocmulgee. To avoid entanglements with the pushing whites, the red people had abandoned their once-populous towns on the river and retreated westward. The Upper Creeks were now remotely situated on the Alabama, Coosa, and Tallapoosa rivers in Alabama territory, while the more neighborly Lower Creeks were established on the waters of the Flint and Chattahoochee. [1]

The Indians dwelling nearest the Ocmulgee frontier were on the waters of the Flint River less than forty miles away. [2] Directly west of the white settlement of Hartford stood several villages occupied by Uchee Indians under the influence of Timothy Barnard, a white trader who had taken an Uchee woman as his wife. Barnard's Trading Post stood on the west side of the Flint River near present-day Oglethorpe in Macon County. Down the Flint in the vicinity of modern Lake Blackshear, extended a row of villages inhabited by elements of the Chehaw Tribe. The principal center for the group was the town of Chehaw, or Au-muc-cul-le, situated on Muckalee Creek eight miles beyond the Flint. [3]

On the waters of the Flint River below the Chehaw villages, lay settlements of Lower Creeks, chiefly of the Oswichee, Hitchiti, and Ocmulgee tribes. Their villages extended from the lower end of Lake Blackshear down to an area below today's Albany. [4] Then, scattered around the point at which the Flint and Chattahoochee rivers merge to form the Apalachicola, were settlements of Seminole Indians. Although most of the Seminole towns were in Florida, some extended up into the southern part of Georgia. [5]

Even though the Indians did not have any known permanent settlements on the west bank of the Ocmulgee at this time, they **used** this territory extensively as a treasured hunting and fishing domain. Many well-worn trails led to the Ocmulgee from Indian towns on the Flint and Chattahoochee, from Alabama territory in the west, and from Florida to the south. During the hunting and fishing seasons, the red people made their way from all parts of the Creek Nation to hunt in the woods along the Ocmulgee and to fish in its teeming waters. While the shad were running, the Indians could be seen gathering fish at every shoal from the mouth of the river as far up as the shad could run. [6]

While out on their long camping and fishing expeditions, the red people established camps of a more or less permanent nature along the Ocmulgee and its adjacent streams. Occasionally, at the crossways of their trampled paths, they erected huts made of poles covered with brush and mud. These lonely wayside shelters provided welcome protection from the cold and rain for the weary huntsmen deep within the wilderness. Some of the huts were still standing long after the departure of their primitive red builders.

The Indian huts were described by an early observer as being constructed of round poles, arranged side by side, and extending upward from the ground to form a pointed gable about twelve feet high. The huts were about twelve feet long and ten feet wide. The poles in the structure were arranged in such a manner as to enclose the sides and back, with the front left open. In front of each hut, a long pole rested horizontally within the forks of two upright posts standing in the ground. The horizontal pole was formed from a sapling well studded with limbs. The limbs were cut back to provide short knobs about eight inches long. From these projections, hides and articles of clothing were hung up to dry. [7]

The Ocmulgee River was used extensively for fishing by both the Indians and their white neighbors. Long before the coming of the whites, the red people found the waters of the Ocmulgee an abundant source of fish. To catch the fish in the quantity needed for their sustenance, the red people constructed large fish traps at favorable places within the stream. These novel devices were formed by extending two rows of rocks—one from each bank—into the water at an angle slanting downstream, but with a narrow opening left between the tips. Through this opening, the fish were driven by redskins descending noisily upon them from above, while other Indians stationed below the trap gathered the wriggling fish into nets as they swirled through the opening. [8] The nets commonly used by the primitive fishermen were made of wahoo, or narrow strands of bark peeled from the elm tree, and skilfully woven by the hands of the natives.

The construction or use of fish traps in the Ocmulgee River was specifically forbidden to the white people by the Treaty of Washington. Under the terms of the treaty, the whites could use nets to catch their share of fish in the stream, but were required to draw their nets to the east bank. The Indians, in turn, would pull their nets to the west bank. Violations of this agreement by either party brought sharp clashes between the rival fishermen.

With their respective domains resting upon a common boundary, the whites and Indians engaged in some degree of intercourse, although seldom trusting each other completely. The differences in race, background, and interests presented barriers not easily surmounted. The red people were avid traders and eagerly sought any place on the frontier offering opportunities for the exchange of goods. Under the terms of the Treaty of Washington, the United States Government established a trading post at Fort Hawkins to serve the Indian trade. With its large factory, Fort Hawkins soon became the leading commercial center on the Ocmulgee.

The frontier town of Hartford, likewise, rose to a position of importance as an Indian trading place. Strategically located on the Ocmulgee at the Uchee Shoals, Hartford was the focal point for a network of important Indian trails fanning out from the shoals into the Creek Nation beyond.[9] Along these paths, the red people freely ventured to the frontier settlement to exchange the products of their simple civilization for clothing, cooking utensils, ammunition, tools, trinkets, and other articles treasured by the Indians.

The Indian trails converging at the Hartford trading center fell into a well-defined pattern. Leading directly westward from the Uchee Shoals to the Uchee villages near Barnard's settlement was a branch of Barnard's extensive system of trading lanes.[10] Running southwestward from the shoals to the Chehaw villages near the upper end of Lake Blackshear was the Slosheye Trail.[11] Proceeding from Hartford southwestward toward the Indian villages clustered around the Chehaw town of Au-muc-cul-le was the Lower Uchee Path.[12] Upon reaching the Flint River, these noted trails joined other native thoroughfares leading westward to the Lower Creek towns on the Chattahoochee, and southward down the Flint to the Seminole settlements. These well-trodden pathways provided convenient access to the trading center of Hartford, and greatly expedited the exchange of goods between the frontier post and the Creek Nation.

Jacksonville, in Telfair County, was doubtlessly an Indian trading place during its frontier years. A main prong of Barnard's Trading Path led from the seacoast by Beard's Bluff on the Altamaha and on to Barnard's establishment on the Flint. As it traversed the Ocmulgee country, the trail swept around the Big Bend just below Jacksonville, and a spur of this busy thoroughfare led to the frontier settlement. [13]

Indian trade was not limited to the larger settlements. At other accessible places on the Ocmulgee stood wayside posts serving both the white and red people. At intervals along the river were shallow fords, rocky shoals, or rising bluffs, which provided crossing places for fording or ferriage by means of flatboats or dugout canoes. A number of trading establishments arose at these river crossings where the red people could come from the Creek Nation to secure their coveted goods. At Durham's Bluff in Twiggs County was a flourishing post frequented by Indians in large numbers. [14] Then, in the lower corner of Twiggs County at Buzzard's Roost Bluff, near today's Westlake, stood a large trading house operated by Richard Smith, an early trader from Burke County. [15] At this conveniently-located post, Indian trails coming through the Creek Nation from three directions converged to cross the Ocmulgee. Known as Polk's Trail, Middle Trail, and Little's Trail, these avenues provided good passage for the Indians to come and go on their trading missions. [16]

Another trading post was Horne's, located in the lower part of Pulaski County. The post was apparently erected in 1816 by Michael Horne, an early comer to the scene. Situated at a bluff on the Ocmulgee a short distance below the mouth of Cedar Creek, the post maintained communications with the Creek country through Horne's Path, a lane leading westward along the lower waters of Cedar Creek toward the Flint River. [17] The Ocmulgee was doubtlessly ferried at Horne's by a ferry operated by Stephen Mitchell, a Pulaski County pioneer.

A very likely place for another frontier trading house was on the east side of the Ocmulgee, in the northwest corner of Old Telfair County, where the Indian path known as the Oswichee Trail crossed the river opposite today's Abbeville.

Well stocked with homespun, shawls, ammunition, knives, looking-glasses, and other seductive articles, the frontier posts presented such an array of tempting attractions for the redskins that they sometimes imprudently broke into the storehouses and made off with large quantities of stolen goods. [18] Such incidents, coupled with provocative intrusions upon Indian territory by indiscreet whites, precipitated troublesome boundary clashes.

In addition to trading at established posts or wayside stores, wandering bands of red people oftentimes dropped in to trade at the isolated homes of the white newcomers. These pioneers, far from the security of blockhouse or river settlement, did not have the same enthusiasm for intercourse with the Indians that the owners of commercial establishments enjoyed. The silent, stealthy approach of redskins brought anxiety to the bravest of men and downright terror to the women and children. Most pioneers drew little distinction between friendly Indians endeavoring to trade, and rampaging savages seeking victims for their flaming firebrands and crushing tomahawks. [19] To the uneasy whites, all redskins looked alike, and they were anxious to complete with the utmost speed any transactions to hasten the departure of their fearful visitors.

No sooner had the Anglo-Americans extrenched themselves on the Ocmulgee than they began to devise ways of extending avenues of communication out into the Creek Nation. Under the terms of the Treaty of Washington, the United States had gained the right to open a horse path through the Creek Nation from Fort Hawkins southwestward to Fort Stoddart on the Mobile River in Alabama territory. American citizens were to have the right at all times to pass peaceably along this avenue. The Creek chiefs were to keep ferries at the rivers for conveying men and horses over the difficult streams. At the same time, the red people were to establish at suitable places houses for the accommodation of travelers through the Indian country. The prices for ferriage and entertainment would be regulated by the Indian Agent.

The Government lost little time in acting upon the provisions for a pathway. An ancient thoroughfare known as the Lower Trading Path had long traversed the route. Now, this trail was used as the base for a white man's way. At first, the horse path was little more than a narrow lane permitting travel for horsemen, but with the increased demand for transportation along the vital artery, it was widened to provide passage for wheeled vehicles. The important thoroughfare was known as the Federal Road. [20]

The new roadway met a pressing need for a line of communication between the Georgia frontier and the new settlements arising in the old Southwest. Through Georgia's cession to the federal government of her western lands in 1802, and through the purchase of the Louisiana Territory the following year, a vast new area was opened for settlement in the territory later organized into the states of Louisiana, Mississippi, and Alabama. As the new lands were opened for Americans, streams of immigrants began to pour in from Virginia, the Carolinas, and Georgia. Before the Federal Road was created, the Creek Nation, lying between the Ocmulgee River and the Southwest, had formed a barrier to migration through Georgia; but now that the barrier was pierced, large caravans could be seen wending their way over the Ocmulgee and through the Creek country to the settlements beyond. [21]

Other travelers found the Federal Road useful. For the roving red people in the Creek Nation, the road provided a welcome way to the trading center at Fort Hawkins. From within their own country, they could bring the products of their primitive order to be exchanged for the many appealing articles provided at the factory by the white man's civilization. In turn, itinerant white traders welcomed the road as an open avenue into the heart of the Indian country, the very source of the red people's trade.

Responsible authorities found it prudent to exercise caution in permitting wayfarers to enter the Creek Nation. It was imperative that trouble makers who could so easily upset the balance of peace be kept out. To assure tranquillity among whites and Indians alike, anyone proposing to enter the Nation was required to obtain a passport from the Georgia Governor or the Indian Agent. [22] The Creek Nation was a semi-sovereign domain within itself, and the mode of entry demanded observance as such. One applicant for a passport significantly indicated his intention of journeying into "the foreign country of West Georgia." [23] Passports were granted only to those giving promise of good conduct while sojourning in the Indian country. In seeking the required passport, the applicants were expected to furnish references of good character from local officials or others in a position to vouch for them.

The earliest passports were usually issued to persons entering the Nation to trade, collect debts, or recover stolen horses and slaves; but, after the opening of the Southwest to settlers, many passports were granted to prospectors who wished "to view the country" with the intention of settling there. [24] Once the stream of migration commenced, floods of immigrants secured passports for themselves, their families, and their slaves. By 1810 large caravans from the Carolinas were coming through Georgia and rolling along the Federal Road toward the new country.

By 1812 the Federal Road had become a heavily-traveled highway. In a report covering the amount of traffic for a period of five months ending on March 16, 1812, the Indian Agent listed the impressive number of 120 wagons, 80 carts, 30 chairs, and 3 four-wheeled carriages, with a total of 3726 persons availing themselves of passage along the busy roadway. [25]

Poised upon the Ocmulgee at the Federal Road crossing, Fort Hawkins was the chief gateway to the Creek Nation. At this place, all manner of wayfarers gathered to make final preparations for the long journey through the Indian country. Here, amid an atmosphere of excited expectancy, mingled traders, immigrants, preachers, adventures—a motley array of humanity—with eyes set upon the hazy realm beyond the Ocmulgee. Ahead lay the open road.

The frontier settlement was a place of feverish activity. To provide food and shelter for the many wayfarers, houses of entertainment were established. As early as 1812 a Milledgeville newspaper published an advertisement proclaiming the virtues of "a house of Accommodation at Fort Hawkins for the benefit of travelers passing through the Creek Nation." Operated by John Jerreson, the establishment offered refreshments and forage "to those going to encounter the wilderness." At the same time, the prospective wayfarer was assured that "the road has recently been cleared out, is safe and pleasant. [26] This enticing pronouncement painted a much rosier picture of the conveniences of the Federal Road than had been portrayed two years before, when the Georgia House of Representatives had issued the warning: "For the benefit of travelers, we state that it now is, and has been the policy of the Creek Indians to prevent carriages of every kind from passing through their territory." [27] Apparently a transformation had taken place in the unfolding thoroughfare in the short period intervening between the two pronouncements.

With peaceful relations between the whites and Indians always in a state of delicate balance, responsible leaders of both races were anxious to avoid any incident which might upset the peace. For this reason, every effort was made to protect white travelers from annoyance or attack by impetuous warriors while crossing Indian territory. At the same time, the leaders endeavored to prevent any untoward incident on the frontier which might provoke the Indians to mischief. Since Fort Hawkins was a common meeting ground for both parties, it provided fertile soil for discord.

In spite of all efforts to maintain a state of tranquillity, conflicts arose at Fort Hawkins. In the early part of 1810, an affray erupted at Furlow's store. A white man and an Indian were killed, and another red man was seriously wounded. Mr. Magnan, the Assistant Factor, hastily notified the Governor of the incident, fully aware of the ominous results which could follow. Magnan was fearful for the safety of the frontier, as well as for the welfare of white wayfarers pursuing their precarious way through the Creek country. The trader urged an inquiry into the affair to guard against "the vengeful disposition of the Indians by which the innocent suffer." [28] The Governor promptly dispatched Eleazer Early to Fort Hawkins to communicate with Captain Smith, commanding officer of the fort, and with Benjamin Hawkins, Indian Agent. After investigating the affair, Early was able to make the reassuring report that the conflict had been resolved without further violence. [29]

After the successful establishment of the Federal Road, efforts were made to open other American avenues into the Creek Nation. In 1811 the Georgia General Assembly requested the Governor to address the President upon the subject of opening a road to extend westward from Hartford until it intersected the Federal Road at an undetermined point in the Nation. The following year, the same body reaffirmed the appeal with a resolution proposing that the road from Hartford should cross the Flint River at or near Barnard's Trading Post, then proceed the most direct way to intersect the Federal Road. [30]

As war clouds darkened, the task thrust upon Georgia of protecting her exposed frontier brought increased needs for avenues penetrating the Creek country. Governor Early endeavored to shield Georgia's western frontier by establishing a military outpost on the Flint River forty miles in advance of the Ocmulgee boundary. In order to erect and supply the outpost, General David Blackshear carved out a road leading from Hartford, through the Indian country, to the Flint stronghold subsequently known as Fort Early. [31]

Another military roadway traversing the Creek Nation was the Blackshear Road leading from the Ocmulgee River near Jacksonville to Trader's Hill on the St. Mary's River near the seacoast. Laid out by General David Blackshear and constructed by his brother, Major Elijah Blackshear, this frontier pathway provided a vital connection between the Big Bend of the Ocmulgee and the coastal section of Georgia. With limited military forces to ward off possible attack upon two fronts, Georgia authorities designed this strategic roadway as an avenue along which troops could be shuttled back and forth between the western and the southeastern war fronts. After several years of sporadic efforts to construct this frontier artery, the road was finally completed in 1814. [32]

An early roadway was established leading from the Jones County boundary on the upper Ocmulgee, through the Creek Nation, to Coweta Town on the Chattahoochee. By 1819 a ferry operated by Collin Pope had been stationed at the Ocmulgee crossing. Pope made known through the pages of a Milledgeville newspaper the advantages of the route using his ferry, described as being fourteen miles above Fort Hawkins on the direct way from the upper part of Georgia to the Creek Agency. By using Pope's Ferry, travelers were assured they could save one day's time on their westward journey. [33]

A very long avenue proceeding through the Indian country led from the Jasper County frontier to Coweta Town on the Chattahoochee, and from thence to Pensacola on the Gulf of Mexico. This roadway became the object of serious concern in 1813 when it was identified by Benjamin Hawkins as the route along which contraband goods were being smuggled from Pensacola, through the Creek Nation, and into Georgia. Notifying the Governor of this illicit practice, the Indian Agent quoted the Creek chief, Big Warrior, to the effect that four wagons were on the way to Georgia, and that other goods had been left at the homes of Indians in the Nation. Slaves, too, were reported as being illegally transported into the upper part of Georgia along the road to Jasper County. [34]

Although the white settlements ended abruptly at the Ocmulgee River, outposts of the white man's world extended far out into the Indian country. By the Treaty of Colerain, the United States had gained the right to hold small reservations of land inside the Creek Nation. Taking advantage of this provision of the treaty, Benjamin Hawkins, Indian Agent, established a permanent Agency on the east bank of the Flint River at the Federal Road crossing. In time, the military post of Fort Lawrence was erected upon the opposite bank of the river from the Agency.

At the Indian Agency on the Flint, Hawkins was well situated for the dual task of serving the interests of the United States Government and of the Indians dwelling under his care. Here, the Agent was conveniently accessible to the white settlements on the Georgia frontier and to the Indian towns within the Creek Nation. Through well-defined thoroughfares, Hawkins had open lines of communication with the Upper Creeks on the Coosa and Tallapoosa, and with the Lower Creeks on the Flint and Chattahoochee. At the same time, the waters and trails of the Flint provided convenient channels connecting the Agent with the Uchees, Oswichees, Chehaws, and Seminoles, whose habitations clung to the Flint and its adjacent streams below the Agency. From his strategic post, Benjamin Hawkins was able to detect noticeable signs of discord arising among the red people and their white neighbors.[35] Through his judicious dealing with all parties, the Agent was able, for the most part, to keep their paths "white and clean."

Forty miles down the Flint from the Creek Agency stood another important outpost of American civilization. This was the large trading post of Timothy Barnard.[36] Having long dwelt among the red people, Barnard was a respected and influential leader of the Uchee Indians who occupied settlements in the vicinity of his post and on the Chattahoochee River to the west. Barnard carried on an extensive trade with the Indians, and, from his establishment, well-beaten trading paths extended to the white settlements on the Altamaha, the St. Mary's, and the Ocmulgee. Along these busy avenues, products of the white man's civilization were conveyed to Barnard's Trading Post, there to be distributed throughout much of the Creek Nation by means of other pathways leading to the Indian towns on the Chattahoochee and beyond. The thoroughfares running to and from Barnard's served as vital channels of communication between the world of the whites and the domain of the red people. Occupying a position of such influence, Timothy Barnard rendered invaluable aid to the Indian Agent in maintaining peace among the whites and the Indians. [37]

Down below Barnard's, on Kinchafoonee Creek, stood another huge trading establishment operated by Jack Kinnard, a half-breed who exercised undisputed dominion over vast commercial holdings. From Kinnard's Post, deep within Lower Creek territory, long trading lanes led to Colerain on the St. Mary's, to St. Augustine in Spanish Florida, to Barnard's on the Flint, and to the Indian country centered around Coweta and Cusseta on the Lower Chattahoochee. Through his strong American and Indian connections, Kinnard was in a position to keep open the avenues of intercourse between the whites and the Indians. [38]

With all manner of white people swarming into the Creek Nation, with legal passports or as flagrant trespassers, a certain amount of discord occurred among the whites themselves. At times, the portion of the Creek country adjoining the Georgia boundary line became the scene of intrigue and lawlessness. Taking the form of all manner of offenses from the trivial to serious acts of violence, the misdeeds of white Americans upon Indian soil called for stern measures.

The State of Georgia took decisive steps to maintain law and order within the area by setting up a system for the trial of offenders. Claiming legal jurisdiction over the "unlocated territory," the General Assembly, in 1814, passed an act attaching the territory to the jurisdiction of the courts of Jasper County. [39] It soon became apparent that the intended purpose could not be carried out effectively because of the immense size of the area covered. To overcome this difficulty, the General Assembly then divided the territory into well-defined realms of judicial responsibility, with each division assigned to the courts of the frontier county nearest which it was located.

The unlocated territory lying between the boundary line established by the Treaty of Fort Jackson, and the Blackshear Road leading from the Big Bend at Jacksonville to Trader's Hill on the St. Mary's River, was placed under the legal jurisdiction of Montgomery County. [40]

The area extending from the Blackshear Road up to the Oswichee Trail leaving the Ocmulgee River near the upper Telfair County line, and running southwestward to the Flint River, was added to and made a part of the courts of Telfair County. [41]

The territory stretching northward from the Oswichee Trail to the Uchee Trail, known as the Blackshear Road leading from Hartford on the Ocmulgee to Fort Early on the Flint, was attached to the judicial system of Pulaski County. [42]

The land extending from the Uchee Trail up to the Federal Road leading from Fort Hawkins on the Ocmulgee to Fort Mitchell on the Chattahoochee River, was placed under the care of the Twiggs County courts. [43]

The unlocated territory lying between the Federal Road and a road leading from the house of Zachariah Phillips, Sr., was placed under the jurisdiction of the courts of Jones County. [44]

The upper Ocmulgee country, extending from the Phillips line up to the Cherokee boundary, or a path running from the High Shoals of the Apalachee to the Standing Peachtree on the Chattahoochee, called the Hightower Trail, was reserved to the courts of Jasper County. [45]

With nothing but the narrow waters of the Ocmulgee River dividing the domains of the white and red people, peace was always uncertain. For the most part, responsible Georgia officials, principal Creek chiefs, and the Indian Agent strove to maintain a state of tranquillity along the precarious boundary line. Among the leaders was an awareness of the serious consequences which some untoward incident could set into motion.

But, in spite of the striving for peace upon the frontier, elements of discord were mounting. The eager whites were pressing hard against the boundary separating them from the coveted lands beyond the Ocmulgee. Among them were agressive individuals with little regard for treaties or the rights of their red neighbors. At times, callous whites violated the boundary line to encroach upon Indian territory. At first, the trespassers limited their intrusions to hunting, fishing or grazing; but, emboldened by their success, they were soon clearing land, planting crops, and giving the appearance of permanently occupying lands known to belong to the Creek Indians.

For their part, the red people were bitterly resentful over the encroachments of the pale intruders from the east. Among the Indians were impetuous young warriors who made sporadic raids upon the frontier, carrying off livestock and destroying property. Increasingly hostile redskins threatened to go on the warpath, to apply the firebrand to the houses of the frontiersmen, and to stain their tomahawks with the blood of the occupants.

The paths between the whites and Indians had been kept generally "white and clean," but now ominous forces were moving within the mysterious land beyond the Ocmulgee.

CHAPTER XIII

DISTANT DRUMS

Indian troubles were rising along the Ocmulgee. After anxious years of dwelling in domains separated only by the narrow waters of the river, the whites and Indians were moving toward a deadly conflict which threatened to engulf both sides of the dividing stream. Since the arrival of the first white settlers along the Ocmulgee, with the hazy land of the Creek Indians rising beyond, a sense of deep foreboding had hovered over the country. As the year 1812 moved along, the mood of uneasiness grew into a state of acute alarm. Beyond the turbulent Ocmulgee, deep in the heart of the Creek Nation, ominous forces were in motion threatening to spread destruction over the thinly-settled Georgia frontier.

The Lower Creeks, inhabiting the waters of the Chattahoochee and Flint rivers, were considered relatively friendly toward the white Americans. Dwelling in close proximity to the frontier settlements, they had gradually taken on much of the civilization of their neighbors. The United States Government, through its Indian Agent, had endeavored to transform the red people from the roving life of huntsmen to the settled way of farmers. The Government perceived the inevitable need for Georgia's growing population to expand into the lands held by the Indians, but attempted to prevent this expansion from working undue hardship upon the red inhabitants. The Indians' mode of living, based largely upon hunting and fishing, required vast areas of land to provide sufficient food for their people. If the huntsmen could be led to adopt an economy based upon the intensive use of the soil for planting and grazing, less land would be required for their sustenance. To this end, the Government offered favorable inducements to the Indians for learning good agricultural practices. Benjamin Hawkins had worked diligently among the Creeks, instructing them in the use of land, raising livestock, developing orchards, and establishing permanent homes. Hawkins had brought into the Nation the implements needed in agriculture and simple industry, as well as instructors to teach their use.

In his efforts to win the Indians to the white people's civilization, the Agent had attained marked success among the Lower Creeks. Hawkins ventured the opinion in 1812 that nine-tenths of them had left their old towns and established themselves as farmers on the creeks and rivers where land was fertile and the range favorable for livestock. Many of the women had become adept at spinning, weaving, and other domestic arts commonly practiced by their white neighbors. [1]

But among the Upper Creeks a spirit of resistance was more pronounced. Dwelling upon the waters of the Alabama, Coosa, and Tallapoosa, far from the settlements of Georgia, the Upper Creeks continued to follow more closely the customs of their forefathers. With their livelihood more dependent upon hunting and fishing, they were less amenable to cessions of land than were the Lower Creeks. Their opposition to the increasing demands of the whites for more territory was growing. By 1812 the hostility of the Upper Creeks toward the white man's land-grabbing civilization had reached a perilous state.

The mounting hostility of the Upper Creeks was given marked impetus by the timely rise to power of the great Shawnee leader, Tecumseh. Of Alabama background, Tecumseh was born in the valley of the Miamis where his parents had migrated about the middle of the eighteenth century. Early in life, he embarked upon a crusade against the inroads of the white man's civilization. It was the contention of Tecumseh and his brother, the Prophet, that Indians should be Indians and nothing but Indians. As true Indians they should hold in reverence the beliefs and customs of their forefathers, and should continue steadfastly in their hallowed ways. [2]

Tecumseh exhorted his red brothers to reject the artificial civilization of the white people and return to the primitive economy of their forebears. The fiery chieftain denounced the encroachments of the whites upon the ancient domain of the Indians, and renounced all treaties by which the intruders had gained a foothold. Tecumseh contended that these lands were held in common ownership by all red people, and that no tribe, or group of tribes, could bargain them away. [3]

To expel the grasping whites, and to regain the lost domain of his Indian ancestors, Tecumseh advanced an ambitious plan. All tribes, from the Great Lakes to Florida, should unite into one confederation thereby creating a force with power to destroy the despised whites and drive them from the land of the red people. For four years, Tecumseh was on the move, going from place to place and from tribe to tribe, exhorting all red men to join in his daring campaign. [4]

While Tecumseh was engaged in his zealous crusade, another significant force was unfolding, designed to pitch the Indians against their white neighbors and to endanger the very existence of both. This was the conflict mounting between the United States and England. For some time, trouble had been brewing between England and her former American subjects, stemming from the war in which England and France were currently engaged.

Caught between two struggling powers, the United States tried to follow a course of neutrality, favoring neither belligerent, but maintaining the right to trade freely with both. But America's position of neutrality was disputed by England and France alike, with both countries contending that trade with the enemy constituted a breach of neutrality. Both combatants attempted to impose restrictions upon American shipping and threatened to seize any ship found trading with the enemy. This policy of interference with its shipping brought about a series of incidents which the United States maintained violated the principle of freedom of the seas. With a superior navy, England eliminated France as a threat to American shipping, but in doing so, confined the conflict upon the seas to herself and the United States. After repeated indignities, culminating in actual attack upon its ships, the United States, on June 18, 1812, declared war upon England.

The mounting trouble between the United States and England occurred simultaneously with Tecumseh's drive to crush the white Americans. Finding themselves with a common cause, the British and Tecumseh were drawn into a mutual alliance. Taking advantage of the animosity which the red people bore against the Anglo-Americans, the British endeavored to stir the embers of discord. Sending agents into the Creek Nation, the British attempted, through extortion and bribery, to incite the redskins to active warfare against their white neighbors. Most of the Lower Creeks stood firm in their resistance to the subtle overtures, but many Upper Creeks and Seminoles fell prey to the machinations of the British agents.

Strengthened by British support, Tecumseh was rapidly gaining ground in his crusade. Since the Creek Confederacy was one of the strongest Indian powers in America, the shrewd chieftain deemed it necessary to win the Creeks to his cause. Leading a party of dancing and prancing warriors, Tecumseh set out in person to win the support of the leaders of the Creek Nation. Proceeding to Tuckabatchee, a capital seat of the Nation, he arrived at a time when a Great Council was in session attended by the venerable Indian Agent, Benjamin Hawkins. [5]

Since his appointment as Indian Agent, Hawkins had attained marked success in making friends with the red people and gaining their confidence. The peaceful relations existing between the white Americans and the Indians during these years were largely due to his wise and devoted service. Long had he kept the paths "white and clean," but now evil tides were flowing in upon the Nation which even the sagacious Benjamin Hawkins could not stem.

The presence of the renowned Tecumseh created an air of keen anticipation among the red men assembled at Tuckabatchee. Hints were dropped here and there each morning that before the day ended, the walls of the council house would resound with the mighty voice of the eloquent speaker. But the subtle chieftain daily withheld his furtive scheme.

On the first night after the Agent had left the scene, a great throng of red people assembled in the Round-house. Now, with his audience tense with suspense, the famous chieftain came forth to deliver his long-awaited exhortation. Rising to heights of eloquence, Tecumseh pleaded with his red brothers to abandon the ways of the white man and return to the ancient life of Indian warriors. With telling persuasion, the Shawnee argued that, after the whites had despoiled the Indians' hunting grounds, they would subject the red people to slavery. The impassioned appeal of the fiery speaker fanned the fires of hatred glowing in the breasts of his listeners into a furious flame. Before the night was over, many of the assembled warriors had resolved to thrust high the red club, symbol of war.[6]

Tecumseh's dramatic appeal for the Creek Nation to take up arms against the Americans brought about a sharp division among the red people. The Lower Creeks, having tasted the sweets of their white neighbors' civilization, displayed little inclination to return to the primitive ways of their forefathers. For the most part, they were little impressed with the wild harangues of Tecumseh and his threats to destroy his enemies through supernatural powers which he claimed for himself and his aides, who called themselves "Prophets."

In rejecting Tecumseh's appeal, the Lower Creeks were supported by some of the Upper Creeks. Big Warrior, Chief of the Tuckabatchees, opposed the fanatical uprising, but most of the Upper Creeks were swept along the red paths of war. Thus, among the divided Indians arose a peace party and a war party, and the lines were sharply drawn.

As the days moved ominously along, dark clouds hovered over the Creek Nation. The hostiles were furtively proclaiming their determination to take up the sharp hatchet and spill the blood of their enemies. The mystical red sticks were moving from town to town, and the war spirit was rapidly mounting. Nightly, the squares were echoing the haunting rhythm of "The War Dance of the Indians of the Lakes."

Then a fateful blow fell.

Arthur Lott was moving his family from the Georgia frontier to Mississippi Territory. While on the Federal Road deep in Indian country, the party was suddenly attacked by rampaging Red Sticks. Lott was savagely slaughtered. [7]

When Benjamin Hawkins learned of the atrocity, he recognized the precarious position which the Red Sticks had thrust upon the Indians and whites alike. Hoping to prevent a general conflagration before it was too late, the Agent directed the Creek leaders to dispatch a party of loyal warriors to seek out and execute the murderers. [8] This act etched still deeper the spirit of hostility embedded within the breasts of the Red Clubs.

Shortly after the attack upon Arthur Lott, a party of hostiles was returning from a visit with Tecumseh's Shawnees in the North. Erroneously informed that war had erupted between the Indians and whites, the hostiles fell upon a group of white settlers near the mouth of the Ohio River and massacred several families. [9] This savage act provoked a wave of anger among the inhabitants of the neighboring territory. The governments of Georgia, Tennessee, and Louisiana began to prepare for action against the threatening Red Sticks.

Benjamin Hawkins, deeply concerned over the turn of events, urged the Creek chiefs to avoid retaliation by delivering up the miscreants for punishment. [10] The chiefs promptly executed some of the warriors who had taken part in the unwarranted atrocity. Not to be outdone, the infuriated Red Sticks struck back by slaying members of the enforcement party. Civil war was sweeping the Indian country. [11]

In the struggle now spreading among the red people, the friendly towns of Tuckabatchee and Kialigee were attacked and destroyed. The occupants fled for protection to the Lower Creek town of Coweta. Coweta Town and other loyal towns on the Chattahoochee then became the chief targets of hostile attack. The Chattahoochee settlements were now the first line of defense for the endangered Georgia frontier. [12]

CHAPTER XIV

ECHOES ALONG THE OCMULGEE

The throbbing beat of war drums far out in Indian country was echoing along the Ocmulgee. The frenzied Red Sticks were now threatening to advance to the frontier, crush it, and drive the inhabitants back to the Savannah River. The white settlers along the frontier were fully persuaded of the designs of the whooping warriors and lived in daily dread of their horrible fulfilment.

Other dangers threatened the Ocmulgee frontier. Along with the booming drums in the Creek country to the west, came ominous rumblings from the Seminoles in the south. [1] Like the Upper Creeks, the Seminoles had long harbored a smoldering resentment toward the Georgians, whom they considered brazen intruders upon the Indians' rightful domain. The impact of Tecumseh's crusade had touched these fierce redskins and aroused them to a state of heated animosity. Coinciding with Tecumseh's sweeping movement, British agents were establishing themselves among the Seminoles, gaining their friendship, and winning their support for England in her struggle against America. The Spaniards in Florida were traditional enemies of the Americans and could be expected to harbor any British forces planning to invade Georgia from that quarter. [2]

Still another danger presented itself to the defenseless frontier. On the waters of the Flint River to the west and southwest were situated numbers of villages of Lower Creeks, chiefly of the Uchee, Chehaw, Hitchiti, and Ocmulgee tribes. Some of these villages lay in close proximity to the hostile Seminole towns located on the lakes and streams of southern Georgia and northern Florida. Many Lower Creeks and Seminoles were so closely related that they occupied the same villages, making it difficult to distinguish between them. While most Lower Creeks were considered friendly, those intermingling with the Seminoles were displaying the same spirit of hostility, and it was feared that other hitherto loyal tribes would be won over to the war party. [3]

Some of the Lower Creek villages extended up the Flint River above Lake Blackshear, only forty miles from the Big Bend of the Ocmulgee. From their Flint River villages opened numerous trails leading to vulnerable points on the Ocmulgee. The hostiles could stealthily advance along these avenues and fall upon any part of the exposed frontier which their cunning minds might select. The white settlers were so thinly scattered along the river that every cabin stood in danger of the flaming torch, and the occupants exposed to the ravages of the deadly tomahawk.

The commencement of hostilities between the United States and England brought an immediate demonstration of hostility from the Indians. Within a matter of days, a band of marauding redskins appeared along the Big Bend opposite Telfair and Pulaski counties. Crossing over the river to the white side, the intruders embarked upon a series of depredations which sent a wave of alarm up and down the Ocmulgee.

On a July night, a party of hostiles, accompanied by a Creek known as "Winter Jack," was prowling along the white side of the Big Bend in Telfair County. Stealthily, the marauders made their way to the home of Philip Brown located on the west side of the River Road a mile above present-day Hopewell Church. Creeping up to the frontier home, the redskins broke into a cowpen. Here, giving way to a common Indian trait, the intruders slipped out a choice horse and sought to make their escape. But Philip Brown was aroused and went out to investigate. Discovering his loss, the pioneer rushed for help to the homes of Andrew Posey and William Henley. The neighbors promptly responded, and the small party sped in pursuit of the Indians.

The trail led north along the River Road for a mile or so, until the road struck the Oswichee Trail. The fleeing marauders had turned west at this juncture and were retreating along the path toward the Ocmulgee River.

As the white men followed the Oswichee Trail in swift pursuit, they soon came to a place where the red men had paused to observe a rite common among Indians after stealing a horse from a white person. At this point on the trail, they had skinned a large tree of its bark and cut into the exposed surface the brand of the stolen horse. This act was usually performed when the redskins reached a spot at which they considered themselves safe from their pursuers. The brand was carved into the tree so that if Seminoles later took the horse from the Creeks, the Creeks could repossess the horse by using the carving to prove that they had stolen it first! [4]

From the carved tree, the white pursuit party continued along the Oswichee Trail until they reached the east bank of the Ocmulgee. Here, to their dismay, they found that the Indians had forced the horse into the water and escaped to the safety of the Creek Nation on the opposite bank. [5]

Shortly after the raid upon Philip Brown's home, a party of Creek Indians appeared at a trading house in the frontier town of Hartford. Here the red men bought all the gunpowder they could get and conveyed the kegs over the Ocmulgee into Indian territory. After all the powder had been purchased but one keg, the proprietor became suspicious and refused to sell the remaining keg. Confronted with his refusal, some of the redskins seized the proprietor and held him while the others carried off the last keg. The inhabitants of Hartford were intensely aroused at this overt act and sent a party in pursuit of the raiders. [6]

Other depredations followed, and wild rumors spread along the Ocmulgee. Frenzied preparations were made against Indian attack. The inhabitants of Hartford hastily commenced erecting a blockhouse, and Clement Lanier raised a volunteer force for the defense of the frontier settlement.[7] In Telfair County, a group of civil and military officials, fearing that their county would be depleted of its fighting men for use elsewhere, petitioned the Governor to consider the defenselessness of their thinly-settled frontier so exposed to the mercies of the redskins, and leave the men to protect their own homes.[8]

The troublesome Indians continued to roam the Ocmulgee country for awhile, but no general conflict occurred. As the uneasy days passed, the panic subsided, but an air of anxious waiting hovered over the Ocmulgee.

Early in 1813, the Georgia frontier again became the scene of sporadic raids by bands of plundering Indians. Striking along the Wayne-Camden line at the southern tip of the boundary, the hostiles created such a commotion that Governor Mitchell thought it prudent to send a military force down to investigate. [9] A detachment of cavalry under command of Captain Richard H. Thomas was ordered to the scene. Rendezvouing at Hartford, the force set out down the Indian side of the Ocmulgee piloted by Benjamin Brown and William Goodson. As the men moved along the river, they scoured the land for any hostile redskins gathered there. Discovering signs of pilfering, but encountering no Indians, the detachment returned to Hartford. From evidence collected on the march, the officials concluded that the depredations had been committed by Indians of the Chehaw Town. [10]

As the year moved on, Indians continued to plunder exposed parts of the Ocmulgee boundary line. Late in the summer, a party of six was skulking near the plantation of William Goodson, five miles below Hartford where the River Road crossed Limestone Creek. Accosting a black slave, the intruders searched his pockets for valuables, and left him in a state of wide-eyed terror. The prowlers then raided the plantation, stole fruit from the orchard, and finally departed, taking with them a valuable horse. Having done their mischief, the raiders fled to the safety of the Ocmulgee River a mile away, with William Goodson and Captain Mewborn in vain pursuit. [11]

During the summer of 1813, the war spirit within the Creek country continued to mount. Confined chiefly thus far to civil strife between the hostile and loyal Creeks, the conflagration now threatened to flare into open warfare against the whites themselves.

The influential Hoboheilthle, Micco of the Tallassees, had embraced Tecumseh's cause and was the acknowledged leader of the Red Stick warriors. Spurning the plea to discard the red clubs, the chieftain boldly proclaimed his determination to march from Tuckabatchee to Coweta Town and destroy all loyal Creeks. Having gained this objective, he would then descend upon the people dwelling upon the Ocmulgee frontier, overwhelm them, and march on to the Ogeechee, far to the east. Pausing on the Ogeechee for a brief rest, the hostile Micco would lead his warriors triumphantly to the seacoast of Georgia. All north of Hoboheilthle's line would be destroyed by his British allies, with whom the scheme had been secretly planned. This fearful plot was revealed by runners coming directly from the Upper Creek enemy country. [12]

The disclosure of the scheme for their destruction by an avalanche of merciless redskins brought an unprecedented state of alarm to the Ocmulgee inhabitants. Fearful rumors spread without limit, and panic followed in their wake. Many people fled from the exposed frontier to seek safety in the counties of eastern Georgia. Those remaining sought speedy measures for the protection of their families and firesides. Painfully aware of the inadequacies of their own numbers and resources in holding the long line of defense, they urgently called upon Governor Mitchell for assistance. From Hartford, Captain Richard H. Thomas warned that there was no longer any doubt of the certainty of war, and urged measures for arming the militia, particularly the portion most exposed to danger. [13]

Lieutenant Colonel Allen Tooke viewed the situation with such alarm that, on August 4, 1813, he dispatched a hasty message to the Chief Executive, portraying the seriousness of conditions on the Pulaski frontier. The place of deposit for arms at Hartford was so exposed, and armed men so scarce, that Tooke feared a slight attack would make the settlement "easy prey to savage rapacity." The officer foresaw disaster unless a force could be stationed at Hartford adequate for the defense of the town and the frontiers of Pulaski County. Tooke revealed that scouting parties were having difficulty in distinguishing between friendly Indians and the prophets. Numbers of hostiles were coming "under the cloak of friendship to act as spies." The frontier leader proposed that no Indians be permitted to come into the settlements except at Hartford, where they should "be designated by a certain badge of friendship previously agreed upon, or by a special license to trade." Word had reached Hartford that three Lower Creek towns had been "taken in" by the prophets' talk, and numbers had come in, some painted, eager to buy gunpowder and war paint. It appeared that the red traders were securing these for enemies instead of friends. Tooke suspected that the redskins were "waiting a fit season for their horrid purposes." The officer summarized the situation by stating that "things are beginning to wear a serious aspect, the people in great confusion, and very clamorous for prompt measures of defense." [14]

Governor Mitchell lost no time in responding to the appeals of the Ocmulgee residents. Upon receiving the critical report of Lieutenant Colonel Tooke, he promptly issued orders to Brigadier-General David Blackshear, military commander in the threatened counties, to proceed to the frontier and "adopt such measures as will afford some security to the inhabitants, until the troops now ordered to be in readiness are marched to the attack of the Indians."[15] General Blackshear, a resident of Laurens County, was thoroughly familiar with the problem of defense now confronting him and took decisive steps to meet it.

To provide protection against the hostile Indians beyond the Ocmulgee, Blackshear devised a plan of defense based upon the establishment of a line of forts along the east side of the river. Each fort would be erected at a suitable place on the boundary, from Fort Hawkins down to the confluence of the Ocmulgee with the Oconee. In this manner a chain of defense would be forged which the General hoped would prove impregnable. With his plan mapped out, Blackshear dispatched orders to the officers commanding the militia in Twiggs, Pulaski, and Telfair counties, directing them to execute the plan without delay. [16]

Fully aware of the urgency of the impending crisis, the officers hastened to comply with their orders. In Twiggs County, Lieutenant Colonel Ezekiel Wimberly immediately called out a force to erect and garrison the proposed forts. With Fort Hawkins already established as the upper anchor, Wimberly proceeded to construct in Twiggs County three forts at intervals of ten miles along the river. Each fort was designed to provide a stockade 100 feet square, rising eight feet above ground, the whole enclosing two blockhouses. Upon completion, every station was garrisoned by a force consisting of one subaltern, a sergeant, one corporal, and fifteen privates, with a captain in command of the whole. The garrisons served in regular reliefs, with each relief replaced every week with a similar force. [17] The Twiggs County bastions were named Forts Telfair, Twiggs, and Jackson. [18] Rations for Forts Telfair and Jackson were furnished by William Jemison, while Fort Twiggs was supplied by Drury Williams. [19]

In Pulaski County, the frontier strongholds were erected under the command of Lieutenant Colonel Tooke. Since Pulaski embraced a longer boundry on the Ocmulgee than Twiggs, it was necessary to provide four stations for ample protection. The forts followed the same plans and specifications as those erected in Twiggs County. [20] The first post below the Twiggs line was Fort Pike, located in the vicinity of Beaverdam Creek, near the site of the newly-built Mount Horeb Church. Downstream, the next station was placed near Hartford, and named Fort Mitchell. Six to ten miles below Hartford was erected the third military post, known as Fort Green. In the lower part of the county, near the site of Old Daniels Church, stood Fort Laurens. Rations for the Pulaski forts were furnished by Major James M. Taylor. [21]

Three forts were established in Telfair County under the command of Major Josiah D. Cawthon. The Telfair stations were slightly smaller than those in the upper counties. Each military post was designed to provide a strong stockade ninety feet square, rising eight feet from the ground, and enclosing two blockhouses. [22] On the line of the Ocmulgee below Pulaski County, the first station was Fort Adams. This stronghold was situated at a point designed to provide protection to the upper part of Telfair County, and the men who garrisoned the fort dwelt in the Copeland and Temperance settlements. [23] Ten miles below Fort Adams stood Fort Clark. Most of the men stationed at this post were residents of the China Hill and Jacksonville area. [24] The last military station in Telfair County was Fort McIntosh. This frontier post was located in the lower part of the county, and the men engaged in its construction and defense lived in the Horse Creek territory. [25]

The garrisons serving the Telfair forts were somewhat smaller than those in the upper counties of Twiggs and Pulaski. Telfair was more sparsely settled and did not have as many men available for military service as did the neighboring counties. The garrisons assigned to each station consisted of a subaltern, one sergeant, a corporal, and twelve privates. Operating in reliefs, each detail was replaced with a similar force every twelve days. [26] Provisions for the Telfair forts were provided by Ziba Fletcher of the Temperance settlement. [27]

In addition to the line of military posts extending along the white side of the Ocmulgee, the plan of defense called for two horsemen stationed at each fort to serve as mounted spies. It was their task to cross over to the Indian side of the river and reconnoiter the territory extending down to the next station below. In this manner the likely avenues of approach could be scoured for any signs of hostile redskins. Should indications of danger be discovered, the horsemen were to ride hastily to the threatened station and warn the occupants against surprise attack. [28] At the same time, the inhabitants dwelling within the paths of danger could be warned to flee to the safety of the stockade.

With a chain of military strongholds thus linked along the thin frontier line, it was necessary to establish an avenue of communication between the isolated posts. Troops must be moved from place to place, and while stationed within the forts, must be supplied with food and other materials. To afford a means of ready communication and transportation, a roadway must be carved along the east bank of the Ocmulgee, linking all stations from Fort Hawkins down to Fort McIntosh. A primitive path had long existed on this river line in the form of an old Indian thoroughfare known as the River Trail. Sections of the trail had been cleared by the earliest white settlers and widened into a crude roadway known as the River Road. [29] Long stretches, however, were still inadequate for the needs arising from the exigencies of war. To meet these needs, obstructions were removed, and undeveloped sections opened at an increased rate.

The completion of the forts, and the assurances of the Governor that the frontier would be protected, greatly relieved the fears of the white settlers on the Ocmulgee. Some who had fled to the interior now returned home. General Blackshear was convinced that the small frontier forts, with their meager garrisons, had saved the exposed inhabitants from a dreadful fate. [30]

If the forts served the purpose attributed to them by General Blackshear, then they were established just in time. Hardly had the last blockhouse been completed than the Creek War erupted in full force. Until this moment, the war had been limited mostly to a struggle between two factions of the Creek Nation; but suddenly, the blow fell devastatingly upon the whites themselves.

For some years, white people had been settling along the waters of the Alabama River near the southwestern terminus of the Federal Road. In the face of growing Indian troubles, a crude stockade was erected at the home of Samuel Mims to afford some means of protection to the settlements. On August 30, 1813, a

large assembly of white refugees, soldiers, and slaves was encamped within the walls of the stockade. Unaware of immediate
danger, the occupants were caught off guard by a lightning-like
assault by a horde of frenzied savages. Breaking into the stockade, the redskins overwhelmed the confused assemblage and
massacred men, women and children with a degree of brutality
seldom witnessed. [31]

The massacre at Fort Mims so aroused the country that the
states nearest the scene were called upon to take up arms against
the Red Clubs. The states in the most favorable situation for
military action were Georgia, Tennessee, and Louisiana. [32]
Through united effort, a strategy was devised by which a three-
pronged attack would be launched upon the heart of the Upper
Creek country. The Georgia forces would drive westward; the
Louisiana army would move northeastward; and the Tennessee
troops under command of General Andrew Jackson would advance southward. In this way it was designed that the Red Stick
forces would be crushed within the jaws of American military
might.

The United States Government, in September, 1813, called
upon Georgia for a levy of troops as her part in the proposed campaign. Resolved to carry the war to the hostiles upon their own
soil, Georgia's governor responded with a call for 3600 men. The
troops were ordered to rendezvous at Camp Hope near Fort Hawkins directly on the Ocmulgee frontier. Here the Georgians were
placed under the command of General John Floyd of Camden
County. Within a short period, military units from virtually all
parts of Georgia were marching to the frontier outpost. Although
the first class militia from the Ocmulgee counties were in the
call, the men dwelling on the most exposed portions of the boundary were kept in readiness in case of actual invasion of their own
domain. [33]

With his army assembled and ready to march into the heart
of the Creek Nation, General Floyd's first step was to establish
a plan of defense for the upper portion of Georgia against invasion
from the south. To accomplish this, Floyd planned a line of forts
extending from Fort Hawkins westward into Alabama territory.
On his march along the Federal Road, the General executed his
plan by erecting Fort Lawrence on the Flint River across from
the Creek Agency, Fort Perry in western Georgia, and Fort Mitchell on the west side of the Chattahoochee in Alabama territory.
Fort Mitchell, situated in friendly Lower Creek country, was designed to serve as a base from which the Georgians would launch
their campaign against the Upper Creeks. [34]

The Georgia forces concentrated at Fort Mitchell were soon poised for their offensive. On November 29, 1813, a detachment struck at the hostile towns of Autossee and Tallassee, located on the Tallapoosa River. Supported by a body of Lower Creeks led by William McIntosh, General Floyd's men overran the defenses of the Red Sticks and burned the towns to the ground. During the assault, the old Tallassee king was killed, and General Floyd was wounded.[35] Having been badly mauled in the affray, the Georgians fell back to nurse their wounds.

Again, the Georgia forces struck at the Red Sticks on January 27, 1814, attacking the town of Callibee at night. Again, the whites reported a sorely-won victory.[36]

While the war was being taken to the heart of the Upper Creek country, the necessity of defending the Ocmulgee frontier continued. Now that the main body of Georgia Militia was engaged in Alabama territory, the Seminoles, urged on by British agents, were in a position to strike the frontier from the south. The hostile Seminoles had won over numbers of Lower Creeks dwelling on the Lower Flint to increase their ranks to a formidable force. With the bulk of Georgia's defenders encamped beyond the Chattahoochee, the Seminoles and their allies could advance up the Flint in the rear of the militia and fall upon the weakened frontier.[37]

Again, the line of forts so recently erected along the Ocmulgee proved their worth. Without them, the frontier would have had little protection, and the inhabitants no place of refuge. Once more the forts were garrisoned, and again the Indians withheld their onslaughts as the forms of the strongholds loomed above the troubled waters of the Ocmulgee.

Within the land of the hostile Creeks, events were moving toward a climax. The Red Sticks were losing ground under the pounding power of the American forces commanded by General Andrew Jackson. Suffering defeat after defeat, the hostiles finally prepared for a last stand. Withdrawing into a horseshoe-shaped bend in the Tallapoosa River, the Indians set up across the narrow neck of the horseshoe a fortification which they proclaimed impregnable. But the red men underestimated the military might of the whites. Cutting off the Red Sticks' means of escape by water, Jackson's men launched a direct assault upon the fortification. The barricade was broken. The whites then charged at the hapless Indians trapped within the river bend. The fury of Jackson's men was unleashed upon the struggling redskins in an orgy of destruction.[38] As darkness descended, a mass of broken warriors lay upon their once-hallowed ground, and the presence of death hovered over the ill-fated horseshoe.

The defeat of the Red Sticks brought a period of tranquillity to the Ocmulgee world. As spring moved into summer, the inhabitants were able to resume to some degree their normal pursuits. Fields were to be cleared and ploughed, planting must be hastened, livestock demanded attention, and the endless tasks of pioneer living must be met.

Back in the Creek Nation, General Andrew Jackson was preparing to wring from the hapless Indians another cession of land. Calling a council of friendly chiefs to his headquarters near the junction of the Coosa and Tallapoosa rivers, Old Hickory forced upon them the Treaty of Fort Jackson. Under the weight of Jackson's dominating power, the red men ceded to the United States a large portion of their Alabama lands and a long strip of their hunting grounds in Georgia. The latter comprised the territory lying along the Florida boundary and stretching northward to the approximate sites of today's Fort Gaines, Ocilla, and Jesup. Included in the ceded land was the Tallassee County, long a source of contention between the Indians and the whites. [39]

Jackson's treaty had the effect of creating a wedge between the Alabama Creeks and the unconquored Florida Seminoles. Doubtlessly, the astute warrior hoped to cut the hostiles into separate pockets and prevent them from uniting forces to continue the war.

CHAPTER XV

HOLDING THE FRONTIER

By late summer, Indian troubles were again threatening the Ocmulgee. The Upper Creeks who had eluded Jackson's grasp in Alabama territory, had escaped into Florida and found refuge among the kindred Seminoles. The hostile parties had joined forces and declared their determination to continue the war against the Americans. The slaughter of their comrades at Horseshoe Bend, and the harsh terms forced upon the Creeks by Andrew Jackson brought deep resentment to the Indians. [1] The united hostiles vowed that they would not lay down the red club until they had driven the white intruders from their hallowed domain. In their tenacious struggle, the natives were supported by British agents now firmly entrenched within their councils.

Again, the frontier felt the weight of Indian depredations. Late in the summer of 1814, hostiles invaded the white side of the Ocmulgee and struck at the home of John Rabun. Rabun, who lived directly on the river seven miles below Hartford, was working in a cornfield unaware of danger. Suddenly, three redskins arose from their hiding place in the corn. One of the intruders fired at Rabun and wounded him in the back. Taking instant flight toward his house, the wounded man was pursued by the whooping savages. As he attempted to cross a fence, Rabun was fired upon by two other Indians and wounded in the shoulder. Managing to reach the house, Rabun seized his gun and attempted to return the fire. But at this moment, his hysterical wife flung her arms around him and thwarted his effort.

Leaving John Rabun seriously wounded, the invaders proceeded to the neighboring home of John Bolling, which they thoroughly ransacked. Then, stealing a horse from Bolling's lot, they set out to plunder the premises of John Frokock, not far away. [2]

On the morning after the raid, a club was found on the ground where Rabun was attacked. The strange object was inscribed with a number of odd figures, among which was a representation of seven men in a line of march, and a musket with fixed bayonet. These provocative symbols were interpreted to mean that there were seven Indians in the party and that they belonged to a town which had received British muskets. [3]

This savage act, demonstrating the designs of the redskins and their British allies, set off another wave of alarm which was echoed as far away as the capital seat of Milledgeville and the distant city of Augusta. The incident was given a prominent place upon the pages of newspapers published in both places. The prevailing view was that the Indians committing the outrage were dissatisfied with the terms of Jackson's treaty, and that their boldness had been increased by the appearance of a British force in Florida. The presence of British troops in their midst was giving encouragement to the hostiles and increasing their numbers.

The belief that the frontier troubles were instigated by the British was confirmed by Benjamin Hawkins from reports coming to him at the Indian Agency. Hawkins informed Governor Peter Early that the British had ten vessels off the coast of Florida and were "using all stratagems within their power to deceive the Indians and unite them to the British cause." The British, Hawkins stated, were training a body of Indians and Negroes in military tactics "for purposes hostile to the Americans." [4]

Governor Early was anxiously concerned for the welfare of the inhabitants along the Ocmulgee. The Chief Executive sought to relieve them of needless apprehension, but wished to keep them in readiness for any unfavorable development. Writing to Major Josiah D. Cawthon of Telfair County, Early acknowledged that some of the people were leaving the Telfair frontier, and that considerable dread existed because of the attempt of a hostile party to commit murder in neighboring Pulaski County. The Governor had reasons to believe that the intruders belonged to a body of enemy forces collected at the mouth of the Apalachicola River in Florida, but that they had returned to that quarter. Early assured Cawthon that the people on the frontier had little cause to fear the Indians dwelling near them, as they were "from intent or inclination decidedly friendly." To avoid undue risk, however, Governor Early instructed Major Cawthon to employ a few trusty spies to ride ten or fifteen miles over on the Indian side of the Ocmulgee to reconnoiter. In this way, the scouts could cover the trails of any threatening parties approaching from below. Cawthon would instruct the spies to be discreet and to avoid any overt act. [5]

The Florida Indians were in a state of turmoil. A British sea force had put in at Apalachicola. From this point the force had moved on to Pensacola where it had landed supplies. Coming on shore was a British agent, Edward Nicholls, who immediately commenced inciting the red people against the Americans. [6] With British aid, the Red Sticks who had eluded Jackson's clutches in

Alabama territory, had united with the Seminoles to create a formidable force. The recent raids in Pulaski County had apparently come from this source. The Georgians feared that the incursions were forerunners of a massive assault upon the frontier from the hostile alliances in Florida.

The alarm sweeping the Ocmulgee was intensified by a warning from Christian Limbaugh, Assistant Indian Agent, at Fort Mitchell on the Chattahoochee, to Lieutenant Colonel Allen Tooke at Hartford. According to reports coming from Limbaugh from down the Chattahoochee, the Seminoles were planning an attack against Fort Mitchell or Hartford, with Hartford or that vicinity the likely target. Tooke, on September 8, relayed this warning to General Blackshear, apprising him of the state of affairs, and appealing for assistance in defending the frontier. To meet the immediate emergency, Tooke called out an Ensign's command for Forts Pike, Green, and Laurens and garrisoned Fort Mitchell at Hartford with a larger force.[7]

With the Pulaski forts occupied by sizable defensive forces, Governor Early again faced the old problem of providing protection for a long frontier line at lower costs in manpower and money. Convinced that one strong force, firmly entrenched at a strategic point within the Creek Nation well in advance of the boundary line, could afford ample protection, the Governor ordered General Blackshear to execute a plan to this effect. Under Early's orders of September 17, Blackshear would send "some prudent officers with a patrol of cavalry, consisting of twenty privates, armed with guns, to explore the country between the Ocmulgee opposite Hartford, and the Flint River, at, below, and above Hitchee Town." The object of the expedition was to ascertain if any hostile Indians were lurking in that quarter; and to determine the best route for a road from Hartford to the Flint River, striking the river below the mouth of We-cuy-wau Creek. Richard H. Thomas, Captain of the Pulaski Cavalry, was chosen for this timely service. [8]

The need for an expedition into the Indian country was made more acute by the development of a new trouble zone. Enemy forces were reported concentrating at Perryman's, on the east side of the Chattahoochee River, twenty miles above the Florida line. The number of hostiles at this place was increasing, and the Indians were being supplied with arms in preparation for a possible assault upon the lower part of the Georgia frontier. [9] Governor Early perceived the necessity of crushing this concentration of enemy forces before their plans could be executed. But circumstances arising at this very moment disrupted the Chief Executive's plans. [10]

General Andrew Jackson was now facing the British on the Gulf of Mexico near Mobile, and a major clash appeared imminent. In anticipation of the approaching struggle, the United States Government, on September 24, 1814, called upon Georgia to furnish 2,500 troops. Governor Early received orders from the War Department to set the troops in motion as soon as possible. Even though fearful for the safety of his own frontier, the Georgia governor complied and ordered the commanders to march their forces with all speed to Fort Hawkins. From Fort Hawkins the troops would proceed westward to Fort Jackson in Alabama territory for General Jackson's use. [11]

To meet the quota set for Georgia by the War Department, it became necessary to take the first class militia from the frontier counties thus leaving the Ocmulgee line weakened in the face of mounting danger. Aware of the reduced defenses, the cunning redskins appeared to be choosing this critical moment for their long-awaited attack.

Increasingly ominous rumors issued from the land of the Seminoles. From his Agency outpost, Benjamin Hawkins, on October 30, dispatched to Governor Early a warning of impending attack. From several quarters, Hawkins had learned that the Seminoles were gathering at Perryman's "for mischief." They were reported to be preparing war food. The Indians were said to be under orders "to strike on this side when the British are ready to strike on the other." The warriors were to be ready by full moon when a large party would march off somewhere for "mischief." It was supposed that their target would be the Georgia frontier below Fort Hawkins, and probably in the vicinity of Hartford. An informant had heard the Indians say that they had been illtreated near Hartford, and "the day was not far off when they would be revenged." [12] Hawkins ordered Christian Limebaugh to collect all friendly Indians possible, place them at outposts, and hold them in readiness.

Six days later, Hawkins hastened a more ominous warning to the Georgia governor. A Black had just arrived at the Agency with word that Carr's Ned, a free Black on the way from Hartford, had fallen in with a large body of hostiles. The enemy made a quick prisoner of Ned, but upon his telling them he was going to join the British, they released him. [13]

Faced with the prospects of red warriors at the very gates of Hartford, Governor Early hastily ordered Colonel Allen Tooke to "use all means within your power for repelling, pursuing, and destroying said party." [14] In accordance with this command, Captain Richard H. Thomas was ordered to keep his cavalry ready for immediate defensive measures. At the same time, Colonel Wimberly of Twiggs County was instructed to co-operate with Colonel Tooke. The first class militia from the frontier counties were now retained for the defense of their own lines. To prevent a surprise attack, a cavalry detachment was sent to patrol the Indian country along the Big Bend of the Ocmulgee for a distance of fifty miles below Hartford.[15]

Now, a wave of fear and bewilderment swept across the frontier and extended into the executive halls at Milledgeville. The "large" body reported at the gates of Hartford was found to consist of only twenty-eight Indians and instead of being at the very threshold of the settlement, proved to be at a safer distance. [16] The Indian Agent's warnings of threats inside the Creek Nation frequently proved to be exaggerated or distorted. Governor Early, in his eagerness to protect the frontier, found himself in the frustrating position of issuing orders for specific measures, only to find it necessary to countermand his orders in the light of later information. With conflicting reports reaching him so rapidly, it was impossible to effect any plan of action before a contradictory report would necessitate a change of strategy. The Governor and the frontier officers were bewildered in their efforts to afford protection to the confused residents of the Ocmulgee.

Mysteriously, the anxiously-awaited attack did not come. After a period of suspense and uncertainty, the Governor concluded that whatever danger may have existed had now subsided. On November 16, Early ordered Colonel Tooke to discharge most of the men mustered into service to meet the crisis. On the same day, the writer for the *Georgia Journal* ventured the guarded opinion that the Indian alarms were gradually subsiding. No hostile force had been discovered near the frontier, but the cautious writer thought it prudent to warn the people to keep on the alert. [17]

A week later, the Milledgeville journalist attempted to analyze the situation according to the best information available. It was not known who had induced the enemy to return without doing mischief. The British were still continuing their "most infamous attempts to incite the Indians against us." They were reported offering $1000 for every trader, cow buyer, or other American found in the Indian country, and were offering a like sum for capturing Negroes. Having been foiled in their latest attempts against the frontier, the enemy had set up a new plan of operation. The revised strategy was to attack American convoys after the Georgia troops had passed through on their way to join General Jackson in the west. At the same time, the redskins would launch an assault upon the frontier below Fort Hawkins when the bulk of the army was no longer available for its defense. [18]

Trickery was afoot. Three Seminoles had gone to Fort Lawrence, opposite the Indian Agency on the Flint, and given themselves up to the military authorities there. The Indians claimed to be part of the hostile body recently reported on the frontier, but had been forced to flee in consequence of an affray with some British soldiers in the party. Suspecting some design, the commanding officer at the fort sent the captives under guard of three men to Fort Hawkins. On the way, the Indians loitered along until nightfall; then, at a signal, they rose up against the guards, wounded one with a knife and made their escape. In the light of this intrigue, Captain Barnard, the half-breed Uchee, with eighty friendly warriors was ordered to remain below the Agency to scout as a cover for the unsettled frontier line. [19]

CHAPTER XVI

PUSHING INTO THE INDIAN COUNTRY

The repeated threats against the Ocmulgee were retarding the general war effort. Faced with an impending invasion of British forces on the Gulf coast, General Andrew Jackson was in dire need of the Georgia troops. But Georgia's fighting men were delayed by dangers threatening their own homes. To resolve the dilemma, Governor Early entered into an exchange of views with General Jackson and General John McIntosh, now commanding the Georgia troops awaiting the opportune time to join Jackson.

From this exchange, emerged a strategy designed to remove the threat against the frontier. Governor Early would send a detachment into the Seminole country to destroy the hostiles within their own towns and villages. A deposit for supplies would be established on the Flint River within striking distance of the enemy now concentrated at the juncture of the Flint and Chattahoochee. From this base, a powerful offensive would be launched against the hostiles. The chosen site would be so near the enemy settlements that the troops could march without wagons, strike the hostiles, and return to their base. The strategy was essentially the same as that previously employed by General John Floyd's Georgians in their campaign against the Red Sticks, using Fort Mitchell as their base. [1]

A force under the command of General David Blackshear would be detached from the main army for the task. At the same time, the main army, commanded by General John McIntosh now at Fort Hawkins, would march on to the aid of Andrew Jackson at the discretion of McIntosh. After Blackshear had disposed of the troublesome Indians, he would return to his depot and regulate his movements as General McIntosh directed. At the appropriate time, a body of horsemen would be sent to overtake Blackshear at the Flint depot and join in the march against the enemy. The expedition would be further augmented by a body of friendly Indians recruited and led by Colonel Benjamin Hawkins. [2]

At Camp Hope near Fort Hawkins, General David Blackshear made final preparations for his anticipated campaign. On December 14, 1814, he received his marching orders from General McIntosh. Blackshear would advance with Colonel Wimberly's

Regiment directly to Hartford. Upon reaching the frontier post, he would proceed to open a roadway through the Indian country the most direct way to the Flint River forty miles away. The object of the march was "to deter any hostile or marauding party of Indians from committing acts of violence or making depredatory excursions on the frontiers of Georgia, most exposed to their savage fury, making every effort at the same time to arrive at the Flint River . . . ."

Upon reaching the Flint, Blackshear would "select a proper situation as a place of deposit for provisions, and throw up a small breastworks with pickets about it, and with blockhouses at right angles of the same, about sixteen or eighteen feet square... sufficient to secure the work from assault on every side." A subaltern's command would occupy the works until otherwise ordered or relieved.

Blackshear was admonished to proceed cautiously as he crossed the Ocmulgee and entered the Creek Nation. If he detected any signs of a collected enemy along his route, he would be careful to have his detachment march in regular order, either in two or three columns, "keeping an advance guard and rear guard out with double flankers in front, center, and rear, to prevent surprise ambuscade." As a safeguard against night attack, the General would fell trees and throw up entrenchments wherever he camped.[3]

With his orders outlined, General Blackshear promptly proceeded to effect plans for the fulfilment of his mission. Mindful of the need for haste in putting the army over the Ocmulgee when they reached Hartford, Blackshear sent Lieutenant Dean ahead of the main force to construct a river flat for passage.[4]

On the morning of December 17, 1814, with all preparations made, General Blackshear gave orders to strike tents and take up the line of march. Proceeding in two columns, the troops set out down the Ocmulgee for Hartford.

The army reached the frontier settlement on December 22, and pitched tents at Camp Blakeley. Blackshear was eager to cross over the river and set out upon his expedition, but disappointment awaited him. The party sent ahead to construct the flatboat had been unable to complete the task. The men had encountered difficulty in securing the necessary tools and complained that the ones available were of poor quality. While waiting for the completion of the ferry, Blackshear instructed Captain Richard H. Thomas to hold his troop of horse in readiness to march upon notice.[5] At the same time, the General ordered

Captain Groce to keep alerted his Pulaski militia, which would be reinforced by men from the frontier districts of neighboring Twiggs County. [6]

The flat was finally completed, and the task of transporting the troops across the Ocmulgee was begun on Tuesday, December 26. Owing to some obstructions in the river, the operation was not concluded until three days later. As soon as a sufficient number of men could be put over the stream, they were sent on to clear the road and to build a bridge over the first creek, the most important on the route. [7]

As soon as the entire force had crossed, Blackshear dispatched a communication to General McIntosh apprising him of the fact. The message was sent to Timothy Barnard at his trading post on the Flint, there to be relayed by Indian runner to McIntosh. In his report Blackshear complained bitterly about the lack of supplies available at Hartford for the expedition. Provisions for men and livestock were meager. There was not more than one day's forage for horses, or hogs; no soap, nor any rations except flour, hogs, and salt; and no contractor to furnish the necessary supplies. [8]

In the face of such dismal prospects, the men pressed onward. Leaving Hartford on the morning of December 31, the soldiers took up the line of march into the Creek Nation of Indians. Blackshear hoped to reach his destination within six days, but many difficulties lay ahead. [9]

The route through the wilderness followed the old Uchee Trail, an Indian path leading from the Uchee Shoals at Hartford southwestward to the Flint River. While an avenue of the dimensions of the Uchee Path would afford passage for footmen and horsemen, it was not of sufficient width to accommodate wheeled vehicles. To convert the primitive trail into a military roadway, it was necessary to increase the width by cutting down trees and clearing the debris. Hacking their way into the interior of the Indian country, the men were increasingly exposed to the danger of ambuscade.

As the toiling soldiers pushed deeper into the wilderness, they encountered an increasing shortage of supplies. The Quartermaster Department was having trouble in procuring enough food and forage for men and animals. Moreover, the problem of transporting the supplies over a raw new road through a barren wilderness in mid-winter was almost insurmountable. The number of wagons, and men to drive them, was woefully short. The chief responsibility for supplying the army fell upon the youthful and bewildered Assistant Foragemaster, Alexander McDonald of the Georgia Militia. Provisions were to be procured at Fort Hawkins and conveyed down to Hartford. At Hartford, they were ferried across the river by means of the flatboat used to transport the troops over the stream. Once across, the supplies were hauled laboriously by wagon along the newly-cut road to the army pushing on ahead. [10]

From his post at Hartford, McDonald was striving to keep the supplies moving to the army now trudging deeper and deeper into the interior of the Indian country. At the same time, he sought to obtain such additional provisions as could be found in the vicinity of the frontier settlement. The constant danger under which the farmers had been forced to live, with the necessity of frequently abandoning their fields to rush to blockhouses for military duty, had greatly hampered farming operations. So, as McDonald foraged for supplies, he found them in scarce quantities and at such distances that it was necessary to haul them as far as ten or twelve miles into Hartford. To speed the supplies to Blackshear's advancing men, McDonald used all available wagons in shuttle fashion, moving them from supply base to army, and back again. [11]

In the face of steadily mounting troubles, a crushing blow fell upon McDonald. On January 3, he ruefully notified General Blackshear that the flat, the main link in the supply line, had sunk. Five wagons had started over the ferry, four loaded with corn, the other with ammunition and blacksmith's tools. The first wagon landed safely, but as the second drew near the opposite bank, the flat went under. Not only had the priceless ferry broken from its course, but it had drifted downstream. The bewildered McDonald was "at an entire loss to know what to do." [12]

Beset with gnawing hunger and hardship, the determined soldiers pushed stubbornly ahead. On January 3, they pitched tents at "Twenty-six Mile Creek," where Blackshear bluntly responded to McDonald's woeful report of the sunken flatboat. By January 6, the army encamped on "Thirty-six Mile Creek." At this point, deep in Indian territory, General Blackshear issued orders to his men to refrain from firing on any Indian accosted, unless the Indian should display some "manifest intention of hostility, or refuse to answer when hailed." The soldiers were admonished not to injure any friendly Indians, "especially when bearing a white flag, or other token of friendship." [13]

Blackshear's detachment reached the Flint River on the evening of January 6, 1815. After a long, hard march, the men went into camp on the east bank of the stream in the vicinity of a cluster of Chehaw villages which dotted the opposite bank. Here, the men hoped for a brief respite from their hardships. On the grueling march through the bleak wilderness, in the depth of winter, with little food and less comfort, many had sickened, and one had died. Nothing but a soon-to-be-forgotten mound of freshly-turned earth remained to mark the place where the solitary soldier had come to the end of his journey. But little cheer awaited the weary men at the wilderness rendezvous. The winter weather was miserable; the army was without forage and extremely low on rations. Sickness continued to plague the camp and, before long, two more soldiers dropped from the ranks in death.[14]

On the day following his arrival at the Flint River, General Blackshear commenced building his supply depot. At the same time, he unloaded all wagons and, except for three or four which he retained for hauling building materials, sent them rolling back to Hartford to convey other articles of deposit for the outpost. [15] Here, in addition to the men already with him, Blackshear must assemble a force of 100 infantrymen and the same number of cavalry troopers. But, to meet the needs of such numbers, the General faced a critical scarcity of supplies.

The army was now deep in Indian country, forty-one miles from the nearest white settlement. To this remote spot on the Flint River, the soldiers had completed a military roadway entirely through the wilderness. General Blackshear firmly believed the cutting of this strategic thoroughfare an accomplishment of merit, and contended that the road would serve as an excellent avenue of communication for a critical period. [16]

With the walls of Fort Early rising above the waters of the Flint River, the next phase of David Blackshear's expedition lay ahead. After the outpost was completed, it would serve as the base from which Blackshear's army would launch an assault upon the enemy forces to the south. The men would march down the Flint River to its junction with the Chattahoochee to form the Apalachicola. At the same time, a party of friendly Lower Creeks commanded by Colonel Benjamin Hawkins would proceed from Fort Mitchell down the Chattahoochee to a common rendezvous. After uniting forces, the allies would launch a concerted drive against the hostiles concentrated in the Apalachicola territory. In this manner, it was hoped the massing of enemy forces against the Georgia frontier could be thwarted in its initial stage.[17]

The proposed strategy had evolved from information secured by Benjamin Hawkins as to the strength and activity of the enemy concentrations on the Apalachicola. As the Agent received information through Indian runners in the Seminole country, he would relay it to General John McIntosh, who would then plan his strategy while keeping in touch with Governor Early. After decisions had been made, they were dispatched for execution to General Blackshear, operating directly in the field.

With Blackshear now at his Flint depot planning to advance against the foe, a series of complications arose destined to shatter his well-laid plans. Reports previously coming through the Indian Agent told of heavy enemy concentrations on the Apalachicola, with indications that these forces would be directed against the Georgia frontier. Later reports revealed that the British had sailed on toward New Orleans, with the implication that this would be the target of invasion. The British were now reported to be facing General Andrew Jackson in overwhelming numbers. Jackson needed all reinforcements possible, and General Mc-Intosh was preparing to march the main body of Georgia troops to Jackson's aid. With this development, came reports from Benjamin Hawkins that the hostiles now before Blackshear's army had dwindled to a mere handful.

In the light of the changing situation, Governor Early reluctantly ordered General Blackshear to abandon his expedition and hastily rejoin McIntosh, now proceeding toward New Orleans. Early suggested the feasibility of Blackshear's taking a short cut westward by penetrating to Barnard's Post, and from there directing his course toward Coweta Town on the Chattahoochee. The Governor had been advised that wagons and carts had repeatedly traversed this primitive pathway. [18]

Governor Early's orders reached Blackshear on January 8, and found him busily engaged in constructing Fort Early on the Flint. The General obediently took steps to comply. [19] But, while executing his revised plans to rejoin General McIntosh, Blackshear received another order directly from McIntosh, evoking another change in strategy. Now, instead of marching his entire force, Blackshear would send only one battalion to rejoin McIntosh. With the remainder, Blackshear would proceed upon his mission to subdue all hostile elements within his quarter. He would be supported by Colonel Hawkins and his body of Indian warriors now numbering some 700. Blackshear would march down the Flint, while Hawkins proceeded down the Chattahoochee, and both would meet at the confluence of the two rivers. [20]

In order to reach his destination, it would be necessary for Blackshear to march his troops through the territory occupied by a number of Lower Creeks, chiefly of the Chehaw, Hitchiti, and Ocmulgee tribes. Most of these were believed to be friendly, but through close association with the Seminoles, some had turned hostile. Hoping to prepare the Indians in that quarter for the alarming spectacle of a large body of marching soldiers, and to gain their support for the whites, the Indian Agent penned an appeal to the chiefs to give Blackshear all possible assistance. The message would be carried by Blackshear himself and would be delivered in person upon his arrival at the settlements of Jack Kinnard and at the Chehaw town of Au-muc-cul-le.

Addressing himself to Kinnard and the chiefs of Au-muc-cul-le, Benjamin Hawkins informed them that Blackshear's army was coming among them to protect and secure the loyal Indians on their river and to punish the mischief makers. The Agent ordered the Chehaws to "point out sixty warriors under two chiefs" to act with General Blackshear until they could meet Hawkins. The Agent warned the chiefs to be very particular about spies. They knew all the friendly and hostile Indians and, if any hostiles, or spies, came among them, they were to point these out to the white chief. The red warriors were to be as quick as the white soldiers to apprehend and destroy the enemy. [21]

At this critical moment, still another reversal arose, and Blackshear's precarious expedition was suddenly terminated. In the midst of his final preparations to advance, an urgent appeal came from General McIntosh to halt the campaign and rush his entire force to rejoin McIntosh. Blackshear's men were desperately needed to move with the main Georgia army in support of General Andrew Jackson, now facing a critical moment at New Orleans. [22]

This final order climaxed a long series of contradictions and confusions suffered by General Blackshear. Baffled in the execution of his long-awaited mission, David Blackshear now gave way to a temper which had reached the boiling point. He laid the blame squarely upon the shoulders of Benjamin Hawkins and his Indian informants.

Dispatching a heated epistle to Governor Early, Blackshear bitterly denounced Hawkins for his conflicting reports as to the size and movements of the hostiles on the Apalachicola. At first, they had been pictured as so overwhelming that a strong force should be sent against them. Shortly afterward, the enemy was reported as negligible in strength, thus making Blackshear's long, toilsome expedition appear useless. What had previously been described as a massive force threatening the frontier of Georgia was now portrayed as an overwhelming force directed at General Andrew Jackson at New Orleans. Blackshear had no confidence whatsoever in the reports of the Indian Agent, nor in the Creek warriors under Hawkins' command. Blackshear viewed the Indians as more of a hindrance than a help, and bluntly stated that their presence among his ranks would not only make it necessary for his men to fight the enemy, but to stay forever on the alert to avoid being scalped by their supposed friends. [23]

General Blackshear was at "Camp Twelve Miles East of Flint River" when he received the final order to abandon his expedition and rejoin the main army. In compliance with this latest directive, the frontier general set his command in motion toward the Ocmulgee. Marching back along the roadway which he and his faithful men had so recently carved from the wilderness and thereafter to bear his name, General David Blackshear retraced his steps to Hartford.

CHAPTER XVII

MARCHING DOWN THE RIVER ROAD

A new crisis suddenly descended upon Georgia. General Blackshear had marched his army but five miles above Hartford when a startling dispatch was placed in his hands. Georgia was being invaded by the British! A large flotilla had loomed off the Atlantic Coast and landed a force at a vulnerable point. The Governor had received intelligence that two ships-of-the-line, seven frigates, and a number of smaller vessels had entered St. Andrew's Sound and made a landing on Cumberland Island. From this foothold, the enemy was preparing to advance along the defenseless coast line. [1]

At this critical moment, Georgia had no military force of any consequence in the area to repel the intruders. Only General Blackshear's small army was in a position to reach the place of invasion in time to offer any reasonable defense. In desperation, Governor Early was now calling upon Blackshear to shape his course without delay to the point of danger. The Governor feared that before any other forces could be collected and organized the British, through the aid of Negro insurrections and Indian massacres, "would have produced their full measure of ruin." [2]

General David Blackshear now faced a baffling dilemma. Confronted with two contradictory orders, he was forced to make a crucial decision. At that moment, he was actually in the service of the United States Government and subject to the commands of a superior officer. His superior officer, General John McIntosh, had ordered him to march with all speed to join his own command on its mission to aid General Andrew Jackson in the southwest. Now, with his own home state invaded, Blackshear was under orders from Georgia's Chief Executive to advance in haste to repel the invasion from the southeast. The Governor, however, exercised command only over the state militia, and had no authority to issue an order contrary to that previously issued by an officer of the United States Army. Nevertheless, in the desperation of the moment, Governor Early had appealed to Blackshear to rush to the defense of his own state, despite the previous order of General McIntosh.

Torn between two loyalties, the General must make a difficult decision. Should he comply with the command of his superior officer and march westward, leaving his own state to the mercies of an invading foe, or should he heed the plea of the harassed Georgia governor and go to the defense of his own people? Whatever struggle may have gone on in the mind of the General, his decision was prompt and clear. Without further ado, Blackshear turned his column squarely about and set his march toward the endangered Georgia seacoast. [3]

To expedite Blackshear's advance to the scene of conflict, Governor Early advised him of the best route to follow. Two avenues presented themselves. The shortest and most direct was the new military road constructed the previous year by Major Elijah Blackshear, brother of the General. This route led inland from Hartford directly to Jacksonville on the Big Bend of the Ocmulgee. The other avenue was the River Road, which followed closely the curving left bank of the Ocmulgee down through the counties of Pulaski and Telfair. This road crossed the Oconee barrier at Bell's Ferry near the juncture of the Ocmulgee with the Oconee to form the Altamaha. From the Oconee crossing, the River Road continued along the north bank of the Altamaha to Fort Barrington, fifteen miles above the coastal town of Darien, now in the path of enemy invasion.[4]

Governor Early advised General Blackshear to follow the River Road in preference to the shorter way. He feared that the new road might prove to be impassable for wagons during the rainy season. The River Road had the advantage of leading through an inhabited country rather than a sparsely settled wilderness. Moreover, by following the route of the Ocmulgee and Altamaha rivers, the troops would be in a position to receive supplies by means of river boats navigating the streams.[5]

Following the Governor's suggestion, General Blackshear directed his column down the River Road. Marching back through Hartford, the army continued five miles farther, then stopped to go into camp. From this encampment, on January 21, Blackshear penned a hasty order to Farish Carter, contractor, for 30,000 rations to be delivered at Hartford. Since the troops would proceed along the river lines, Carter would keep them supplied by waterway. At the same time, the General dispatched orders to Captain Lane, calling upon the Ordinance Department for 500 rounds of good powder and at least 10 reams of cartridge paper to be transmitted without delay.

From the same camp, Blackshear sent General McIntosh an explanation of the circumstances which had caused him to change his march. Blackshear expressed confidence in McIntosh's approval, but declared his willingness to abide by any order to the contrary. [6]

Before striking tents the following morning, General Black-shear dispatched a message to Governor Early, apprising him of his course of action. The General voiced concern over the poor quality of powder and stated the likelihood of depending, from necessity, upon the bayonet. Blackshear was confident that the country through which the army was passing abounded in provisions, and that the river calculated to raft them down should avert undue hunger in the ranks. [7]

Despite Blackshear's expressed optimism, he soon encountered his old trouble in securing supplies for the army. Again, the contractors and the Quartermaster Department were not up to the demands placed upon them. The youthful Alexander Mc-Donald was still struggling to provide the marching troops with provisions and forage, but was experiencing his usual frustrations. At this critical time, the services of John Willcox, an early settler on the Ocmulgee, proved most valuable. Willcox operated a boatyard on the Ocmulgee where he constructed river boats to be used in transporting supplies for the needy army. [8]

General Blackshear continued his march down the River Road. He was now following the familiar route along which he had once established a line of forts to protect the frontier inhabitants from hostile attack. Behind him, stood the forts of Twiggs County and Forts Pike, Mitchell, and Green in Pulaski County. As he proceeded down the Ocmulgee, he would come to Fort Laurens in the lower part of Pulaski. Then, entering Telfair County, Blackshear's army would pass, at ten mile intervals, the ramparts of Forts Adams, Clark, and McIntosh, all standing as silent sentinels beside the River Road.

Some of the men marching in the ranks were inhabitants of the frontier counties. As they swung along the River Road, their eyes fell affectionately upon familiar scenes by the wayside. Occasionally, one would find himself passing his own homestead, with members of his family and neighbors standing along the way, eager for a glimpse at their own soldier boy. The army, with its military pomp and color, presented a spectacular scene as its ranks stepped briskly along the remote frontier way. At clearings and settlements, the people gathered to gaze at the might of the army marching boldly to meet the foe.

As the column entered Telfair County, the men tramped across the old Oswichee Trail, then marched for a short distance over a stretch of road which had been the scene of early conflict. For it was along this path that Philip Brown had pursued the marauding redskins whose raid upon his home marked the first known act of the war directed against the Ocmulgee frontier. A short distance ahead loomed the form of Fort Adams, a haven of refuge for the people dwelling in the upper part of Telfair County.

Reaching a small stream a few miles below the Temperance settlement, the army halted and went into camp. Here, within the stillness of the night, the life of a weary soldier ebbed away. The next morning, as his comrades moved onward, they left a lonely grave upon a rise of ground above a trickling stream, thereafter to be known as Soldier's Branch. [9]

A short distance beyond Soldier's Branch, the marching men came to Fort Clark, already an unique shrine on the River Road. Here, within the walls of the stronghold, the inhabitants were gathering in times of danger for protection and companionship. Inside one of the blockhouses, with a sense of their need for Divine protection, the refugees were holding worship services. Upon this site would arise a meetinghouse bearing the significant name of Blockhouse Church.

Two miles below Fort Clark stood an eminence upon which was being established for Telfair County a seat of government to be called Jacksonville, in honor of the noted figure now playing such a vital part in the current conflict and some day to become President of the United States.

Marching on past Fort McIntosh, on the night of January 8, the army camped at Little Ocmulgee River, having taken five days to reach this place since leaving Hartford, seventy-three miles away. From Little Ocmulgee, General Blackshear penned to Governor Early a progress report of the expedition up to this point. Blackshear had proceeded by forced marches which he intended to keep up until he reached Fort Barrington. Supplies were critically low. On the previous day, the army would have been completely without provisions except for a singular occurrence. A river boat, laden with supplies bound for the coast, had made its way down the Ocmulgee some distance below the marching column. As the boat continued downstream, the crew became alarmed lest it be drifting into danger. The cautious boatmen deemed it prudent to turn the vessel about and pull upstream for safety. They had proceeded but a short distance when they encountered the frontier army on the river bank. Blackshear, being in dire need of food for his hungry men, authorized the Quartermaster to buy the entire cargo at once. Although delayed in crossing the Little Ocmulgee, the General expressed confidence that the army would reach Bell's Ferry, on the Oconee, by the next day. [10]

While moving toward the scene of invasion as rapidly as possible, Blackshear received alarming reports of trouble ahead. General John Floyd, now stationed at Savannah, hastened word that the British had pillaged the town of St. Mary's and had destroyed the fort at Point Petre. The enemy then seized all vessels in the St. Mary's River and withdrew to Cumberland Island. Floyd estimated the strength of the intruders at 2,000, of which over 400 were reported to be black. He anticipated that the hostiles would proceed up the coast to Darien, and from thence launch an attack upon the city of Savannah. General Floyd was anxiously awaiting the arrival of Blackshear's forces to block the enemy's drive. [11]

Although exerting every effort to hasten his march, Blackshear soon found his way impeded by "a multitude of wagons flying from the horrors of invasion and insurrection." The enemy had taken over most of the area between the St. Mary's River and the Altamaha, and many of the inhabitants were fleeing in frantic haste. The traffic jams thus created on the narrow road rendered the streams, bordered by swamps, almost impassable. The progress of the struggling troops was so retarded that Blackshear feared he would not be able to provide the distressed citizens the speedy relief so urgently needed. [12]

The strength of the frontier army was gradually increasing in numbers. The sick and convalescent left behind in Hartford were rejoining the force, and new cases of sickness were rare. By the time of his arrival on the coast, Blackshear expected a "gradual augmentation" to the number of 900. [13]

From a camp located 118 miles below Hartford, Blackshear communicated to General Floyd his hopes and difficulties. Two days later, the army was in camp 132 miles below Hartford. From this point, General Blackshear notified Captain A. A. Massias that he would arrive at Fort Barrington that evening. In his dispatch, he revealed the joyful news, just received by messenger, that on Monday last, a *feu-de-joie* of nineteen guns had been fired at Fort Hawkins in celebration of the great victory gained by General Andrew Jackson at New Orleans. [14]

Reaching the seacoast after a long, forced march, with few supplies for his men and livestock, General Blackshear set about restoring the spirits of his faithful troops. The weary army was in camp at Darien when the ranks were suddenly electrified by a joyful proclamation. The Treaty of Ghent was declared: England and America had made peace: The war was over!

CHAPTER XVIII

SMOLDERING EMBERS

The treaties growing out of the War of 1812 brought little peace to the Ocmulgee. The Treaty of Ghent ended hostilities with England, and the Treaty of Fort Jackson was designed to prevent further Indian troubles, but in spite of these paper agreements, another crisis was arising. Along the boundary between Georgia and Spanish Florida a situation was smoldering which would soon erupt in full force. The impact of this eruption was destined to reach the Ocmulgee frontier and to precipitate a bitter feud between a Georgia governor and a future president of the United States. This stubborn conflict was the Seminole War.

The Seminoles were a body of Indians made up of many elements. The nucleus around which they developed was the ancient tribe known as the Oconees. From very early times these people occupied a position on the Oconee River near Rock Landing, just below the site of Milledgeville. After the Yamassee War of 1715, the Oconees became alarmed over the encroachments of the white people and abandoned their seat on the Oconee.[1]

For a time, the Oconees dwelt among the kindred Creeks, but finding life there unsuited to their roving ways, they migrated to Florida where they established themselves about 1750.[2] In their new homeland, the Oconees settled among remnant elements of the Indian tribes occupying Florida at the time of De-Soto's expedition. Eventually, these parties, augmented by other fugitive or roving bands, emerged into the people known as Seminoles.

Troubled relations had long existed between the Florida Indians and the Americans. Even before the founding of Georgia, the Spanish Province of Florida had provided a haven of refuge for runaway slaves from South Carolina. Long after slavery was introduced into Georgia, the Blacks continued to flee from their masters to seek asylum beyond the Florida border. Once across the line, the Negroes came within the dominion of a sympathetic Spanish Government. The Florida Indians, likewise, received the runaway Africans hospitably and offered them sanctuary among their own towns and villages. Thus deprived of their costly slaves, the white slaveholders harbored a spirit of resentment toward both the Spaniards and the Seminoles.

With relations already strained between the Georgians and their Florida neighbors, border conflicts frequently occurred to further aggravate matters. When Tecumseh embarked upon his southern campaign, exhorting resistance against the white Americans, his inflammatory appeal found a warm reception among the Seminoles. Tecumseh's fiery crusade, aided by persuasive British agents entrenched among the Seminoles, created an atmosphere of such volcanic nature that violence was inevitable.

So, when the Creek War commenced, the Seminoles sided with the Red Sticks against the white Americans. All during this fierce conflict, the pioneers on the Ocmulgee lived in constant dread of attack from this coalition of hostile powers. The defeat of the Red Sticks at Horseshoe Bend, and the cessation of open hostilities with England, aroused hopes that the Indian troubles were over — but now the hostiles were threatening again.

Although most of the Red Stick warriors had been dealt a deadly blow during the Creek War, a small but dauntless remnant escaped into Florida to find a ready haven among the Seminoles. Led by the Prophet Francis and Peter McQueen, the red Sticks denounced the Treaty of Fort Jackson and vowed to continue the conflict until the bitter end. In this cause, they were strongly supported by the kindred Seminoles.

By the Treaty of Fort Jackson, General Andrew Jackson had wrung from the reluctant red people a large area of land which embraced their ancient and beloved Tallassee County. The territory acquired in Georgia consisted of a wide strip extending across the lower part of the state, from the Wayne County line westward to the Chattahoochee River, and from the Florida border northward to a point centered around present-day Ocilla. The ceded territory was a favorite hunting ground for the Creeks and Seminoles and was the site of many of their towns and villages. In their resentment over the loss of their beloved land, and at the manner in which it was wrested from them, the Red Sticks and Seminoles manifested their determination to drive the white intruders from the land.

Having enjoyed an alliance with the British in their mutual struggle against the white Americans during the late war, the Indians still clung to the belief that England stood ready to help them regain their lost domain. This conviction was given encouragement by a group of British agents remaining among the red people after the war ended. One such agent was Colonel Edward Nicholls, a prime agitator and leader of enemy forces during the war. After peace was declared between England and America, Nicholls remained in Florida where he continued his intrigues among the Seminoles whom he appeared to consider his own special charges. In the spring of 1815, Nicholls proclaimed a high-sounding treaty of offense and defense between the Seminoles and Great Britain. In this movement, Nicholls apparently acted upon his own initiative, with little authority from England. The red people, nevertheless, were led to believe they had full British support in their resistance against the Americans. [3]

Among his intrigues, Colonel Nicholls repaired an abandoned British fort on the Apalachicola River some distance below the juncture of the Flint and Chattahoochee. Through a series of tragic events, this stronghold became known as the Negro Fort. Shortly after restoring the bastion, Nicholls sailed to England with a deputation of Indians for the apparent purpose of gaining the support of the British Government for his singular treaty with the red people. In departing, Nicholls left the fort abundantly stocked with arms and ammunition for the use of his Seminole charges. [4]

Shortly after the departure of Colonel Nicholls, the fort was taken over by a strong band of runaway Negroes who entrenched themselves within the walls of the formidable bastion. From this renegade stronghold, the belligerent Blacks presented a serious threat to the inhabitants of southern Georgia and to the inept Spanish Government of Florida. [5]

In the meantime, the United States Government was proceeding with plans to establish the boundaries of the territory acquired through the Treaty of Fort Jackson. But, as the surveyors commenced their surveys, they were threatened by Indians still dwelling within, or near, the territory in question. As a safeguard for the Georgia-Florida boundary, a military force under the command of General Edmund Pendleton Gaines was sent to the troubled land. Upon his approach, Gaines viewed the smoldering situation with such alarm that he took the prudent step of authorizing the erection of a military stronghold near the juncture of the Flint and Chattahoochee some distance above the Negro Fort. The new outpost was named Fort Scott. [6]

In order for Fort Scott to serve as an effective military base, it was necessary for it to be supplied with provisions and military materials. The most direct route for conveying the supplies was by boat from New Orleans and Mobile, along the Gulf coast, and up the Apalachicola River. A well-laden convoy was dispatched along this route. The hazardous course led under the very guns of the Negro Fort. As the convoy approached the outlaw bastion, it received a blast of fire from the fort's arms. In swift retaliation, the gunboat fired a hot shell which, by rare chance, landed in a magazine inside the fort. The terrific explosion which followed shattered the Negro Fort and killed most of its occupants. [7]

The destruction of the Negro Fort removed one source of danger from the troubled Florida border, but it set into motion other events of far-reaching effect. The incident focused attention upon the apparent impotence of the Spanish Government in keeping order within its Florida domain. The failure of the Spanish officials to quell the Negro uprising, along with their lack of restraint upon the Seminoles, convinced many Americans that the Spanish could not be depended upon to maintain order within their own land, and led to a demand for the annexation of Florida to the United States.

The Negro Fort incident aggravated the troublesome situation already developing along the Florida border. Through circumstances surrounding the event, the Indians became acutely aware of the presence of Fort Scott, and other American military outposts, standing upon land which they considered their own. With these forbidding bastions frowning down upon them, the Seminoles feared that the time was rapidly approaching when all of their treasured domain would be taken from them by the land-grabbing Americans. [8] This alarming prospect produced among them a state of desperation boding no good for their white neighbors.

Brooding over the never-ceasing advancement of the white Americans, the Seminoles grasped at any straw offering hope for repelling the intruders. During the year 1817, their spirits were bolstered by the arrival of a British trader, Alexander Arbuthnot, who immediately espoused the cause of the red people. From thenceforward, Arbuthnot worked tirelessly for the Seminoles. Serving as spokesman for the red wanderers, the trader sent a barrage of appeals and protests to the British Government, the Spanish Government, and the American Indian Agent. [9]

The war clouds hovering over the troubled land were darkened by the appearance among the Seminoles of another British adventurer to further inflame their sullen mood. This impetuous agitator, Robert Ambrister, was a former associate of Colonel Edward Nicholls whose name was anathema to American patriots. Upon his arrival in Florida, Ambrister threw himself headlong into the smoldering Seminole intrigue. Openly advocating a resort to armed force, the reckless adventurer led the Seminoles down the red paths of war. [10]

As the year moved uneasily along, the state of hostility between the aggressive whites and the sullen Indians increased in intensity. Foolhardy parties on both sides were encroaching, burning, and killing. The breaking point was near.

Amid mounting animosities, General Gaines was engaged in negotiations with the Seminole chiefs. Placing the blame solely upon the Indians, Gaines demanded an end to their marauding attacks. The Seminole chief, Kenhagee, with equal determination, insisted that the white people cease their aggressive actions toward the Indians. [11] An impasse was reached which only a resort to arms could breach.

First to feel the weight of American arms was Fowltown, a Seminole settlement located fourteen miles east of Fort Scott. Standing upon territory ceded at Fort Jackson, Fowltown faced abandonment, with its occupants doomed to removal. With their familiar homesites approaching extinction, the inhabitants vowed they would hold on to their land at all costs. The chief boldly warned Colonel Twiggs, Commandant of Fort Scott, to keep hands off all territory east of the Flint River, which he vociferously claimed as his own. General Gaines promptly sent a runner to summon the defiant chieftain to Fort Scott for a talk. The adamant chief refused to budge. [12]

General Gaines then dispatched a military party to Fowltown to bring in by force the chief and his warriors. The detachment, under command of Colonel Twiggs, reached the town just before dawn. As the whites approached, brisk firing erupted from both sides. Seeing that they were opposed by an overwhelming force, the red people fled the scene, leaving their abandoned settlement in the hands of the victors. [13]

The infuriated redskins struck swiftly back. Ten days later, a boat occupied by troops, soldiers' wives and children was making its slow way up the Apalachicola River to Fort Scott. When almost within sight of the fort, the boat was ambushed by a band of frenzied savages. Surprised and overwhelmed, the occupants were mercilessly slaughtered. Men and women alike were scalped, and the brains of the children were dashed out against the sides of the boat. Few escaped. [14]

Other atrocities followed in rapid succession, and before the year was over even Fort Scott was threatened. In the face of the mounting crisis, General Gaines urgently appealed to the federal government for vigorous support. But, by an odd quirk of circumstances, the Secretary of War, not yet having received Gaines's message, ordered the General to proceed from his critical post to Amelia Island where a body of revolutionaries was adding to the border troubles. So, at this crucial moment, the smoldering field was left without a general commander. [15] But not for long.

When apprised of the seriousness of the situation, the Secretary of War ordered General Andrew Jackson to take immediate command of the troops on the Georgia frontier. [16]

Meanwhile, with Jackson's aid yet a matter of the future, the American forces within the troubled land were experiencing severe difficulties. Fort Scott was now occupied by a garrison under the command of Lt. Col. Arbuckle. With the fort's supply lines cut off by the enemy, this force was facing such a serious scarcity of food that Arbuckle feared the fort would fall.[17]

Seventy miles up the Flint River from Fort Scott was stationed a detachment of Georgia militia under command of General Thomas Glasscock. This force was attempting to protect the Georgia frontier through the same strategy employed by General David Blackshear during the late Creek War. By placing troops on the Flint River forty miles in advance of the Ocmulgee boundary, Glasscock hoped to arrest any attack upon the frontier before it could get started.

On January 18, 1818, General Glasscock's army was encamped in the vicinity of Blackshear's old fort, eight miles above the nearest Chehaw Indian town. Finding Fort Early somewhat deteriorated, Glasscock's men erected a stockade upon the site to provide a stronghold sufficient for frontier defense.[18] Being dependent upon the Blackshear Road for communication with the white settlements on the Ocmulgee, the troops at Fort Early were again placed in a difficult position for securing supplies. During the torrential winter rains, the road became so boggy that supply wagons were unable to get through to the outpost. It then became necessary to send supplies by means of packhorses, a slow and tedious procedure.

In an effort to find sorely-needed provisions, a small party was sent down the Flint River to the Chehaw settlement known as Fulemmy's Town. While the whites were there, a body of hostile Indians in charge of Chenubby, a chief of the Fowltown Tribe, made its appearance near the town. Fearing attack, the leader of the military party hastily dispatched an appeal to Fort Early for reinforcements. During the night, Major Thomas Woodward led a small relief force to the aid of the stranded militia.[19]

With the coming of the dawn, it was discovered that the hostiles had departed, moving toward Fort Early and the Ocmulgee settlements beyond. Major Woodward's detachment pursued the Indians until late in the day when, having seen only the trail of the elusive redskins, the men returned to Fort Early. At the fort, they were informed that Major Morgan had been out with another party of militia and had come across the trail of the Indians. Following until nightfall, Morgan's men came within sight of the enemy six miles from Fort Early. The next morning, a friendly red man came into camp with the disturbing report that the hostiles had broken camp and were moving toward Hartford.[20]

This turn of events brought grave concern to General Glass-cock, for he knew that at this very moment, a pack train was making its way from Hartford to his camp. The General feared that the provision train would be waylaid by the redskins with disastrous results. During the evening of January 22, Glasscock ordered Major Franklin Heard to take five men and proceed hastily toward Hartford to meet the approaching convoy. [21]

Setting out along the Blackshear Road, the party soon came to Cedar Creek. Proceeding two miles east of the creek, the militia party met the pack train, plodding along unaware of the presence of danger. Major Heard hastily warned Captain Leigh, commander of the convoy, of possible trouble. Then, with five men, Heard set out ahead of the provision train to scout the uncertain path. The pack train, guarded by twenty men under command of Cornet Issac Brown, followed at a distance [22]

Reaching Cedar Creek, the advance party halted to adjust a loose strap which was about to fall. Captain Thomas Leigh and Private Samuel Loftis continued on into the swamp. Major Heard called out to Leigh to warn him of danger ahead. Leigh responded that he "thought not," and moved on. As they approached the opposite bank of Cedar Creek, Leigh and Loftis suddenly received a blast of fire from hostiles lying in ambush amid the sheltering growth of the swamp. Both men fell dead upon the spot.[23]

From the sound of the volley, Major Heard judged that there were from twenty to thirty Indians in the attack. The Major wheeled his horse sharply about and galloped back to the provision train. Upon his orders, the entire procession fled to the shelter of Blackshear's old breastworks mercifully at hand on the east side of Cedar Creek. From this refuge, Captain Strother and John Bridges slipped downstream, hoping to cross over to Glasscock's camp for assistance. [24]

After nightfall, reinforcements reached the stranded party. The provision train then continued on its way. When the men reached the scene of the ambush, they found, to their horror, that the savages had scalped Loftis and cut off Leigh's head. The soldiers' mutilated bodies were borne by their companions to Fort Early, six miles away. [25]

CHAPTER XIX

OLD HICKORY TO THE FRONT

Within days after the ambuscade at Cedar Creek, General Andrew Jackson was on his way to the Ocmulgee frontier. Upon receipt of his orders at home in Tennessee, Old Hickory promptly prepared for an expedition to the Seminole War front. Arrangements were made for a rendezvous at Fayetteville, not far from Jackson's residence. From this place, the main Tennessee forces, under command of Inspector-General Hayne, would proceed to Fort Jackson in Alabama territory. Arriving there, they would replenish their supplies and hasten on to Fort Scott. Jackson would leave earlier and proceed to Fort Scott by the way of the Ocmulgee frontier.

On January 22, 1818, General Jackson, accompanied by a guard of two companies, left Nashville for Georgia. Proceeding by the way of Monticello in Jasper County, he reached Fort Hawkins on the evening of February 9.[1] Marching on down the east side of the Ocmulgee River, Jackson arrived three days later at the frontier settlement of Hartford. Here he found awaiting him General Gaines, with a force of Georgia Militia recently raised for the expedition. Encouraged at the promptness with which the Georgia troops had assembled, Old Hickory was led to hope he would be able to make a speedy march to Fort Scott.[2] But, at this crucial moment, torrents of winter rain descended upon the frontier, flooding streams and rendering roads impassable.

General Jackson remained at Hartford for seven days. During this period, he made final plans for his campaign against the Seminoles. At the same time, the famous leader was afforded the opportunity of observing frontier life as it was lived at the outpost settlement of Hartford, directly across the Ocmulgee River from the Creek Nation of Indians.

Tidings of the arrival of the hero of New Orleans and Horseshoe Bend brought a surge of excitement and hope to the troubled frontier. Now the Seminoles would share the fate of the Red Sticks! And Old Hickory was ready for action. Here, at the gateway to the Indian country, the battle-scarred warrior stood poised for a crushing assault upon the Seminoles and their allies.

On a wintry day in February, Jackson's troops crossed over the Ocmulgee River and stepped upon the soil of the Creek Nation. Marching with an air of determination, they set out through the wilderness toward Fort Early on the Flint. But the torrential rains had so flooded the countryside that the men found the streams out of their banks and the ground so "rotten" that movement was painfully slow. As the column proceeded along the Blackshear Road, Jackson soon saw that the road was impassable for vehicles. Tenaciously, Old Hickory ordered the soldiers to abandon wagons and convey their baggage upon the backs of the wagon-horses. [3]

Like a slowly-crawling snail, the column of humanity wound its way along the boggy thoroughfare. Within a mile of Hartford the men crossed a small branch completely out of its banks. Three miles farther, and they came to Big Creek where they went into camp. On the next morning, after marching six miles, the troops crossed a creek at the foot of a flinty hill. Continuing on past the site of Friendship Church, the column crossed over the spot where Cordele would some day arise. Another march, and the toiling soldiers reached Cedar Creek where they viewed the scene of the grisly attack upon Glasscock's provision train. Six more weary miles, and the army reached Fort Early. [4]

At Fort Early, bitter disappointment awaited Andrew Jackson and his footsore, hungry men. Jackson had intended to use the Flint station only as a wayside stop on his way to Fort Scott. Here he expected to find awaiting him enough food to meet his immediate needs and to provide a reserve sufficient for the march to Fort Scott. [5] But, from the beginning of hostilities with the Seminoles, the military forces had encountered serious difficulty in securing provisions for their isolated outposts—and now the pinch was sorely felt.

In an effort to improve matters General Gaines had worked out a plan whereby supplies would be sent from Fort Hawkins, along the Federal Road to the Creek Agency on the Flint. Here they would be loaded upon river boats and sent downstream to supply both Fort Early and Fort Scott. To prevent enemy attack upon the vessels, they were designed in such a novel manner as to render them "ball-proof." Two provision boats were scheduled to reach Fort Early by the time of Jackson's arrival—but they had not come. Now General Jackson found himself at a remote outpost deep in Indian country, with a large body of hungry men, but "without a barrel of flour or a bushel of corn." [6]

To add to the mounting difficulties, an urgent communication was received from the commandant of Fort Scott warning that unless he received food for his starving garrison, he would be compelled to abandon the post. In a desperate effort to prevent such a calamity, General Gaines took twelve men, placed them on board a boat laden with such emergency rations as he could procure, and set out down the Flint River for the relief of Fort Scott. [7]

Faced with a compelling mission, but without sufficient provisions for the task, Old Hickory resolved to march on to Fort Scott. At least, he had "pork on foot," and hoped to secure some corn at friendly Indian settlements along the way. So, on February 27, 1818, General Andrew Jackson set his column in motion down the Flint River toward Fort Scott. Proceeding four miles along the east bank of the stream, the troops crossed over at a ferry. Continuing on along an Indian trail, they reached the Chehaw town of Au-muc-cul-le, located on Muckalee Creek eight miles beyond the Flint River. The town consisted of from fifteen to twenty cabins, with a large council house in the center. The red inhabitants received the soldiers cordially. Not only did the Chehaws furnish the whites with all the corn they could spare, but the warriors joined the ranks of Jackson's army to go against the foe. [8]

From the Chehaw Town, the column wended its way toward Fort Scott. About five miles from Au-muc-cul-le, the army crossed Kinchafoonee Creek three miles below Kinnard's old trading establishment. On the south side of the creek, the men observed the remains of an ancient town of considerable size. Still marching generally southward, the army struck Echenoche Creek five miles from its juncture with the Flint and crossed a branch of the same stream four miles farther along. From this crossing, the path followed the Flint River all the way to Fort Scott sixty miles below the Chehaw Town. The fort was situated on the west bank of the Flint about eight miles above its confluence with the Chattahoochee to form the Apalachicola River. [9]

On the evening of March 9, Jackson's weary men reached Fort Scott. Here Jackson found his worst fears fully realized. Within the walls of the fort was a garrison of starving men. Ominously, nothing had been heard from General Gaines and his river boat with its emergency cargo. [10]

Now, at this outpost in a hostile land far from supplies, Andrew Jackson faced a critical decision. Should he remain at the protective stronghold, or move deeper into enemy territory? With starvation stalking the ramparts, there could be but one outcome if he chose to pause. To push forward was to risk the danger of the unknown. Never one to remain indecisive, the indomitable Old Hickory faced his column directly toward the enemy, and sounded the command to march.

CHAPTER XX

HOSTILE FLAMES REACH THE FRONTIER

The flames of the Seminole conflict were touching the Ocmulgee frontier. Five days after Jackson's army departed from Fort Early, an incident occurred on the Ocmulgee which set off a series of confrontations between the white pioneers and the hostile redskins, culminating in a bitter feud between General Andrew Jackson and Governor William Rabun of Georgia.

Throughout the era of Indian troubles on the Ocmulgee, the portion of the frontier lying upon the Big Bend was especially vulnerable to savage attacks. The territory on the Indian side of the Big Bend was of particular value to the red people as an abundant hunting ground. At certain times of the year, the Indians came from all parts of their country to the Ocmulgee River to hunt along its wooded banks and to fish in its teeming waters. From the Indian settlements on the Flint and Chattahoochee, well-worn pathways led directly to the Big Bend. Reaching the vicinity of the stream, the paths divided into an intricate network of hunting trails winding through the wilderness and penetrating the deepest recesses of the river swamp. At certain places, the trails met in crossroads fashion. Occasionally, at the crossways, primitive pole huts could be found, offering shelter to the roving huntsmen.

The land along the Big Bend proved as alluring to pushing white settlers as to red hunters. Although without legal right, over-eager whites began to cross over the Ocmulgee and establish homes within the network of Indian pathways. Now, with hostile Indians stalking through the woods and with new pioneer cabins arising defiantly in their paths, a situation emerged pointing toward inescapable confrontation.

In the spring of 1818, as the Seminole troubles were reaching a climax, a large body of Indians appeared on the Big Bend opposite Telfair County. Taking advantage of the isolated settlers, the savages drove off livestock, applied the firebrand to houses, and threatened all who fell within their paths. [1]

On the third of March, Joseph Burch and a young son, Littleton, crossed over the Ocmulgee from Telfair County to the Indian-infested side. Reaching a spot near present-day Oscewichee

Springs, the pair commenced erecting a shelter. After nightfall, the father and son continued their camping activities without any sense of impending danger. Suddenly, from the darkness beyond the light of the campfire, came a deadly blast. The marauding savages had crept stealthily upon the unsuspecting whites and opened fire. Joseph Burch was killed instantly, and Littleton was seriously wounded. The merciless savages then fell upon the hapless pair and scalped the dead father and the living son. Although conscious and suffering the pain of the scalping knife, the quick-witted youth feigned death to preserve his life from his assailants. Concluding that young Burch was dead, the Indians departed with his bloody scalp. [2]

The wounded lad mustered enough strength to stagger through the darkness toward the river. Reaching the bank of the stream, he endeavored to relieve the burning pain of his scalped head by applying a poultice of damp moss to the raw wound. Then, somehow, the weakened boy crossed the treacherous Ocmulgee to the safety of the white side. Setting out from the river bank, Littleton Burch dragged his wounded body to the home of John Willcox, situated on the River Road two miles above Temperance. The Willcox family warmly welcomed the lad to their fireside and administered all possible aid to his wounded body and sorrowful spirit. [3]

The startling news of the Indian attack spread rapidly along the Ocmulgee. Tidings of the tragic event were received with mingled alarm and anger. With redskins on the warpath just beyond the narrow Ocmulgee, the whites feared the savages would slip across the stream and fall upon their habitations. The faint of heart fearfully fled to the safety of the interior, but the courageous ones grimly held their ground.

The first concern of the aroused inhabitants was to seek safety for themselves and their families. With their homes so widely scattered along the Big Bend, each home was in danger. In accordance with pioneer custom, doubtlessly, many abandoned their homes and sought refuge behind the sheltering walls of Fort Adams close at hand. The area most seriously threatened lay along the east bank of the Ocmulgee in the Copeland and Temperance settlements. It was on this front that Fort Adams was erected when the frontier faced a similar threat during the late Creek War. [4] Many of the veterans who had built and garrisoned the post were still dwelling in the neighborhood of the station. Among these were Jehu McCall, Joseph Fletcher, Griffin Fletcher, John Fletcher, William Griffin, Benjamin Mitchell Griffin, Moses Rountree, William Rountree, John McAnnally, William Studstill, Norman McLeod, Lain Posey, John Posey, and Major Josiah D. Cawthon.[5] It was upon the shoulders of these pioneer military men that the burden fell of once more protecting the inhabitants from a newly-rising peril.

Littleton Burch reached the Willcox home on the fifth of March. Doubtlessly, the next two days were spent in rounding up the scattered settlers and getting them into the stockade of Fort Adams. With the women and children safely lodged inside the stronghold, the next step lay ahead. The marauding savages must be pursued and destroyed. All able-bodied men must rally to the call.

By the eighth of March, thirty-four Telfair citizens had assembled for action. From the neighborhood of China Hill, Temperance, Hopewell, and Copeland they had come. Most were soldiers in the Creek War or more recent recruits of the Telfair Militia. Major Josiah D. Cawthon assumed command, with Captain Benjamin Mitchell Griffin second in command.[6]

Setting out from the vicinity of Fort Adams, the little force marched resolutely toward the Ocmulgee to seek redress. Reaching the river opposite Jordan's Bluff, the men crossed over by fording or ferrying the stream.[7] On the southwest side of the Ocmulgee, the men found themselves at the crossway of four well-beaten Indian trails.[8] At this place stood a simple Indian hut offering shelter to red huntsmen while following the trails. Running up and down the edge of the river swamp was the ancient River Trail. Then, leading away from the River Trail in a south-westerly direction was another path. This trail followed a direct line to the bank of Big House Creek five miles away. Crossing the creek about a mile above the old Barrentine Ford, the trail curved westward and continued on toward the Flint River.[9] From visible signs left by the redskins, the whites concluded that the Indians had taken this path. Major Cawthon set the party in pursuit along the Indian trail. As the men moved along, they saw numerous signs of depredations recently committed by the red intruders. The Indians had burned several houses and driven off large numbers of cattle and hogs belonging to the white dwellers.[10]

It was evidently late in the day when the Telfair men crossed the river and darkness descended upon them before they had proceeded very far from the crossing place. Deeming it prudent, no doubt, the men went into camp while still at a safe distance from the foe.[11]

Early next morning, the whites resumed the chase. Three miles southwest of the crossing at Jordan's Bluff was the head of a small branch. Rising from a bubbling spring, the branch flowed a distance of a mile, then merged with the main run of

Big House Creek just above Barrentine Ford. Near the spring, at the crossway of three Indian trails, stood another hunter's hut similar to the one at Jordan's Bluff. [12] The trail of the redskins pointed directly toward this Indian campsite. Tradition has it that as the Telfair forces approached the branch head, the Indians were having breakfast in their camp scattered around the hut. But the cunning redskins were not caught off guard.

As the Telfair men drew near, they suddenly found themselves face to face with an advancing foe. Here the whites and Indians met head-on. As the opposing parties advanced, firing erupted from both sides. Along the gentle slope rising from the branch head, the fighting raged for nearly an hour. Both opponents fought in savage fashion, firing from behind trees, logs or other objects affording shelter from the withering enemy fire. [13]

As the fierce combat continued, it soon became apparent that the whites were outnumbered and were facing a force of forty to sixty fiercely-fighting savages. Gradually, the numerical superiority of the Indians turned the tide of battle. The whites, outflanked, were forced to drop back. At first, the retreat was orderly, but as the ferocity of the attack reached its peak, the whites broke ranks. From this moment, it was every man for himself. The routed Telfair men employed every conceivable means of avoiding capture or death. One wounded white struggled down the branch and eased himself into a small lake known as Jones's Pond. Here, the refugee was able to avoid detection by submerging his body in the water with only his nose protruding for air. [14]

In the fiercely-fought battle, seven whites were killed and three wounded. Four Indians were known to be dead. Among the Telfair men killed in action were Captain Benjamin Mitchell Griffin, William Mooney, William Morrison, _____ Nobles, and Michael Burch, an older son of Joseph Burch, the martyr. The wounded were Moses Rountree, John Lawson, and Mark Willcox, young son of John Willcox. [15] In addition to the dead and wounded, other Telfair County men known to have participated in the affray were Redding Hunter, Daniel Drawdy, John Willcox and another son, James Lea Willcox. [16]

In the retreat, Thompson Nathaniel Statham found Mark Willcox lying upon the ground seriously wounded. Statham and Willcox were bitter enemies and not on speaking terms. It was even rumored that they were carrying guns for each other. But, when Statham saw his rival lying helpless and in danger of losing both life and scalp, he was unwilling to leave young Willcox to the mercy of the savages. Placing the wounded youth upon his back, Statham carried him all the way back to the boat landing. [17]

Some of the men retreated to the boats and rowed to the safety of the Telfair side of the Ocmulgee. Others were lost in the wilderness, or remained in hiding. Major Cawthon was among the missing and even reported killed in battle,[18] This, however, was an erroneous report, for on the tenth of March, Cawthon was back in Telfair County, from whence he dispatched an account of the historic event to Governor William Rabun. [19] At the same time, Major Cawthon urgently appealed for assistance, fearing the troubled frontier would break.

From this struggle between white pioneers and red warriors at the head of an obscure wilderness branch, the stream was known thereafter as Breakfast Branch. [20]

On the day after the skirmish, Lieutenant Colonel Richard H. Thomas, now commanding the Pulaski County Militia at Hartford, received a short dispatch from Isham Jordan of Telfair County, reporting the dreadful news. Thomas immediately relayed Jordan's communication to Governor William Rabun in Milledgeville. [21] Rabun hastily authorized Thomas to support the bruised frontier by calling out all available forces to scour the country in search of the enemy. [22] By the thirteenth of March, a force under Captain Benjamin S. Lanier of Pulaski County and a company of cavalry commanded by Captain James Harrison of Twiggs County were in the field. On the next day, a detachment of drafted men led by Captain William Pace of Pulaski County was ordered to the frontier.

Among the military forces dispatched to the defense of the Telfair frontier was a company from Laurens County commanded by Captain Jacob Robinson. This small party was destined to play a peculiar role in the unexpected turn of events soon to follow. Seeking to relieve the threat of danger on the Big Bend, Governor Rabun ordered Captain Robinson to the Telfair front where he would relieve a detachment from Pulaski County commanded by Captain Furney F. Gatlin. Robinson's men rendezvoued at Dublin on March 13, and set out for their assigned post. [23]

Reaching the Big Bend of the Ocmulgee, Captain Robinson stationed his men on the southwest side of the river near the scene of the recent Indian depredations. Here, at an unprotected place, the soldiers erected a fort which was placed under the care of a guard of infantry. [24] While his men were encamped beyond the Ocmulgee, Captain Robinson crossed back over the river to the boatyard of John Willcox near the Temperance settlement. At the boatyard, according to Robinson, the Captain conferred with Willcox about having a boat built for himself.

For this act of seeming negligence, Jacob Robinson would be called into account. [25]

After fourteen days on the Telfair frontier, with no signs of further Indian depredations, Captain Robinson decided to march his detachment back home. According to his report, supplies were running low, and he intended to return for replenishment. From their station on the Big Bend, the men proceeded back upstream to Hartford. [26]

Upon reaching Hartford, Captain Robinson encountered Captain Obed Wright, who was in command of a small force of Georgia Militia at the frontier post. From Captain Wright, Jacob Robinson learned of a plan for an expedition against the Indians who had caused the trouble on the Big Bend. Without hesitation, Captain Robinson volunteered to join the expedition. [27]

CHAPTER XXI

A BITTER FEUD ERUPTS

In the face of their many troubles, the Telfair inhabitants had appealed to Governor William Rabun for assistance in protecting their lives and property. The defeat of the military force at Breakfast Branch brought another wave of panic along the Ocmulgee. The alarm, although felt along the entire frontier line, reached its height in the area of the Big Bend. Lying within the arc formed by the Ocmulgee in its downward sweep, Telfair County occupied the most exposed position on the frontier. Having borne the brunt of depredations and defeat, the Telfair people were filled with fear and fury. The resolute ones, daring to remain upon their endangered lands, were undergoing daily dislocations in their pattern of living. With the season for planting at hand, many were forced to remain forted in and were unable to get on with their seasonal labors. Hopefully, the Telfair citizens awaited assistance from their governor.

The appeals of the troubled pioneers fell upon sympathetic ears. Fully aware of the precarious position occupied by the white citizens, Governor Rabun resolved to give them protection. The bulk of Georgia's military forces were now with General Andrew Jackson. Rabun was convinced that, with Georgia's own frontier under attack, Jackson should take steps to provide the needed protection. Accordingly, on March 21, the Governor hastened an appeal to Jackson for assistance. Informing the General of the attack upon the Burch campers, with the resulting skirmish at Breakfast Branch, and the state of alarm engendered by these events, Rabun requested that some of the Georgia troops be stationed near the Big Bend and at the most assailable places below. [1]

The Governor's appeal was hastily dispatched by courier to General Jackson, now marching southward away from the endangered Ocmulgee.

On the same day that the whites and Indians met in combat at Breakfast Branch, Jackson's army reached Fort Scott. It was here that Rabun's plea was placed in the hands of the crusty warrior. But Old Hickory was unmoved by the plight of Georgia's Chief Executive. Beset with troubles of his own, Jackson now stood at the gateway to the Seminole country. Poised for attack, it was unthinkable to him that he should divert any of his forces for what he considered an insignificant purpose. Jackson simply ignored the plea of Georgia's governor.[2]

Stung by Jackson's rebuff, Rabun resolved to plan his own course of action. Through reports which he considered reliable, Rabun concluded that the recent attacks upon the Big Bend had come from two Chehaw villages situated on the Flint River a few miles below Fort Early. These villages were named for their chiefs, Phillemmee and Hopaunee, who had long harassed the Georgia frontier with their depredations. The majority of the warriors were said to be painted in war paint, and cattle recently driven from the Big Bend had been seen in their villages.[3]

Governor Rabun resolved to take decisive action. He was sure that any attempted defensive measures would prove ineffective. The initiative would still remain with the opponents. The clever redskins knew the weak points on the frontier and could choose the time and place to strike best suited to their own designs. Instead of a weak defense, Rabun favored a strong offense. The power of the hostiles must be destroyed at its source — within their own settlements.

At this opportune time, there was stationed at the key frontier post of Hartford a small force of Georgia Militia under the command of Captain Obed Wright of Chatham County. Wright's detachment was a remnant of the troops which had joined Jackson's army at Hartford and marched with him toward the land of the Seminoles. Governor Rabun decided to use Captain Wright's party as the core around which he would assemble a force to advance against the hostile Indian villages.[4] To bolster Wright's command, Rabun ordered Captains Dean and Childs to bring their details from the frontier stations to join Wright's party. At the same time, two companies of cavalry were assigned to the forces gathering at Hartford.[5] It was while these preparations were being made that Captain Jacob Robinson's command arrived at Hartford from the Telfair front. Being informed by Captain Wright of the proposed plan, Captain Robinson, although without authority, volunteered the services of his detachment for the expedition.[6]

Deeming General Jackson's army too far away to afford any protection to the Ocmulgee, Governor Rabun ordered Captain Wright to proceed against the hostile villages of Phillemmee and Hopaunee and utterly destroy them.[7] Wright willingly took steps to comply.

On April 21, with some 270 effective troops, Captain Obed Wright set out from Hartford for the Indian settlements on the

Flint River. Proceeding along the well-trodden Blackshear Road, the men made a quick march and reached Fort Early the next day. As he approached the fort, Captain Wright encountered "several persons of veracity" who informed him that the old chieftain, Hopaunee, whose town had turned hostile, had recently taken his abode in the neighboring Chehaw town of Au-muc-cul-le. This was the town in which General Jackson had received such a cordial welcome on his way to Fort Scott. Wright's informants continued with the intelligence that, although some of the Chehaws were with Jackson's army, most of them had fallen under the influence of Hopaunee and were now hostile.[8]

Believing the information to be reliable, Captain Obed Wright immediately changed his plan of attack. Instead of continuing on down the Flint to the villages of Phillemmee and Hopaunee, he would cross over the river and proceed directly against the Chehaw Town eight miles beyond.[9]

Upon reaching Fort Early, Captain Wright discussed his plan with Captain Bothwell who was in command of the fort. Bothwell tried to convince Wright that Hopaunee was a loyal friend who, that very day, had brought to Fort Early a public horse which had been lost. Unconvinced, Captain Wright persisted with his plan of attack. In accordance with his general orders, he called upon Captain Bothwell for support. Bothwell reluctantly furnished additional troops, but refused to go along himself.[10]

According to Captain Wright's account of the events which followed, the force crossed the Flint on the night of April 22, and advanced cautiously toward the Chehaw Town. When within a half mile of the town, the advance guard captured an Indian who was attending a drove of cattle. Mr. McDuffie, a member of Wright's party, readily identified some of the cattle as his own property. This circumstance further pointed the finger of guilt at the occupants of Au-muc-cul-le.[11]

Reaching the Indian town, Captain Wright directed an immediate attack, but with positive orders not to injure the women and children. As the militia rushed upon them, the red people hastily took refuge inside the houses, from whence, through the crevices, they fired a number of shots at the whites. Finding the Indians thus inaccessible to their charge, the militia set the houses on fire, in consequence of which a number of occupants were burned to death. Wright estimated that between forty and fifty Indians perished in the affray; but a considerable number of warriors made their escape by fleeing to the safety of a thick swamp near-by. While searching through the town, the Georgians discovered a large supply of gunpowder which they promptly destroyed. As a final appraisal of the situation, Captain Wright stated, "The town was completely desolated without the loss of a man." [12]

Having thus destroyed the Chehaw Town, the forces of Captain Obed Wright recrossed the Flint the same evening and returned to Fort Early. From thence, they marched back to Hartford.

In the meantime, General Andrew Jackson had directed his expedition against the Seminole towns deep within the Spanish domain of Florida. Indian resistance to such strong odds was feeble as Jackson's army overwhelmed the hostile settlements, dispersed the natives within the swamps, and left their towns in ashes. Learning that some of his enemies had taken refuge inside the walls of the Spanish fort at St. Marks, Old Hickory promptly seized the fort and executed the leaders of the Seminole cause.

Having overrun all elements within his path, and deeming General Glasscock's Georgia troops no longer needed, Jackson dispatched the men back to Hartford to be mustered and discharged.

On his way to Hartford, Glasscock followed a route leading near the Chehaw Town. Being in need of beef, and remembering the generosity of the Chehaws on his march down to Fort Scott, General Glasscock sent a small party to the town in search of food. Arriving at Au-muc-cul-le just four days after Wright's attack, the men found the Indian town burned and deserted. [13]

Upon reaching Fort Early, General Glasscock hastily dispatched to General Jackson the details of Wright's assault upon the Chehaw Town, as they appeared to him. Glasscock stated that after Wright assumed command of the militia at Hartford, "he obtained certificates of several men on the frontier that the Chehaw Indians had taken part in a skirmish on the Big Bend. He immediately gained orders from the Governor to destroy the towns of Philemmee and Opaunee." When Wright's forces reached Chehaw, stated Glasscock, "An advance was ordered, and the cavalry rushed forward to commence the massacre. Even after the firing and murder commenced Major Howard, an old chief . . . came out of his house with a white flag in front of the line. It was not respected. An order was given for a general fire, and nearly 400 guns were discharged at him before one took effect. He fell and was bayoneted; his son was also killed . . . seven men were killed, one woman, and two children . . . ." [14]

When Andrew Jackson received Glasscock's communication, he blazed with fury. Decisively, he dispatched Major Davis to

Hartford to arrest Captain Wright and deliver him in irons to the military authorities at Fort Hawkins. Then, with anger at white heat, Old Hickory sat down, pen in hand, and vented his anger at Governor Rabun with these words: "I have this moment received by express the letter of General Glasscock . . . detailing the base, cowardly, and inhuman attack on the old women and men of the Chehaw village, while the warriors of that village were fighting the battles of our country against the common enemy . . . ."

Warming up to his subject, Jackson threatened: "That a Governor of a State should assume the right to make war against an Indian tribe, in perfect peace with and under the protection of the United States, is assuming a responsibility that I trust you will be able to excuse to the government of the United States, to which you will have to answer . . . ." Then, striking at Captain Wright, Jackson fired: "But it is still more strange that there could exist within the United States a cowardly monster in human shape that would violate the sanctity of the white flag when borne by any person, but more particularly when in the hands of a superannuated chief, worn down with age. Such base cowardice and murderous conduct as this transaction affords has not its parallel in history, and shall meet with merited punishment . . . ."

Now, aiming his blast directly at Rabun, the irate General commanded: "You, sir, as Governor of a State within my military division have no right to give a military order whilst I am in the field . . . Captain Wright must be prosecuted and punished for his outrageous murder . . . I call upon you as Governor of Georgia to aid into effect my order for his arrest and confinement . . . ." [15]

William Rabun was not the man to bear Jackson's denunciation in silence. Long had the harassed Governor grappled with the thankless task of striving to provide protection for a difficult, defenseless frontier line. Well did Rabun recall the desperation of the appeal which he had so urgently sent to Jackson for assistance. The callousness of Jackson's rebuff still burned in Rabun's memory. And now Jackson had the audacity to direct to Georgia's governor this dispatch reeking with abuse.

William Rabun, himself a man of decisive action, promptly dispatched a blistering reply: "Had you, sir, or General Glasscock been in possession of the facts which produced this affair, it is to be presumed, at least, that you would not have indulged in the strain so indecorous and unbecoming." Taking Jackson to task for his indifference toward Georgia's plight, Rabun reminded him: "I had . . . stated the seriousness of our bleeding frontiers to you, and requested you in respectful terms to detach a part of your overwhelming force for our protection . . . to which you never deigned to reply."

Then, giving Jackson a taste of his own bitter medicine, Rabun thundered: "You state, in a very haughty tone that 'I as a Governor of a State within your military division, have no right to give a military order whilst you are in the field.' Wretched and contemptible, indeed, must be our situation, if that be the fact. When the liberties of the people of Georgia shall have been prostrated at the feet of despotism, then, and not till then, will this imperious doctrine be tamely submitted to."

Now, asserting his own adamant position, the Governor bluntly stated: "You may rest assured, that, if the savages continue their depredations on our unprotected frontier, I shall think and act for myself in that respect. You demand that Captain Wright be delivered in irons to your agent, Major Davis. If you, sir, are unacquainted with the fact, I beg leave to inform you, that Captain Wright was not under your command . . . ." [16]

Upon receiving Governor Rabun's sharp retort, Old Hickory, his dander still up, replied: "I am not disposed to enter into any controversy with you relative to respective duties, but would recommend an examination of the laws of our country, before you hazard an opinion on the subject." Riled at Rabun's accusation of "military despotism," the old warrior retorted: "'The liberties of the people prostrated at the feet of military despotism' are cant expressions for political purpose. The better part of the community know too well they have nothing to apprehend in this quarter. The military have rights secured them by the laws of our country as well as civil, and in my respect for those of the latter I will never permit those of the former to be outraged with impunity."

Adding sarcasm to anger, Andrew Jackson jabbed: "Your letter . . . on which you . . . dwell with so much force, you must have been aware could not have reached me in time to produce the object required. 'The situation of our bleeding frontiers' at that time was magnified by the apprehensions of a few frontier settlers, and those who had not understanding enough to penetrate the designs of my operations."

Again directing his wrath directly at Rabun, Jackson demanded: "Whilst you are so tenacious of your executive powers, it may be necessary to explain upon what authority Captain Wright received instructions to call for reinforcements from Fort Early, garrisoned by militia who you will not deny were at that time in the service of the United States and under my command." [17]

Undaunted, Governor Rabun responded in kind: "I find that the same angry disposition which . . . dictated your letter . . . is still rankling in your breast. It is very certain that I have never assailed your feelings, or wantonly provoked your frowns, and I flatter myself it is equally certain that I shall never find it necessary to court your smiles."

Having made himself poignantly clear on this point, the Governor continued with his own touch of sarcasm: "You recommend an examination of the laws of our country before I again hazard an opinion on the subject. Your advice is good and should be attended to . . . by all public officers. I hope you will permit me to recommend to you that before you undertake another campaign, you will examine the orders of your superiors with more attention than usual." Here, Rabun was referring to the public clamor sweeping the United States over Jackson's invasion of Spanish Florida, seizing Fort St. Marks, and executing its occupants, which Jackson's critics claimed he did without authority from federal officials.

Driving this point still deeper into a tender spot, Rabun taunted: "You assert that 'the better part of the community know too well that they have nothing to apprehend from military despotism,' and in proof of this assertion it might be well for you to have called my attention to your late proceedings at St. Marks and Pensacola, as affording conclusive proof of this point."

In loyal response to Jackson's sarcastic reference to the Georgia frontier, Georgia's governor answered: "The situation of our bleeding frontiers, you say, 'was magnified by the apprehensions of a few frontier settlers and those who had not understanding enough to perceive the designs of your operations.' Indeed, sir, we had expected your presence at the head of an extensive and overwhelming force would have afforded complete protection to our bleeding and distressed citizens, bordering on an extensive and unprotected frontier; but our prospects were only delusive . . . ." At this point, Rabun deftly struck at Jackson's apparent egotism by stating: "It would seem that the laurels expected in Florida was the object that accelerated you more than the protection of the 'ignorant Georgians.'"

The harried Governor made one final thrust at the crusty Old Hickory with: "When you shall have explained to me by what authority you sent Major Davis into this state, with orders to apprehend Captain Wright (who was not under your command), and place him in irons, etc., then I shall explain to you the motives which induced me to call for reinforcements from Fort Early." [18]

With this final stroke, the heated correspondence between the two angry officials came to an end. Each sent a complete report of the situation, as he saw it, to the federal authorities in Washington.

The destruction of the Chehaw Town, with its ensuing feud between General Andrew Jackson and Governor William Rabun, created a national sensation. The state and national press gave the events prominent coverage and willing comment. In general, the public was shocked at Captain Wright's act, and he was severely condemned by most. While awaiting legal action against him, Wright escaped and fled to Cuba through the sympathetic assistance of his loyal friend and supporter, Captain Jacob Robinson.

Captain Robinson was brought before court-martial proceedings for certain aspects of his part in the Chehaw affair, found guilty and cashiered; but his conviction was decisively reversed shortly afterward by Governor John Clarke. Robinson insisted to the end that the attack upon the Chehaw Town was justified and gave full expression to his views through the Georgia press. To substantiate his claims, Captain Robinson pointed out that many cattle in the village bore the brands of white citizens dwelling on the Ocmulgee frontier, and that a gun was discovered which was recognized as having belonged to Michael Burch, who was killed in the Battle of Breakfast Branch. Robinson further maintained that some of the Indians in the settlement were painted in war paint, and that a number of British muskets were found on the premises. [19]

Governor Rabun publicly deplored the fact that Captain Wright had violated his orders in changing his objective from the villages of Phillemmee and Hopaunee to the Chehaw town of Au-muc-cul-le. Rabun did not condone the act. At the same time, however, the Governor did not refute the claims of Wright and Robinson that there was apparent hostility in the Indian town.

It appears that those Americans situated at a safe distance from the areas of danger viewed Wright's action with revulsion, but to the harassed pioneers dwelling on the exposed frontier, there was a feeling that all occupants of the Chehaw Town were not entirely innocent.

Governor William Rabun died shortly after the publicized affair was over, and his name was largely forgotten. Andrew Jackson, from the fame and glory gained through his military achievements in the British and Indian wars, went on to become President of the United States. But time could not erase from

Jackson's memory the verbal blistering received from a Georgia governor, arising from a savage Indian attack upon two obscure campers beside the Ocmulgee River.

CHAPTER XXII

THE WHITES CROSS THE OCMULGEE

It has been related that the Americans came to the east bank of the Ocmulgee by the Treaty of Washington in 1805. For the next thirteen to sixteen years, the river was the dividing line between the Georgians with their highly-developed civilization and the Creek Indians with their primitive way of life. During these years, with the two races glaring at each other across the narrow Ocmulgee, inevitable conflicts had occurred, ranging from petty pilfering or trespassing, to the violence of the Creek Indian War.

Having long dwelt under the dread of Indian attacks upon their thin frontier line, and pressed with an acute need for additional lands, the Georgians were eager to remove the red people and to gain possession of the alluring domain beyond the Ocmulgee. Migration to the new world was increasing. Even during the periods of severe Indian troubles new settlers had continued to come, and now that the hostile Creeks had been subdued, a steady stream of immigrants was flowing into the territory along the east side of the Ocmulgee. By packhorse, ox cart, and covered wagon, the pioneers were coming from eastern Georgia, the Carolinas, and Virginia. Casting wishful eyes upon the Indian land beyond the restraining Ocmulgee, the newcomers joined in the rising clamor for more land.

General Andrew Jackson's victory over the Upper Creeks at Horseshoe Bend had brought great satisfaction to the Georgians. Now, with the redskins beaten to their knees, the opportune time had come to remove the Indians completely from Georgia soil and to open their territory to the advancing white settlers. As far back as 1802, when Georgia had relinquished her western territory to the federal government, she had been assured that the Indians would be removed as soon as this could be done peaceably and on reasonable terms. The Georgians believed it was now time for the government to fulfil its overdue promise.

The mood of hopeful expectancy was shattered when the terms of Jackson's treaty reached Georgia. Instead of forcing the removal of the Indians from all Georgia soil, Jackson had secured nothing but a strip of land along the Florida border, far away from the Ocmulgee. The Indians were left in possession of the territory on the opposite bank of the Ocmulgee, the part most coveted by the land-hungry pioneers. The Treaty of Fort Jackson brought disappointment and resentment to the Georgians who had long wrestled with the perplexing Indian problem, and hoped at this time to be rid of the redskins forever.

If the treaty brought dissatisfaction to other Georgians, it cast a pall of gloom over the people dwelling directly on the frontier. All during the years of the Creek War, when others had fled to the safety of the interior, these determined pioneers had clung tenaciously to their posts. Now, harsh as Jackson's terms may have been to the red people, his treaty left the Ocmulgee inhabitants in the same precarious position as before.

The territory ceded by the Indians, known as the Tallassee County, comprised a long strip stretching along the Florida line from Wayne County westward to the Chattahoochee River, and northward to a line extending roughly from modern Jesup westward through Ocilla, and thence to Fort Gaines on the Chattahoochee. Now, lying between the upper boundary of the Jackson cession and the Altamaha-Ocmulgee line, was a long, narrow land wedge of the most strategic value to the inhabitants of the lower Georgia frontier. This slip of land presented a serious problem of defense to the settlers already established on the rivers, and to others moving into the recently-acquired territory south of the strip. This land wedge, still in possession of the Indians, formed a two-edged dagger threatening the white settlers on both sides of its blade. Unhappily aware of their precarious situation, the frontier people now clamored for the acquisition of the strategic strip, and for the removal of all Indians having access to it.

The complaints of the frontier inhabitants echoed through the halls of the State Capitol at Milledgeville. From this newly-created seat of government came a storm of protest over Jackson's failure to remove the Indians from Georgia soil, and a strong demand for the federal government to fulfil its promise to Georgia. In a resolution passed on December 19, 1816, the Senate reviewed the situation and called upon the President of the United States to take measures "as speedily as circumstances will permit, to produce an additional cession of territory, and extinguishment of Indian title, conformable to the stipulations contained in the articles of agreement and cession, entered into between the Commissioners of Georgia and the United States."[1]

Georgia's insistence upon another cession of land reopened an old dilemma for the Government at Washington. Since its agreement to remove the Indians, the Government had undergone considerable pressure from Georgia for the fulfilment of its pledge. The federal authorities recognized the necessity of removing the Indians to meet Georgia's ever-mounting need for land in her westward expansion. At the same time, the authorities were reluctant to push the red people whose domain was gradually being devoured by the American civilization. While wishing to meet Georgia's needs, federal officials were anxious to avoid undue hardship to the ancient owners of the land.

In response to their demands, the President took steps to quiet the Georgians. Benjamin Hawkins, the venerable Indian Agent, died in 1816, and the President appointed as his successor a former Georgia governor, David Brydie Mitchell. The President then authorized the new Agent to enter into negotiations with the Creeks for a cession of some of the land lying beyond the Ocmulgee. Mindful of the wishes of his fellow Georgians, Mitchell took immediate steps to bring about the desired treaty. Meeting at the Agency with a group of representatives from the Creek Nation, Mitchell was able to announce the completion of a new treaty on January 22, 1818. [2]

Under the terms of Mitchell's treaty, the chiefs, headmen, and warriors of the Creek Nation ceded to the United States for the use of Georgia the vital strip lying between the Jackson treaty boundary line and the Altamaha-Ocmulgee line. At the same time, the Indians ceded a large tract of land located upon the headwaters of the Ocmulgee River. In return for the territory gained by Mitchell's treaty, the United States paid to the Indians the sum of $20,000 for the year 1818, and pledged an annual payment of $10,000 over a period of ten years. In addition, the Government agreed to furnish the Nation with two blacksmiths and strikers for three years, in lieu of all former stipulations relating to blacksmiths.

The cession of greatest concern to the residents of the frontier was the strip of land lying between the Altamaha-Ocmulgee boundary and the Jackson treaty line to the south. As defined by Mitchell's treaty, the ceded territory was described as follows:

> Beginning at the mouth of Goose Creek on the Altamaha River, thence along the line leading to the mounts at the head of the St. Mary's River to the point where it is intersected by a line run by the Commissioners of the United States under the Treaty of Fort Jackson, thence along the last mentioned line to where a line leaving it shall run the nearest and a direct course to the head of a creek called Al-cas-ac-a-likie, to the Ocmulgee; thence down the said Ocmulgee to its junction with the Oconee, and the two rivers there forming the Altamaha, thence down the Altamaha to the first mentioned bounds at the mouth of Goose Creek. [3]

In terms of modern Geography, this territory extended westward from the vicinity of Jesup, through Ocilla, and on to a point near Isabella, just northeast of Albany. From this place, the line ran in a northeasterly direction, skirting the headwaters of Big House Creek near Rochelle, and touching the Ocmulgee River about eight miles above Abbeville.

Under the terms of Mitchell's treaty, the United States could survey any line necessary to designate the boundaries of the ceded land at such time and in such manner as deemed proper. Since all other boundaries were already defined, it was necessary to survey only the line marking the northwestern boundary. To the impatience of the Georgians, months passed without any movement on the part of federal officials to survey the territory.

Haste was of the utmost importance to the frontier inhabitants. The ceded territory embraced the troubled land on the outer rim of the Big Bend, an area stretching down the Ocmulgee from a point below Hartford to the confluence of the Ocmulgee with the Oconee. In spite of the treaty, the Creeks and Seminoles were still roaming the familiar trails of their old hunting grounds along the Big Bend. It was just such an intrusion that led to the attack upon Joseph and Littleton Burch, and the resulting Battle of Breakfast Branch, fought upon the very soil included in the new cession. These conflicts, and fear of similar troubles, led Governor Rabun to communicate with federal officials to determine what steps were being taken to run the new boundary line. The Governor politely hinted his desire for prompt action by suggesting his readiness to provide the Georgia Commissioners required for the task. [4]

The federal authorities made no haste to heed Rabun's hint. It was not until November that United States commissioners finally showed up at Fort Hawkins on their way to survey the anticipated boundary line.

Proceeding down the Ocmulgee, the commissioners reached Hartford on Monday, November 3, 1818. At the Hartford outpost, they were supposed to be met by a deputation of Indians to accompany them as a guard. But the Indians had not come. From Monday until Friday, the impatient commissioners remained at Hartford awaiting the arrival of the tardy deputation. But the guard still did not come, nor did they send any intelligence as to the time they could be expected. On Friday, having lost all hope for the services of their Indian escort, the commissioners decided to pursue their own way without a guard, but with the aid of two red men who had come to serve as guides.

Leaving directions for the Indian guard to follow, the men set out down the east side of the Ocmulgee River. Reaching the Copeland settlement in Telfair County, the party was met by Major Josiah D. Cawthon who would pilot the expedition, being described as "a gentleman minutely acquainted with the country we were about investigating." [5]

Major Cawthon was the commanding officer of the Telfair Militia, and it was under his direction that three forts were earlier erected to protect the Telfair inhabitants from Indian attacks directed from the very territory now being secured for white occupancy. The Major, likewise, had led the force of Telfair citizens across the Ocmulgee to seek redress against the marauding redskins who had attacked the Burch campers, with the engagement at Breakfast Branch following upon the land now lying before the explorers. Under the pilotage of Major Cawthon, the party crossed the Ocmulgee twenty-seven miles below Hartford, probably at the same crossing used by the Telfair men on their way to Breakfast Branch.

After crossing the stream, the exploration party proceeded for a distance of eight miles down the southwest side of the Big Bend. Here, they came to a creek called by the Indians Al-ca-sak-a-li-kie, but which the whites, exploring the country some years earlier, had named Big House Creek. [6]

Since the primary purpose of the exploration party was to follow the course of the creek to its headwaters, the mission appeared to be moving toward success; but, at precisely this moment, an element of discord arose. The Indian guides insisted that this was not the stream which they had been instructed to designate on the occasion. The surveyor, William Green, was certain that it *was* the proper watercourse. Reporting this disagreement to the Governor, Green wrote: "This stream, from its position, bearings, length, and direction of its prongs, and indeed most of its localities and circumstances presents a striking significance of its Indian name." The name which the red people had applied to the unique stream beautifully described it: "Al-ca-sak-a-li-kie signifies a kettle boiling in a creek. The creek has numerous springs rising from limestone cavities, surprisingly circular in shape, which by emitting torrents of gas, presents a striking resemblance to a large kettle boiling." [7]

Although convinced from the evidence at hand that the creek before them was the proper stream to be explored, the whites deemed it prudent to heed the words of the Indians, and followed them to a small watercourse five miles below the Blackshear Road leading from Jacksonville to Trader's Hill. The red men pointed out this stream as Al-ca-sak-a-li-kie Creek. To the white commissioners the designated stream appeared more of a gully than a creek. Moreover, it was so far downstream that the use of its headwaters as a boundary line would greatly reduce the size of the ceded territory. The commissioners recalled that Mitchell had specifically stated that the stream agreed upon was the first considerable creek *above* the Blackshear Road, while the waterway pointed out to them was *below* the road. Having to choose between the evidence at hand, or the word of their Indian guides, the commissioners returned to the real Al-ca-sak-a-li-kie Creek to continue their exploration. [8]

With the dawn of the morning on which the explorers prepared to ascend the stream, the Indian guides expressed their reluctance to accompany the white party. They explained that to do so, would expose them to severe punishment from their own people. Wishing to avoid the very appearance of approving the proceedings by their mere presence, the red men took friendly leave and set out for their homes. [9]

Left to their own devices, the whites commenced the task of exploring the watercourse, with the view of locating its headwaters. Beginning at its juncture with the Ocmulgee, the explorers gradually made their way up the stream, tracing the windings as they moved along. The men concluded that the entire length of the creek along its meandering way was twenty miles, but in a direct line would not exceed fifteen miles. [10]

After locating the headwaters of Al-ca-sak-a-li-kie, or Big House Creek, the party began to run the boundary line toward the Ocmulgee River. The course led in a northeasterly direction for a distance of slightly more than nine miles, striking the river some eighteen miles below Hartford. [11] In due time, the remainder of the line was run, and the new territory was made available for the settlement of eager white pioneers.

After Georgia's acquisition of the land lying between the lower waters of the Ocmulgee and Flint rivers, the territory stretching from the Mitchell Treaty line northward to the headstreams of the two rivers still remained in possession of the Creek Indians. With so much of their frontier line still exposed to Indian depredations, and with covetous eyes set upon the remaining lands beyond the Ocmulgee, the Georgians continued to clamor for another cession of Indian territory. Once more, the federal government was called upon to fulfil the terms of its old agreement to remove the red people from Georgia soil.

Again, the government endeavored to pacify the Georgians by seeking another treaty with the Creek Nation. To this end, Daniel M. Forney of North Carolina, and David Meriwether of Georgia were appointed commissioners on the part of the United States to treat with the red people. By agreement, the commissioners met with a delegation of chiefs at Indian Springs for the purpose of entering into negotiations.

Out of the meeting at Indian Springs came another treaty between the commissioners and a body of twenty-six kings, headmen, and warriors of the Creek Nation. Under the terms of the Treaty of Indian Springs, completed on January 8, 1821, the red people ceded to the United States for the use of Georgia most of the territory lying between the Ocmulgee and Flint rivers from the Mitchell boundary northward to the headwaters of the two streams. At the same time, the Creeks retained certain small reserves within the area. Among these were the Indian settlement of Buzzard's Roost on the Flint, 1,000 acres around Indian Springs, and a tract including the home of William McIntosh. In addition, small land reserves were held on the east side of the Flint River near the old trading post of Timothy Barnard for the benefit of the children of the venerable trader. 12

The news of the Treaty of Indian Springs brought joy to the trouble-weary pioneers dwelling along the Ocmulgee. For many trying years their exposed lines had borne the burden of providing a buffer for the interior of Georgia. In the face of daily hardship and danger, when some had sought places of safety and ease, the determined pioneers had held their ground. A new generation had grown up on the frontier in sight of the awesome Indian domain beyond the Ocmulgee. Now, threats of attack from the opposite bank of the stream would no longer bring haunting fears in the night. The Creek Indians would give way to white neighbors of kindred kind. By now the pioneers had grown accustomed to this country with its familiar landmarks. The once-strange wilderness, bearing the footprints of the departing red people, had become the scene of the pioneers' own homes. Many would continue to dwell within their own domain with a new-found sense of security.

But to the new generation, the young who had grown up on the frontier, alluring lands beckoned onward. The spirit of movement was in their restless blood: many would depart from the home-scenes of their youth and venture into the enticing new world beyond the Ocmulgee.

CHAPTER XXIII

NEW WAYS BEYOND THE OCMULGEE

No sooner had the Americans gained possession of the coveted territory beyond the Ocmulgee than they commenced the task of establishing their own way of life upon the hitherto Indian soil. With the white man's civilization firmly planted upon the east bank of the river, the time had come to transplant the growth to the virgin soil beyond. The land must be surveyed, new counties organized, officials chosen, and governments set into motion.

From the territory gained by the Treaty of Fort Jackson and from Mitchell's treaty, two new counties were created whose upper boundaries rested upon the Ocmulgee. These were Appling and Irwin. As originally defined, Appling County extended from Blackshear's Ford near Jacksonville eastward to the Wayne County line. At a very early date, the major portion of the Ocmulgee section was cut off and added to Telfair County, so that Appling County's association with the Ocmulgee world was limited.

The first county beyond the Ocmulgee to be fully identified with the river world was Irwin County. As originally defined in 1818, Irwin covered a vast area stretching from the Ocmulgee River on the north to the Florida line in the south. The portion lying upon the Ocmulgee began at the Blackshear Ford opposite Jacksonville, and extended up the river to a point eighteen miles below Hartford. In its upward sweep, the new county encompassed the historic Big Bend of the Ocmulgee.[1]

As a step toward launching the hopeful new county on its course, the Georgia General Assembly passed an act on December 21, 1819, naming a commission to supervise an election for five Justices of the Inferior Court.[2] After the Justices were chosen, they were to select a county site and hold elections for county officials. Until a suitable courthouse could be built, all courts would be held at the house of David Williams, situated just above Jacksonville, near the juncture of the Ocmulgee River and Sturgeon Creek.[3] The Justices of the Inferior Court were duly elected, and the court thus formed held its first session on July 3, 1820, at the Williams place. The Justices assembling on this occasion were Ludd Mobley, John Sutton, David Callaway, and David Williams.[4]

Under the power vested in them, the Justices proceeded to hold an election for county officers with the result that on May 25, 1820, the following were chosen and properly commissioned: Clerk of Superior Court, William Slone; Sheriff, James Allen; Coroner, David Hunter; Senator, Samuel Boyd; Representative to the General Assembly, David Williams. [5]

As the organization of the infant county progressed, a movement was begun to select a site for the public buildings. At the term of Inferior Court held in July, 1822, an order was passed to move the place of holding courts up to Murdock McDuffie's schoolhouse located on Lot 147 in the 4th Land District. [6] This site was near the juncture of the River Road and the old Fitzgerald Road seven miles below Bowen's Mill, and within two miles of the Ocmulgee River.

Although the Inferior Court was originally empowered to act as a commission for the courthouse and jail, the General Assembly passed an act on December 13, 1823, creating for this purpose a special commission composed of William Folsom, James Crum, Sellaway McCall, Joshua Griffin, and Alexander McDonald. [7] Some difficulty was encountered in procuring a permanent site for the public buildings, so on December 24, 1825, another commission was appointed for the same purpose. But, for some unknown reason, the delay continued. In another attempt, the General Assembly passed an act on December 23, 1830, fixing the county site upon Land Lot 255, at present-day Bowen's Mill, provided title to the land could be secured. In the event of failure, the commissioners were to purchase another lot within two miles of the designated place. The permanent site thus selected would be named Irwinville. At the same time, Robert H. Dixon, Jacob Young, William Bradford, Daniel Luke, and Reuben Marsh were appointed commissioners for the proposed town, with authority to lay off lots and expose them to sale. In the meantime, the courts would continue to be held "at the usual place." [8]

For some unexplained reason, the proposed site at Bowen's Mill was not acquired, for on December 22, 1831, the General Assembly passed still another act, fixing the permanent seat of government upon Lot 39 in the 3rd Land District. [9] The town of Irwinville was eventually laid out on this site, where it has continued to this day.

During the formative years of Irwin, as well as other early Georgia counties, the Inferior Court was an important body which played a vital part in the creation and operation of the counties. The court was composed of five Justices elected by the people. The jurisdiction of the Justices covered civil cases of all kinds, except where title to land was involved. The court tried whites for petit larceny, and slaves for capital crimes. The Inferior Court, likewise, officiated as a court of probate in handling estate matters. In addition to its function as a court, the body held authority over county roadways, which the court established and maintained through the appointment of commissioners for that purpose.

The office of Justice of the Inferior Court was a coveted honor attained by leading citizens in whose ability and integrity the people had confidence. Among the Justices chosen during the formative years of Irwin County were Ludd Mobley, John Sutton, David Williams, Sellaway McCall, Ezekiel Jernigan, Robert H. Dixon, William Bradford, Redding Hunter, James L. Willcox, Jehu McCall, Thomas Drawdy, and Abraham P. Clements. [10]

The first term of Superior Court for Irwin County was held at the house of David Williams on September 21, 1820. The chief function of the infant court at this session was to choose jurors for the next term. The jury was made up of varied elements. Most of the pioneer jurors in the newborn county were men of English, Welsh, and Scotch-Irish descent who had migrated from Virginia, the Carolinas, and eastern Georgia. But, among the first jurors were numbers of Highland Scots who had come from their craggy hills to settle in the new land beyond the Ocmulgee. [11]

When the white pioneers settled on the west side of the Ocmulgee, they became exposed to the same dangers from Indian attack previously endured by the people dwelling on the east side of the stream. As a measure of protection, militia forces were organized in Irwin County at an early time. The most vulnerable section lay along the outer rim of the Big Bend, an area which had long been the scene of Indian troubles. It was here that the attack was made upon Joseph and Littleton Burch, and it was in this area that the Battle of Breakfast Branch was fought. This bloody territory was organized into the 433rd Militia District, and officers were commissioned on October 6, 1820, with Thompson Nathaniel Statham named as Captain. Statham was succeeded in 1823 by Sellaway McCall. [12] These two men typified the military leadership of the new frontier. Statham was a hero in the Battle of Breakfast Branch, and McCall had grown up under the shadow of Fort Adams in Telfair County—long the target area for Indian depredations.

Another very vulneralbe section was the 432nd Militia District, situated on the Big Bend of the Ocmulgee in the lower part of Irwin County, opposite Telfair County. John S. Gilder was commissioned Captain for the district on February 4, 1821, along with Bouser Allen, Lieutenant; and William Hall, Ensign. [13]

After the formation of Irwin County from lands lying between the lower part of the Ocmulgee and Flint rivers, the territory along the northern boundary of the county still remained in possession of the Creek Indians. But, through the Treaty of Indian Springs in 1821, this land, too, was acquired by the Americans who took prompt steps to organize the territory into new Georgia counties.

Irwin's northern neighbor was Dooly County. Dooly was formed from the lower portion of the Indian Springs cession, and embraced such a vast territory that it was known in early days as "The Kingdom of Dooly." Dooly County included an area which had been the scene of much military activity during the Creek and Seminole wars. Within this territory, while it was still a part of the Creek Nation, was erected Fort Early, a frontier outpost which played a vital role in the Indian conflicts. Then, threading its way across the land from Hartford to Fort Early, was the important military roadway cut by General David Blackshear's army during the severe winter of 1814-15. Just three years later, it was over the same path that General Andrew Jackson had marched his forces on the way to subdue the Seminoles and Red Sticks in Florida.

Upon the creation of Dooly County, commissioners were appointed to fix a site for the public buildings. In the meantime, the courts were to be held at the home of Isaac Jones in the Fifth Land District. In 1826, the public site was established on Lot 57 in the 7th Land District at the new settlement of Berrien. Nine years later, the seat of government was removed to Drayton on the Flint River, to be accessible to steamboat navigation on the stream. [14]

The portion of Dooly lying along the west side of the Ocmulgee was cut off in 1826 and added to Pulaski, which had previously occupied only the east side of the river. After giving up its Ocmulgee territory, Dooly County ceased to play a major part in the affairs of the river world.

Dooly's nearest neighbor to the north was Houston County, created in 1821 from lands gained under the terms of the Treaty of Indian Springs. Originally, Houston County was a very large county extending from Dooly on the south to Monroe on the north. The southern boundary line began at a point on the Ocmulgee opposite Hartford, and ran due west to the Flint River, striking the stream in the vicinity of Barnard's Trading Post.

The upper boundary was determined by running a line from the Ocmulgee opposite Fort Hawkins, directly westward to the Flint. Included within the northwestern bounds of the huge country was the old Creek Agency on the Flint River, where Benjamin Hawkins had so long dwelt inside the Creek Nation, and from whence he had sought to keep peace between his Indian charges and their white neighbors. The very inclusion of this old landmark within a rising Georgia county was an indication of the finality with which the white man's civilization was devouring the once-vast domain of the ancient red people. [15]

Upon the creation of Houston County, commissioners were appointed for the purpose of supervising the election of officials required to set the new government into operation. Serving on this formative body were Turner Everett, Daniel Cornwall, Nathaniel McCall, John Keener, Thomas Harvey, Washington Rogers, and Eli Nunn. [16]

Organization of the county progressed rapidly, and on May 6, 1822, the first session of the Inferior Court was held, with Justices Kinchen Curl, Davenport Lawson, John Mathis, and David W. Mann present. At this term it was ordered that, since there was no courthouse in the new county, the Superior and Inferior courts would be held at the home of James A. Everett, situated on Land Lot 16, in the 7th District. [17]

The selection of a seat of government was not long in coming, for on July 7, 1823, the Inferior Court, again in session, designated Land Lot 49, in the 10th District as the permanent site for public buildings. To the town, yet to be laid out, was given the name of Wattsville. At the same time, Joel Walker was authorized to survey the proposed town. [18] By the next year, the name of the county seat had been changed to Perry, in honor of Commodore Perry, naval hero in the War of 1812. The first reference to the town under its permanent name is found upon the records of the Inferior Court for March 2, 1823, at which time John Pollock was appointed commissioner to review and mark out a road leading from Perry to Buzzard's Roost on the Ocmulgee River. [19]

Steps were promptly taken to erect the public buildings, and in 1824, a contract for the construction of a courthouse was let by Justices Daniel DuPree, P. Oliver, and Solomon Simpson. [20]

Efforts to set the Houston Superior Court into operation moved smoothly, and while the courthouse was yet a thing of the future, the first session was held at the house of James A. Everett on May 21, 1822, with Judge Thomas W. Carnes presiding. The primary action taken at this formative term was to draw jurors for the following term. [21]

In the settlement of Houston County, many of the first comers pushed in from the populated areas on the east bank of the Ocmulgee in the counties of Pulaski and Twiggs. Some simply crossed over from their old abodes and settled as near the familiar scenes of their former homes as possible. In the isolation of an undeveloped wilderness, they were thus able to maintain close ties with relatives and friends remaining in the older settlements left behind.

To keep open the channels of communication between the old world and the new, roadways were laid out from various points in Houston County leading to good crossing places on the Ocmulgee, and from thence connecting with the established avenues on the opposite side. Thus, when John Pollock was empowered to lay out a road from Perry to Buzzard's Roost on the Ocmulgee, he was connecting his new home in Houston with his old abode back in Twiggs County. Likewise, one of the earliest settlers in Houston County was Richard H. Davis, who had come from his old parental homestead, located on the east side of the Ocmulgee above Shellstone Creek. On March 2, 1824, Davis, Meredith Joiner, and Amos Chancery were appointed as commissioners to mark a road leading from the River Road on Mossy Creek to Pine Landing on the Ocmulgee.[22] Crossing the river at this place, the new road tied in with the Old River Road on the east bank, a way which led downstream a short distance to the former home of Richard H. Davis, once the abode of his deceased father, Chesley Davis, a noted Revolutionary Soldier.

The broad, fertile lands of Houston County proved suitable for the rising plantation system of the Ante-Bellum Period, and many substantial slaveholders came into the territory, bringing with them considerable wealth and culture. The cultural aspirations of these newcomers were manifested in 1824, when a contract was let for the establishment of the Houston County Academy, with Howell Cobb, James Holt, Charles F. Patillo, Wilson Collins, and Michael Watson as commissioners.[23] Four years later, the Flint Academy was incorporated, and in 1832, trustees were appointed for the Houston County Ocmulgee Academy to be located in either the Tenth or the Eleventh Land District.[24]

Unlike most frontier counties, Houston did not limit its educational efforts to lower levels, but aspired to higher education, as well. A Baptist college for young ladies, founded at an earlier date, was re-incorporated in 1854, with a Board of Trustees composed of such leading citizens as Samuel Felder, Hugh L. Dennard, John Killen, William T. Swift, Samuel D. Killen, Benjamin F. Tharpe, George W. Singleton, Nicholas Mashburn, George W.

Cooper, Laban Segrest, James Barrett, William Summerford, and John T. Cooper. [25]

At the same time that Dooly and Houston counties were created from former Indian lands lying along the lower and middle waters of the Ocmulgee and Flint, Monroe County was formed from the territory situated on the upper waters of the streams. Sharing a common boundary with Houston County on the south, Monroe's northern boundary followed a line leaving the Ocmulgee River at the Seven Islands, opposite Jasper County, proceeding westward for a distance of forty miles, then turning south and continuing directly to the Flint River. [26]

Within the bounds of Monroe County was the Indian Springs Reserve, long associated with the Creek Indians, and the scene of the treaty under which the lands between the Ocmulgee and Flint rivers had passed into the hands of the white settlers. Thus, again, was manifested the extent to which the white man's civilization was swallowing up the landmarks of the old Creek Nation.

The fertile soil of Monroe County was well suited for the cultivation of cotton at a time when the plant was in growing demand. To facilitate the production of cotton in massive quantities, many large plantations arose in the red-hill country. Within a short period of time, the country was populated with substantial planters who brought with them a high degree of civilization. Like neighboring Houston County to the south, Monore sought to encourage education by establishing in 1835 the Forsyth Female Academy, located in the growing county seat of Forsyth. [27]

From the territory on the headwaters of the Ocmulgee, a new county was created and given the name of Henry. [28] Two years after the formation of the headstream county, a seat of government had been fixed upon a convenient site, where a town was duly laid out and given the name of McDonough. Like its neighbors to the south, Henry County soon became important in the production of cotton, with the resulting plantation system rising to a position of prominence.

While the new settlers were spreading into all parts of the Ocmulgee domain, they were concentrating in large numbers at strategically-located Fort Hawkins. Around the walls of the old military stronghold sprang up a populous settlement which acquired the name of Newtown. [29]

Shortly after the west side of the Ocmulgee was thrown open to white settlers, the town of Macon was laid out upon the opposite bank of the river from Newtown. Now, at this open gateway, floods of immigrants surged across the stream into the new Macon settlement. [30]

With its strategic location at the head of navigation, and in the center of a productive plantation system, Macon grew, as if by magic, into the largest metropolis of the entire Ocmulgee world. Within an amazingly short time, streets unfolded, shops opened, warehouses flourished, residences sprawled, and spires pointed upward.[31] So high did the spirit of the mushrooming settlement rise that, even before Macon was officially laid out and named, the proposal was made that the state capital be removed to the new site.[32]

Now, at this thriving settlement, the old and the new stood out in stark contrast. On the east side of the Ocmulgee, the towering blockhouses of Fort Hawkins, long the bulwark of the old frontier were crumbling from decay; but on the opposite bank, silhouetted against the western sky, the tower of a new-born female academy arose to herald a new order.

So, with clearings and settlements spreading throughout the territory between the Ocmulgee and the Flint, the white man's civilization was vigorously transplanted to the land beyond the Ocmulgee.

CHAPTER XXIV

OPEN ROADS BEYOND THE OCMULGEE

As white immigrants advanced into the territory beyond the Ocmulgee, they encountered a pressing need for roadways to reach their destinations, and to connect their clearings and settlements as they arose. With the gradual carving of new avenues through the primitive wilderness, the white man's civilization was pushed along the open roadways.

Since the early comers usually settled as near the west bank of the Ocmulgee as possible, their most urgent need was for a river road similar to the Old River Road long in use on the east side of the stream. The base for such a pathway was to be found in the abandoned River Trail of the recently-departed Indians. The carving of a white man's way could be accomplished by clearing and widening long sections of the well-worn Indian path to permit passage for wheeled vehicles.

Soon after the creation of Irwin County, steps were taken to provide an avenue to connect the clearings and settlements appearing along the Big Bend of the Ocmulgee. In July of 1821, the Inferior Court passed an order to lay out a river road, beginning at the Appling-Irwin boundary line opposite Jacksonville, extending upward across Big House Creek, and continuing on to the northern boundary of Irwin County eighteen miles below Hartford. [1]

From very early times, Big House Creek, where Bowen's Mill now stands, was the dividing line between the Lower River Road and the Upper River Road of Irwin County. Along the Lower River Road, extending from the Appling line up to Big House Creek, the early settlers were Ludd Mobley, John S. Gilder, William Fussell, David Williams, Murdock McDuffie, William Slone, Robert H. Dixon, John B. F. Dixon, John B. Dorminey, Thomas Hunter, and William Bowen. [2]

On the Upper River Road, extending from House Creek to the northern county line, the pioneers were William Barrentine, Jacob Barrentine, James L. Willcox, John Tomberlin, Daniel Luke, Jehu McCall, Sellaway McCall, Abraham Loftin McCall, Frederick Land, Henry Land, Philip Brown, Samuel Stone, Leonard Stone, George R. Reid, Richard Brown, James Brown, Nathaniel Statham, and John Fitzgerald. [3]

After the Treaty of Indian Springs in 1821, other counties were created along the west side of the Ocmulgee, extending above the Irwin County line. In the order of their location upstream from Irwin, the new counties were Dooly, Houston, Monroe, and Henry. Sections of the River Road were carved out simultaneously in these counties to provide a continuous thoroughfare along the west bank of the Ocmulgee from the river's mouth all the way up to its headwaters.

Shortly after the creation of Dooly County, the portion of the county which lay along the Ocmulgee River was cut off and added to Pulaski County. During this changing period, the River Road was continued northward from the Irwin line through the lower part of Pulaski to the site of Hawkinsville, opposite Hartford. Living along this stretch of the pioneer way, and participating in its construction, were Peter L. Livingston, James M. Vickers, James Davis, Benjamin Steagall, and Wiley Williams.[4]

At the site of Hawkinsville, the eastern roads converging upon the old Uchee Shoals were connected with the west River Road by a public ferry crossing over the Ocmulgee from Hartford.[5]

From the public ferry opposite Hartford, the River Road pushed northward into Houston County where early steps were taken to continue the route through the entire length of the county. At the term of Inferior Court held on June 2, 1823, Willoughby Jordan, Robert Thompson, and James McCormick were appointed commissioners to view the ground and lay out a road commencing at the public ferry opposite Hartford, and running as near the Ocmulgee as possible through the lower part of Houston County. At the same time, Daniel Brunson, Michael Watson, and Frederick Watson were appointed commissioners to continue the River Road through the middle portion of the county; and Reddick Bell, James Hardin, and John Clark were authorized to extend the roadway through the upper limits of Houston County.[6] In its upward course, the pioneer path crossed Echeconnee Creek at John Clark's Ferry, and continued on its narrow way to Macon, the thriving new settlement on the west side of the Ocmulgee.[7]

The River Road in Houston County was rapidly settled by pioneer immigrants. Spread out along the route of the newly-carved white man's way were the abodes of: Richard H. Davis, James Gouldwire Davis, Jesse Pollock, John Pollock, Biguas Singleton, Jeremiah DuPree, Isaac Woodard, Thomas Woodard, Simon Bateman, Richard Smith, James Chalker, John Barton, Henry Barton, Allen Barton, Richard A. Singleton, and George W. Singleton.[8]

While the River Road was being formed and populated in the territory stretching up and down the west bank of the Ocmulgee, immigrants were pushing beyond the stream into the interior of the new country. At this time, the old military roadways which were established in the area while it was still a part of the Creek Nation served as open avenues of migration for new settlers. Coming into widespread use were the Federal Road leading from Fort Hawkins through the new land to the old Indian Agency on the Flint; the Blackshear Road running from Hartford southwestward to Fort Early; and the Blackshear military way proceeding from Jacksonville on the Big Bend southeastward to Trader's Hill on the St. Mary's River. During this new period in the expansion of the American civilization, these old thoroughfares were rapidly settled, and continued to serve as open highways to other sections.

But more roads were needed to meet the demands of the rapidly-developing areas beyond the Ocmulgee. The old Ocmulgee frontier was now serving as the base from which venturesome pioneers were pushing into distant parts of the unfolding horizons. New avenues were needed for the immigrants to reach their destinations and to provide communication among their clearings, as they arose.

Again, the Indian trails provided the routes along which new Georgia highways were opened. The old Slosheye Trail leading southwestward from the Uchee Shoals at Hartford to the Flint River was cleared and widened into the Slosheye Road.[9] This once-familiar Indian path now provided an open road between Hartford and Drayton, the new county seat of Dooly County, rising above the Flint River.[10] Early comers who settled along the Slosheye Road, and who took an active part in its conversion into a pathway for the new civilization, were Clayton Bradshaw, John Bradshaw, George Cherry, Harmon Mock, David Wood, and Daniel Mashburn.[11]

Another Indian trail which was converted into a highway for the advancement of the white man's civilization was the Barnard Trail leading westward from the Uchee Shoals on the Ocmulgee to Timothy Barnard's Trading Post on the Flint.[12] The roadway was formed by widening and clearing the Indian path until it reached such dimensions that it could accommodate wheeled vehicles. Eventually, the Barnard Road became a thickly-settled avenue and an open thoroughfare for travelers between Hawkinsville on the Ocmulgee and Oglethorpe on the Flint.[13] Among the pioneer settlers who took part in the transformation of the primitive trail into a white man's highway were Robert Thompson,

Ulysses Crutchfield, Thomas B. Stephens, John Rawls, John Bozeman, and Allen Burch.[14]

Coinciding with the movement of white immigrants into the territory directly west of the Ocmulgee was a pattern of migration from the Big Bend into southwestern Georgia and into the northern section of Florida. With the acquisition of Florida from Spain in 1821, immigrants following this pattern pushed into the newly-opened country and formed settlements in the vicinity of Tallahassee, the rising capital of the former Spanish domain. To meet the need for an avenue of communication between the Big Bend and Tallahassee and to provide access to the lands lying in between, a movement was begun for the creation of a thoroughfare to serve this dual purpose.

Ever sensitive to Georgia's expanding horizons, the General Assembly, in 1822, authorized the construction of a new roadway, beginning at Cunningham's Ford on the Alapaha River, and leading southwestward to the Florida line.[15] John Coffee and Thomas S. Swain, citizens of Telfair County, were commissioned to superintend the undertaking. After some delay, the highway was opened all the way from Jacksonville, across the Ocmulgee River over Swain's Ferry, through today's Alapaha, Nashville, and Thomasville; and on to Tallahassee. The road subsequently became known as the Coffee Road, in honor of one of its chief promoters, General John Coffee.

The Coffee Road, penetrating the very heart of South Georgia, soon became an important avenue along which new settlers took up their abodes, and along which immigrants pressed on into Florida, Alabama, and points westward.

CHAPTER XXV

CHRISTIANITY BORNE ONWARD

As the Americans settled beyond the Ocmulgee, following their treaties with the Indians, they transplanted their Christian order to the land which had so recently fallen to them. Coming from the established sections of the east, the pioneers brought with them their own pattern of civilization, of which their religious order was a vital part. As a natural consequence, the earliest churches to arise upon the west bank of the Ocmulgee were offshoots of the religious system already rooted in the regions left behind.

The most numerous meetinghouses to appear beyond the Ocmulgee were of the Baptist persuasion. Along with the establishment of the pioneer Baptist churches came the need for a traditional bond of fellowship to hold the infant churches together. At first, the meetinghouses united with the old Ebenezer Association, in whose fold many members had formerly reposed.

But the ties between the new and the old were hard to keep. Although sharing a common boundary, the east and west banks of the Ocmulgee fell into two separate worlds which, in some ways, were far apart. Communication between the two sides, by means of bateau or flatboat, was always difficult and, at times, impossible. The river was moody and unpredictable, and during periods of flooding, presented a treacherous barrier to those seeking to cross its swirling waters. This watery gulf separated the new meetinghouses on the western bank from the older eastern churches in the Ebenezer Association.

During the year 1830, in response to the need for a more accessible union, representatives from the western congregations met at Beulah Church in Houston County and formed the Houston Association. The new Association was made up mostly of churches located within the territory lying between the Ocmulgee and Flint rivers. [1]

One of the earliest meetinghouses to arise beyond the Ocmulgee River was Shalem Baptist Church. This newly-formed house of worship was admitted to the Ebenezer Association in 1829 and was apparently constituted the same year. Representing the church at its first meeting with the Association were Jobe E. W. Smith and Wright Howell. [2] The following year, Shalem

165

withdrew from the Ebenezer Association and joined in the formation of the Houston Association.[3] Serving as delegates to the Associational meetings during the earliest years of the church were Probert Collier, L. Hobbs, Matthias McCormick, Thomas B. Stephens, Larry O. Bryant, John Colson, John McKenzie, and James Stephens.[4]

Old Shalem was located on the River Road in the upper part of Pulaski, formerly Houston County. In accordance with the Baptist custom of placing meetinghouses near sizable bodies of water, Shalem was erected upon a hill rising above the banks of Buck Creek. The convenient waters of the neighboring stream were used for baptismal ceremonies.[5]

Of the ministers serving Shalem, only three have been positively identified. These were Ezekiel Bryan, John McKenzie, and James Gouldwire Davis.[6] John McKenzie was known as a leading figure in the formation of the Houston Association and its first moderator.[7] James Gouldwire Davis spent his entire ministry serving the pioneer Baptist churches which arose along the Ocmulgee during the early years of his life. After a long preaching career covering the Frontier Era of the Ocmulgee world, the pioneer minister died preaching in the pulpit at Shalem.[8]

The membership of Shalem Baptist Church was made up of substantial planters who found the fertile western soil well adapted to the plantation system of the Ante-Bellum Era. The agonizing years of the Civil War brought severe loss of life and property to the members of the church. As an aftermath of this tragic struggle, the venerable house of worship was dissolved in 1875 and its past renown has long since been forgotten.

A very early church formed beyond the Ocmulgee was Shiloh Baptist Church, located in Houston County. The exact time of its origin has not been confirmed, but Shiloh was already in existence in 1830 when it was admitted to the newly-established Houston Association.[9] The delegates from Shiloh to this important session of the Association were Ezekiel Bryan and James Gouldwire Davis.[10] Early representatives to other meetings of the Houston Association were Nathan Chancey, Stansell Barbaree, McKinna Howell, Edwin Ellis, Frances Davis, and Thomas B. Stephens.[11]

Like Shalem, its sister church, Shiloh faded into oblivion shortly after the close of the Civil War, doubtlessly as a result of the severe losses suffered by its membership during this critical period.

One of the earliest houses of worship to appear on the west bank of the Ocmulgee was New Hope Baptist Church. This pioneer meetinghouse was erected upon an eminence sloping above the River Road, two miles below present-day Abbeville in Wilcox County. New Hope was constituted in July, 1830, with Wilson Conner, Jordan Baker, and David Wood serving as the Presbytery. [12] In September of the same year, the new Christian church was admitted to the Ebenezer Association, with Daniel Luke and Jacob Barrentine attending the session as delegates. [13] During the next year, New Hope transferred its membership to the Houston Association, then in its infancy. The delegates to this session of admission were Miles Adams and Joseph Davis.[14] The earliest members of New Hope to attend other meetings of the Houston Association were Jacob Barrentine, Miles Adams, Joseph Davis, George R. Reid, James Brown, and Green G. Graham. [15]

New Hope has known the threats of Indian firebrands, the devastation of wars, and the ravages of time, but the venerable shrine still stands upon its lofty eminence, although the casual observer is little aware of the role played by the unassuming old church in planting the Christian order upon the land beyond the Ocmulgee.

In 1832, one of the earliest Christian meetinghouses to arise from the west bank of the Ocmulgee was erected upon an oak-crowned hill overlooking the waters of Big House Creek at the growing settlement of Bowen's Mill in Old Irwin County. Known as Ozias, the pioneer Baptist Church was constituted with Wilson Conner and John Marshall serving as Presbyters. The original members were John McDonald, Randall McDonald, Eliza Hunter, Penelope Hunter, Catherine McCall, Mary McDonald, and Eliza McDonald.[16] In addition to these constituting members, other very early members of Ozias were Philip Brown and wife Jemimah; Samuel Stone and wife Leah; Hardy Hunter and wife Mary; Robert Dixon and wife Lucy; James L. Willcox, Redding Hunter, Steely Goff, Samuel Goff, William Goff, Eliza Goff, Robert Newberry, Malinda Turner, Catherine Newberry, Penelope Goff, Elizabeth Taylor, and Rocelia Barrentine. [17]

Ozias was admitted to the Houston Association in 1838, with Solomon C. Spivey and Elijah Hunter sent as delegates to the meeting.[18] Serving as representatives to the Association for the next ten years, were Elijah Hunter, Solomon C. Spivey, Samuel B. Stone, James L. Willcox, Samuel Stone, and Redding Hunter.[19]

By the year 1854, a shift in population caused the members of old Ozias to move the Church from Bowen's Mill to a sand hill rising between the prongs of Big House Creek, three miles away. At the same time, the name was changed to Bethlehem, the name the historic church has borne for well over a century. [20]

Shortly after the location of Bethlehem upon its sand hill site, a churchyard burial place was begun, with a Hunter child being the first interred. In the years which followed, many of the zealots who first planted their Christian faith upon the soil beyond the Ocmulgee passed from the scene, and their names, like a roll-call of Ocmulgee pioneers, appeared upon the stones weathering in the rustic field: Barrentine, Brown, Bowen, Dorminey, Fitzgerald, Hunter, McCall, Parsons, Reid, Stone, Willcox, Tomberlin—these were familiar names of the early Christian Era beyond the Ocmulgee.

Many of the members of Ozias and New Hope churches dwelt along the River Road—the center of population for Old Irwin County—between the two churches. Before long, a movement was begun to establish a new meetinghouse nearer their homes. To fulfil this purpose, in 1844, Mount Zion Baptist Church was constituted by a Presbytery composed of J. B. Smith and David Ryals. The constituting members were James L. Willcox, Jeremiah Matthews, James Mixon, Joseph Burton, Matthew Mixon, Elizabeth Willcox, Mary Matthews, Mary Mixon, and Rachel Kersey. [21] Coming into membership immediately after the formation of the church were Philip Brown and wife Jemima; Samuel Stone and wife Leah; Hardy Hunter and wife Mary; Robert Dixon and wife Lucy; Jacob Barrentine and wife Elizabeth; William Winderweedle and wife Mary; Jasper Luke and wife Sarah; Richard J. Young and wife Jane; Owen Mulkey and wife Susan. [22]

From its unique location upon a narrow eminence rising between two round ponds, giving the appearance of a pair of spectacles, Mount Zion was affectionately known as "Old Spectacle." [23] The site lay on the west side of the River Road some four miles above Bowen's Mill.

The first building to be erected at Mount Zion was constructed of pine logs, but with a membership made up of substantial planters and slaveholders, the log structure was soon replaced by a durable clapboard building, with lumber sawed at Bowen's Mill. Negro slaves united with the church along with their masters, and a section was provided for their accommodation.

Old Spectacle was admitted to the Houston Association in 1844, with James L. Willcox and David Ryals representing the infant church. [24] Delegates to other early meetings of the Association were Owen D. Mulkey, William Winderweedle, Jasper Luke, Philip Brown, W. F. Willis, Richard Young, Samuel Stone, Miles Fitzgerald, D. M. Suggs, James Mashburn, George M. B. McDuffie, David L. McCall, and Stephen Bowen. [25]

Much of the Ante-Bellum aristocracy of the Old River Road was centered in the membership of Mount Zion Church. During the Civil War, Old Spectacle gave liberally of her fold to the Confederate Army. As the tragic war struck at the heart of the church, many of Old Spectacle's men fell upon battlefields far from the familiar scenes of home and were buried in graves unknown to the ones who remained behind. Throughout this critical period, the membership suffered severe losses in property, health, and life; and as sons, brothers, and husbands perished for a hopeless cause upon scenes far away, many home folk suffered the hardships and heartbreaks of the ones left behind to wait and to wonder.

An early Baptist church taking its name from the stream beside which it was established was Cedar Creek Baptist Church, located on Cedar Creek in the lower part of Old Pulaski, but present Wilcox County. This pioneer western church was created in 1843, with David Ryals and James Reeves forming the Presbytery.[26] Cedar Creek Church united with the Houston Association in 1847, with Berry Hobbs, Martin B. Everett, and J. W. Allen attending the session of admission as delegates.[27] Other representatives to early meetings of the Association were Green G. Graham, Seaborn Whittle, and Anderson W. Miller.[28]

The membership of Cedar Creek Church was made up of a large number of planters dwelling along the banks of the Ocmulgee and two of its tributaries, Cedar Creek and Bluff Creek. At an early time, the members demonstrated their interest in their church by erecting an imposing Ante-Bellum edifice which has long graced the west side of the Old River Road.

During the 1830's, Georgia Baptists experienced a crisis which was strongly felt among the churches along the Ocmulgee. For some years, a controversy had been mounting within the membership over certain innovations coming increasingly into practice among Baptists. Although other factors were involved, generally referred to as "institutions of the day," the issue was largely centered around the subject of missions. In a spirit of missionary zeal, many Baptist leaders had endorsed and propagated a strong movement for the establishment of missions among foreign countries to convert the natives to the Christian faith. Among the missions established in 1823, was Withington, a mission for Indians located within the Creek Nation, which the Ocmulgee inhabitants still viewed as foreign soil. These missionary efforts, however, were opposed by a substantial number of adherents of the Baptist Church.[29]

Now dissension raged inside the Baptist Churches and Associations, bringing discord and division within the ranks. In 1836, the old Ebenezer Association, on the east side of the Ocmulgee, was rent by the withdrawal of the conservative, or anti-mission elements from the Association. [30] The schism now reflected itself within the Houston Association, and dissension was mounting to serious proportions.

With the controversy at its height, the Houston Association opened its session for 1839 at Antioch, located five miles southwest of the thriving new town of Hawkinsville. Chosen to preach the introductory sermon for the grave occasion was the Reverend James Gouldwire Davis, a Captain of Pulaski Militia during the Seminole War, but long since, a minister dedicated to peace. [31]

Seeking to maintain tranquillity among his associates, the pioneer minister preached from the text: "And Abram said to Lot, let there be no strife, I pray thee, between me and thee, and between my herdmen and thy herdmen: for we are brethren." At the end of the conciliatory sermon, realizing that they could no longer continue in unity with such intensely differing convictions, the churches in the Houston Association divided themselves into two bodies: one to continue in the traditional house of their fathers: the other to venture into new pathways. [32]

At the same time that the Christian religion was borne beyond the Ocmulgee by the Baptist denomination, it was also transplanted to the western lands through the Methodist movement. Among the earliest white settlers beyond the Ocmulgee River were adherents of the Methodist faith. Eager to transplant their order to the west bank of the Ocmulgee, these early Methodists followed the usual procedure of holding formative meetings in the homes of the members dwelling at convenient places. From private homes, the movement progressed to brush arbors and then to permanent meetinghouses. During the early period of growth, the Methodist movement was given impetus through the establishment of campgrounds where traditional camp meetings were held at convenient times.

In their efforts to establish their own system of religion on the advancing frontier, Methodist laymen were aided by the much-heralded circuit riders. The circuits beyond the Ocmulgee were thinly settled and covered such vast areas that the circuit riders were kept constantly on the trail to minister to each society once a month.

In spite of the difficulties occasioned by the scattered memberships, few circuit riders, rare meetinghouses, and isolated campgrounds, the Methodist movement grew in strength in the territory beyond the Ocmulgee. Throughout the years, the seed planted by circuit riders and laymen flowered into a vast system of conferences, districts, circuits, and stations bolstered by institutions of learning established to perpetuate the Christian faith through the Methodist establishment.

The early meetinghouses along the Ocmulgee were spread over a wide area extending from the mouth of the river up to its headwaters. Most of the members of pioneer churches dwelt upon small clearings or large plantations, and the meetinghouses were located at places designed to serve a scattered populace.

There were, however, a few settlements where populations were so concentrated that a greater number and variety of churches could be established and maintained. Hawkinsville, Perry, Macon, Forsyth, and McDonough provided favorable conditions for the founding of Baptist and Methodist churches, with an occasional Presbyterian meetinghouse appearing wherever Scots and Scotch-Irish were sufficiently numerous to warrant a kirk of their faith.

Macon, as the outstanding metropolis of the Ocmulgee world, provided the greatest number and variety of denominations. Interestingly enough, however, Macon's very prosperity, with the hustle and bustle of its mushrooming growth, cast its own stumbling blocks in the way of early and widespread support of the Christian order.

Even in the midst of the booming activity of the prosperous settlement, a Macon journalist, writing under the cautious title of "Observer," expressed dismay at the crass secularism displayed by the residents. With the dawn of the Sabbath, the streets were crowded with wagon teams, hauling lumber for new structures. Along with the active laborers, mingled swarms of strollers and loafers. Drunkenness and cursing were prevalent along the teeming streets. Little attention was given to worship services among the motley crowds.

"Observer" commented that with a population of over 400 citizens, hardly 30 saw fit to attend a church. At the meetinghouse itself, an air of rowdiness prevailed. Callous individuals loitered about the entrance and made insulting remarks as the worshipers passed by. Others walked aimlessly in and out of the building without regard for the worship service in progress.

Even inside the sanctuary, disorder still prevailed. "Observer" was shocked by an uncouth character who stalked noisily into the room, brazenly pushed a collection of hats from a bench, irreverently sprawled out upon the bench, and nonchalantly went to sleep.[33]

Nevertheless, signs of religious refinement were soon evident in the Ocmulgee settlement. Before many years had passed, Macon could proudly point to growing churches of the Baptist, Methodist, Presbyterian, Episcopal, and Roman Catholic denominations. Moreover, along with the rising church spires, a Methodist institution for the education of young ladies crowned one of the city's central hills.

Thus was Christianity borne to the land beyond the Ocmulgee River.

CHAPTER XXVI

INDIAN TROUBLES BEYOND THE OCMULGEE

Indian troubles were haunting the pioneer settlers beyond the Ocmulgee.

After the cession of the territory between the Ocmulgee and Flint rivers, the Creeks were left with only a wide strip of land within the boundaries of Georgia. This area, stretching from the Flint westward to the Alabama line, was coveted by the land-hungry whites for its fertile soil, and venerated by the red people as a vital hunting ground and as the site of some of their most honored settlements. The aggressive Georgians, still pressing onward, now sought to gain from the red people this final bit of territory and to remove the Creeks entirely from Georgia soil.

With a determination born of desperation, the Indians firmly opposed any further cession of their dangerously-diminishing domain. But the advancing Georgians, in the face of increasing immigration and overdue federal promises, employed an effective measure to achieve their aim.

William McIntosh, a half-breed leader of the Lower Creeks, had long aided the white people in their struggles against the Upper Creeks and Seminoles. During the Creek War, he had served in the forces of General John Floyd, whose campaign against the Upper Creek towns had helped break the power of the Red Sticks. In the Seminole conflict which followed, McIntosh served as the leader of a party of friendly Indians. His Lower Creek warriors had done most of the actual fighting against the Seminoles in Florida, thereby bringing victory to the American cause. McIntosh had been active in negotiating treaties which had finally brought the white settlers as far west as the Flint River. In recognition of his shrewd ability in helping them attain their goals against the reluctant Creeks, the whites again turned to the astute chieftain for assistance in obtaining a final treaty.

McIntosh proved willing and able. Early in 1825, through a controversial maneuver, the chieftain induced a number of Lower Creeks of varying rank to come to Indian Springs to enter into negotiations for the desired treaty. Through his influence over the assembled red people, McIntosh was able to gain their consent for a cession of most of the territory within the boundaries of Georgia which remained in the possession of the Creek Nation.[1]

The Treaty of Indian Springs brought swift rejection from the Alabama Creeks who maintained that the dubious representatives had no authority to bargain away lands belonging to the entire Creek Nation. Believing themselves betrayed by William McIntosh, the leaders of the opposition party dispatched a vengeance force to dispose of the artful chieftain. Descending upon his abode on the Chattahoochee River, in the darkness of the night, the wrathful warriors set fire to the house and mercilessly butchered McIntosh as he attempted to escape the flames. [2]

The lands upon which the Georgians were now establishing their civilization beyond the Ocmulgee had long comprised a vital part of the Creek Nation. Now, all treaties to the contrary, the red people could not reconcile themselves to the fact that this beloved part of their old world, with its familiar landmarks and enticing trails, was no longer their own. Confined to an area comprising a merc shadow of their once-vast domain, the red people were encountering great difficulty in eking out the barest necessities of life.[3] The gradual disappearance of their abundant hunting grounds before the pioneer's gnawing ax and greedy plough was bringing hunger and despair to the displaced children of the woods. So, from their increasingly remote abodes in Alabama, the Creeks continued to roam their old haunts in the country just beyond the Ocmulgee.

In their roving, the red people frequently encountered the white pioneers now established in new abodes upon land so recently acquired from the Indians. Some of the red men displayed a spirit of amiability toward the white newcomers. The Indians were avid traders and sought out the pioneers to bargain with them. The uneasy whites were usually anxious to agree to any terms to hasten the departure of their fearful visitors. While out hunting, the Indians kept a supply of wild game to exchange for farm products. The red people were fond of watermelons, fruits and milk, and would swap a quarter of venison for one watermelon. When offered game, the whites would politely accept it, but usually it was so unsightly that they would discard the game as soon as they could do so without being observed by the keen eyes of the redskins. [4]

When making their way to the homes of the whites, the Indians approached in awesome silence. Even in large parties their advent was so noiseless that the whites were seldom aware of their nearness until their startling figures appeared in the doorway. Having accomplished the object of their visit, the red people departed as silently as they had come.[5]

If the Indians thought they were well treated by the whites they became loyal friends and at times displayed surprising gentleness, but if they believed themselves the objects of injury, they made bitter enemies and showed little mercy toward the victims of their vengeance. In any case, the redskins were unpredictable, and the sudden appearance of their grotesque figures at the door of a remote cabin brought anxiety to the bravest of men and downright terror to women and children. Regardless of the nature of their visits, the departure of the redskins brought sighs of relief to their white hosts. [6]

The Indians availed themselves of the opportunity of trading with white storekeepers by making long journeys to the settlement stores established along the west side of the Ocmulgee. Among the first white people to venture across the river into the new land were traders, who set up business establishments dealing in an assortment of general merchandise designed to meet the needs of white settlers and of roving red people. Appearing at an early time were stores at Bowen's Mill, at John S. Gilder's, and at Ludd Mobley's, all situated on a section of the Big Bend stretching from House Creek down to the Jacksonville area. [7]

As in days of previous Indian troubles, the territory along the Big Bend in Irwin County was a common haunt for strolling redskins. The woods and streams on the Big Bend and in the country stretching away from the Ocmulgee River had long been a favorite hunting ground for the Creeks and Seminoles. Within this area were remnants of old trails leading from the Ocmulgee to the Indian towns on the Chattahoochee and beyond. Near the apex of the bend in present-day Wilcox County was a vast network of Indian paths running along the Ocmulgee and extending out into the surrounding country. [8] Now occupied by venturesome white pioneers, this territory became the scene of many incidents involving the whites and roving redskins. Some of the incidents, stemming from the ever-present dread of Indians, resulted in ludicrous situations and brought amusing relief to the apprehensive pioneers, while others grew out of circumstances inducing sheer terror.

In the face of continuing Indian troubles, the early settlers beyond the Ocmulgee found it prudent to establish their homes as near the river as possible. In this way they could keep in touch with the inhabitants on the opposite bank, dwelling behind the protective waters of the stream. When the alarm was sounded that hostile redskins were approaching, the white settlers would hastily prepare their homes and property against possible depredations and cross over to the safety of the opposite bank of the Ocmulgee. [9] Here, they would be taken into the homes of their neighbors until the danger subsided. Then the pioneers would return to their home scenes where they sometimes found their fields ravaged, their livestock driven away, and their houses in ashes.

On a stretch of the Big Bend, extending from present-day Abbeville down to Bowen's Mill, there settled a group of pioneers who had come into the new territory from the opposite side of the river in Telfair County. Among these early settlers were the families of Philip Brown, Jehu McCall, Abraham McCall, Nathaniel Statham, John McAnnally, George R. Reid, Samuel Stone, Leonard Stone, Henry Land, Frederick Land, John Gibbs, Dempsey Taylor, James L. Willcox, and others.

Coming into the settlement from more distant places were William Barrentine, Jacob Barrentine, James Barrentine, Daniel Luke, John Tomberlin, Miles Adams, Miles Fitzgerald, and John Fitzgerald.[10]

Closely connected by ties of blood, friendship, or a sense of common danger, these pioneers maintained close communications with each other for protection in times of Indian troubles. When an alarm of danger was sounded, they would hastily assemble at Jordan's Bluff to be rowed across the river to the safety of the Telfair side. Here they would be taken into the homes of relatives and sympathetic friends dwelling in the settlements of Copeland, Hopewell, and Temperance. Thus sheltered, the refugees would remain until the danger was over.[11]

If the Indian scare lasted very long, it became necessary to send a scout back over the river to ascertain the state of affairs. His mission accomplished, the scout would return to bring warnings of continued danger, or to give the signal that all was clear.

On one occasion, when a report reached them that hostile redskins were approaching, the Ocmulgee pioneers hastily made their way to the usual gathering place at Jordan's Bluff. Shortly afterward, they were safely conveyed across the protective waters of the river. Taking customary shelter in the homes of kinsmen and friends, the refugees uneasily settled down to await the outcome of events.

As time passed, with no indication of the state of affairs back home, it was decided that a scout should be sent over to reconnoiter the territory for any sign of Indians. Feigning a boldness which he did not feel, David McCall, oldest son of Jehu McCall, volunteered for the mission. Crossing the river with trembling bravado, the youth reached his abode in safety. After hastily scouting the scene, he decided to go into the house to see if it had been entered or disturbed in any way. Upon entering the house, young McCall found everything in order. As he was about to depart, his uneasy glance happened to be directed toward the hugh fireplace, made of wood framing with cracks chinked with clay. David observed that in one spot, a chink of clay had fallen from the back of the fireplace, leaving a hole through which daylight could be seen. As the scout's attention was drawn to the opening, he was suddenly petrified with fright; for, clearly visible through the opening, appeared a large feather, moving slightly as if in unison with the head of a feather-bedecked savage, who seemed to be peering into the cabin. For what seemed like ages, the frightened youth stood motionless, awaiting some telltale movement from the redskin. But none came. Finally, the scout could stand the suspense no longer. Determined at all costs to learn what fate awaited him, he charged swiftly out the door. Reaching a place within sight of the chimney, McCall cast a fearful glance toward the spot. There, to his amazement, he beheld a pan of feathers, plucked from an old rooster, and left in the rush to flee from the Indians. One large feather stood out above all others; caught in the current of a gentle breeze, the feather was waving to and fro in a manner to suggest the head of a savage to an imaginative and frightened youth.

Greatly relieved at his discovery, David McCall hastened back across the river, where his family anxiously awaited his return. The scout's account of his adventure brought smiles of relief to his listeners and provided an amusing tale to be handed down to later generations of the days when hostile redskins lurked within the shadows of the Ocmulgee forests.[12]

To the pioneer settlers who had moved across the Ocmulgee from Telfair County, Indian troubles were a familiar old story. Many of them had been among the first to come to the river frontier after the territory was opened to whites through the Treaty of Washington in 1805. For many years, they had dwelt upon the frontier with nothing but the Ocmulgee River between them and the Creek Nation. During the early Creek and Seminole wars, the pioneers had lived under the gnawing dread of the firebrand and the scalping knife. It was upon the home of one of their number, Philip Brown, that the first blow had been struck against the Ocmulgee frontier after the commencement of hostilities in the War of 1812.

These pioneers had dwelt within the shadow of the old stronghold of Fort Adams, erected to protect the upper part of Telfair County during the Creek War. Some had served as military leaders guarding the frontier throughout these perilous years. [13] Jehu McCall, who married a daughter of Philip Brown, had been the first commissioned Lieutenant in his militia district as far back as 1810.[14] Later, McCall and others now settled near-by, had served in the detachment which had erected and garrisoned Fort Adams. [15]

Some of the veteran Indian fighters had been in the force of Telfair citizens which crossed the Ocmulgee to seek redress after the Burch attack and had taken part in the ensuing conflict at Breakfast Branch. These old warriors were now settled within the vicinity of the historic stream, and the very sight of its winding course brought back vivid memories of that stirring event. Thompson Nathaniel Statham, upon whose back young Mark Willcox was borne all the way back to Jordan's Bluff, was now dwelling near the scene of his heroic deed.

Now that they were newly settled on the old Indian side of the Ocmulgee, the pioneers were again beset with troubles from their old foes. From the very earliest days of their crossing the river into Old Irwin County, these early comers took an active part in the defensive measures provided through the Georgia Militia, and much of the military leadership came from their numbers in the persons of Captains Jacob Barrentine, Thompson Nathaniel Statham, Sellaway McCall, Samuel Stone, James L. Willcox; and Lieutenants Abraham McCall, Daniel Mack Luke, and Lemuel Taylor.[16]

At times, Indian troubles on the Big Bend became so acute that it was necessary for the able-bodied men to join forces and go after the intruding redskins. Serving in the pursuit parties were Jehu McCall, Abraham McCall, Thompson Nathaniel Statham, James Lea Willcox, Richard Young, Frederick Land, William Winderweedle, Wright Tomberlin, Joshua Luke, and Jasper Luke. As a group, these neighbors and kinsmen "fought and camped and marched from the Everglades in Florida to the Cherokee country." [17]

While the men were away on extended Indian hunts, they left Samuel Brown behind to serve as a scout and to provide protection for the women, children, and old people. In case of danger Samuel was to put his charges over the Ocmulgee at Jordan's Bluff according to custom. During these uneasy times, Brown kept a canoe ready upon a moment's notice to transport the endangered inhabitants to the safety of the opposite bank. [18]

With the men away from home pursuing Indians, the pioneer women carried on the operation of their homes in the face of hardship and danger. Among the ingenious women who proved their ability to cope with the unexpected was Nancy Luke, young wife of Joshua Luke, who lived on the River Road about two miles above present-day Spectacle Church.

One day while her husband was away on an Indian hunt, Nancy was busily engaged with her housework. Glancing out the door of the cabin, she was startled to see a party of redskins approaching in single file. A few days earlier, a bloody massacre had taken place on Big Creek not far away. Nancy fully expected the same fate for herself and her young children. But in the face of danger Nancy's courageous pioneer spirit rose to the occasion. Meeting the fearful visitors at the door, she calmly invited them into the house. Then, surmising that the men were hungry and seeking food, Nancy quickly prepared a meal of cornbread, potatoes, and clabbered milk, to which she cordially bade the Indians partake. The red men ate heartily.

After satisfying their hunger, the redskins marched out into the yard. There, to the astonishment of the onlookers, the warriors staged a wild dance. But, from their gestures, Nancy Luke was made to understand that the dance was a token of appreciation for the hospitality she had shown. Concluding their dance, the red men marched silently away and vanished within the shadows of the forest.[19]

Some of the early settlers erected their cabins at a considerable distance from the Ocmulgee, on neighboring creeks or in the open wilderness. Being too far from the river to gain the security of its sheltering waters, these pioneers were forced to devise other means of protecting themselves from the Indians. In their isolation, the whites found it prudent to unite their efforts by erecting a simple type of refuge known as a "stand." A stand was a squared-off stockade enclosing two or three acres of land. The stockade was constructed of large poles placed side by side in an upright position and firmly braced to give strength to the walls. Within the enclosure, several log cabins were built to provide emergency living quarters in time of need. [20]

When an Indian alarm was sounded, the neighboring settlers would flee from their exposed cabins and assemble inside the stockade. Here, behind its protecting walls, the refugees could live for days in reasonable comfort and safety. In case of attack, the occupants could put forth a united defense, and during anxious days and nights of waiting, they could provide companionship for each other.

One known stand was erected on the south side of the Big Bend about twenty miles below Jacksonville and near the Blackshear Road leading to Trader's Hill on the St. Mary's River. The stockade was designed to provide a haven for the people dwelling within the area of modern Douglas in Coffee County. Among these pioneers were the families of John Peterson and Redding Metts.[21]

On one occasion, a party of hostile Indians was reported moving toward the settlement. Riders were sent out instantly among the scattered inhabitants, urging them to flee to the stand. The response was instantaneous, and within a short time, the area inside the stockade was teeming with frightened refugees.

In their haste to reach the stronghold, some of the people had not gathered sufficient supplies of food and clothing for a long stay. The Metts family was lacking in clothing. Their home stood two miles from the stand on an eminence overlooking Seventeen Mile Creek. Seeking to procure the needed wearing apparel, the wife of Redding Metts dispatched a black woman to the house with instructions to gather the clothing and hasten back to the fort.

Upon the departure of the Negro, the occupants anxiously awaited the completion of her mission and her safe return. But the woman did not come back. As soon as it was deemed prudent, a scouting party was sent out to investigate. Reaching the Metts house, the horsemen found that the place had been ravaged by the marauders, and the faithful servant savagely slaughtered.[22]

CHAPTER XXVII

LINGERING SHADOWS

The towering figure of Andrew Jackson was casting its shadow over the Ocmulgee world. From the primitive paths of the Indian country, the footsteps of the old warrior had led triumphantly to the polished floors of the White House. Now, as President of the United States, Jackson had not forgotten his foes of earlier days on the Georgia frontier and at Horseshoe Bend. With the same crushing diplomacy displayed at Fort Jackson, Old Hickory was determined to remove the Indians from their ancient seats to new lands beyond the Mississippi River. President Jackson's Indian policies were bringing familiar echoes of an old refrain to the Ocmulgee domain.

While conflicts between the early white settlers and Indians had occurred all along, events were moving toward a final climax in the early 1830's. By this time, the Creeks had been officially barred from Georgia soil, and Jackson's efforts to remove them from their Alabama abodes were increasing. But the red people held tenaciously to the last vestige of their Alabama domain and hovered menacingly over the Georgia boundary. At the same time, the Seminoles were violently resisting all efforts to remove them from their Florida lands, and were presenting a threat to the South Georgia frontier. [1]

Dispossessed of their once-bountiful hunting grounds, the Creeks were destitute and desperate. Unable to gain their sustenance from their reduced resources, many turned upon the whites and attempted to supply their wants by raiding and plundering the isolated homes of the pioneers. For their part, the white newcomers, struggling for existence in a primitive land beset with hardships, were of no mind to see the fruits of their labors carried off or wantonly despoiled by the red intruders. [2]

The rising troubles within the Indian country spread toward the Big Bend of the Ocmulgee and surrounding areas where strolling parties of vagabond Indians made mischief. For five months, they roamed over a wide stretch along the headwaters of the Alapaha River, ravaging woods, killing livestock, and robbing fields of corn, peas, potatoes, and sugar cane. By strength of numbers, they were able to impose upon and insult the white people dwelling within the sparsely settled country. Finally, unable to endure the harassment of the redskins any longer, the pioneers collected a small force of fourteen men to drive out the intruders.

Setting out upon the Indian hunt, the whites soon came upon the hostiles firmly lodged within the shelter of a thickly-wooded branch. The little force advanced cautiously toward the entrenched redskins. To their dismay, the whites found themselves outnumbered by the savages who gave every indication of being ready for a fight. As the white men came within range, the redskins suddenly gave a wild whoop and opened fire with eight or ten guns. At this astonishing reception, the whites became alarmed and "turned to go from there." Made bold by their success, the redskins charged after the retreating whites, whooping all the while. By this time, all thoughts of "driving out" the Indians had vanished from the minds of the frightened whites. With surprising swiftness, they departed from the scene without firing a shot! Miraculously, not a man was harmed, although enemy bullets made the bark fly from the trees all about them.

The party of frustrated pioneers was made up of Samuel Storey, Sr., Samuel Storey, Jr., Joseph Sumner, Benjamin Willis, Seaborn Land, Samuel Mixon, Lott Whiddon, Jesse Hobby, John S. Jenkins, David Smith, Seaborn Taylor, and Jonathan Smith. A few days before the encounter, Samuel Storey and John Jenkins had met one of the Indians and talked with him. The redskin informed the whites that his name was Peter, and that he was a member of the party of strolling Indians whom he identified as Chattahoochee Indians. Asked how many were in the hunting party, Peter replied, "Heap Injuns hunting." [3]

Thoroughly alarmed over the turn of events, the white settlers dispatched an account of their difficulties to Governor Lumpkin, and urgently called upon him for protection against "such intruders." [4]

While appealing to the Chief Executive in the distant capital of Milledgeville, the pioneers turned more hopefully to a source of aid nearer home. Across the Ocmulgee River in the old Copeland settlement in Telfair County lived Mark Willcox whose hassles with Indians dated back to the Battle of Breakfast Branch. As a mere lad, he was wounded in this conflict and narrowly missed losing his scalp. In the ensuing years, Willcox had risen through the ranks of the Georgia Militia and would soon become a Brigadier-General in command of the brigade embracing the ravaged territory. In their distress, the Irwin pioneers turned to their old comrade for assistance.

With the reality of his own plight still fresh in his memory, General Willcox promptly responded to the plea of his neighbors beyond the Ocmulgee. Collecting a force of forty men, he crossed the river to drive out the offenders. But, at the approach of such a formidable force, the Indians fled to the larger swamps and eluded their pursuers. The detachment remained upon the scene for several days without encountering the savages or being able to flush them from their hiding places; then, in baffled disgust, the Telfair men returned home. [5]

Upon reaching his abode in Copeland, the ruffled Mark Willcox penned to the Governor a report of his fruitless expedition. In his communication of January 28, 1835, Willcox portrayed the plight of the Irwin County inhabitants dwelling in positions so exposed to Indian depredations. The old soldier lamented that the redskins were "sufficiently strong to bid defiance to the few persons so thinly settled in that country." To portray the hostile actions of the Indians, Willcox recited that a few days before, a party had gone to the home of Mr. Storey and, finding him away from home, had driven his family off and robbed his storehouse of all the supplies they could carry away. [6]

If the account of the one-sided skirmish between the "Indian drivers" and their foes should have suggested a touch of amusement to the people dwelling at a safe distance from the scene, other events were soon to follow completely devoid of any element of humor.

It has been observed that the Indians responded violently to any injury to themselves, real or imaginary. If they became offended at any white person, they were likely to go on the rampage. In retaliating for an offense, the savages did not limit their vengeance to the persons responsible for the injury. Instead, they were likely to strike out at the first white they could reach, and turn the force of their fury upon the most innocent victims.

Near the old boundary line between the counties of Irwin and Dooly lived James Brown, a rugged pioneer noted for his decisive dealings with the Indians. On one occasion, he came upon an Indian stealing hogs from his pen. Unhesitatingly, Brown shot the redskin dead on the spot. From this time on, he was known as "Indian Jim Brown." [7] The act of Indian Jim did not go unnoticed by the observant red people. Shortly after the event, a band of wrathful marauders appeared in the settlement seeking revenge. Not far away, stood a small pioneer schoolhouse kept by Josiah Whitney, a crippled old schoolmaster. The school was attended by a few children from homes scattered about in the Musslewhite settlement. On the day before Christmas in the year 1835, school was in session with the schoolmaster and his pupils following their pursuits unaware of the presence of danger.

Moving directly toward the settlement came the angry savages. Reaching the home of Recy Musslewhite and finding him away from home, they robbed the house and set it on fire. Leaving the house in flames, the hostiles moved on toward the house of Thomas Musslewhite. In order to reach Musslewhite's the savages would pass the little schoolhouse standing in their path. The old schoolmaster looked out and saw them coming. Hastily, Whitney dismissed his pupils and urged them to flee to the surrounding woods. Then, with the last pupil gone, the schoolmaster tried to make his own escape by hobbling hurriedly to the house of Thomas Musslewhite. But the crippled teacher was entirely too feeble to escape the swift redskins. When within sixty paces of the house, Whitney was overtaken. There, the merciless savages fell upon him, shot three balls through his body, and cut his throat from ear to ear.

The school children and a group of women at Musslewhite's watched the grisly spectacle in speechless horror; then they fled to a near-by thicket where they avoided a similar fate by concealing themselves amid the dense undergrowth.

After killing the schoolmaster, the rampaging redskins continued on to the house of Thomas Musslewhite where they killed a dog, plundered the house, and left it in flames.

As soon as the men in the neighborhood could be assembled, they formed a pursuit party and went after the intruders. In the action that followed, one Indian was killed.

The next day was Christmas. On this significant day, the body of the faithful old schoolmaster was laid to rest by his mourning neighbors. [8]

About the time of the attack upon Josiah Whitney, Samuel Storey caught an Indian stealing hogs. Storey was a member of the party of whites which had been routed in the one-sided skirmish with the Chattahoochee Indians, and had no love for redskins. To punish the miscreant, Storey tied him to a tree and gave him a severe flogging with a cow whip.

Again the redskins struck back. In the vicinity of present-day Dakota stood the lonely cabin of Benjamin Willis. The Willis family had settled at an early time on the east side of the Ocmulgee River in Telfair County. Shortly after the opening of the lands west of the river, the family crossed over and settled near the Oswichee Indian trail leading from the Ocmulgee southwestward to the Flint River near old Pindertown. This location placed the Willis home in a position easily accessible to vagabond Indians stalking the trail.

On one occasion, Benjamin Willis left home to install a water wheel for a grist mill near the Ocmulgee River, a task necessitating his absence from home overnight. As Willis later recounted the events: during the night, he was awakened from a terrifying dream. Fearful for the safety of his family, Willis set out on foot for home. Covering the miles in frantic haste, Willis reached the site of his frontier home. There he found his dreaded expectations fearfully fulfilled.

Before Benjamin Willis lay a scene of devastation. Vengeful savages had descended upon his isolated dwelling and massacred his defenseless family. In the ensuing carnage, Peggy Willis, wife of Benjamin, was slaughtered and her body badly mutilated. A daughter had seized an infant child and tried to flee. But her movement did not escape the eyes of the Indians. The girl was swiftly pursued and overtaken a short distance from the house. Here she was slain and scalped. Not content with the havoc they had wrought, the redskins turned upon the infant lying where it had fallen. With ruthless blows, the savages crushed the soft body into a bloody mass. [9]

The victims of the Willis massacre were buried in the virgin wiregrass soil at Dakota, where their graves long served as silent reminders of the days when the early settlers beyond the Ocmulgee lived and died under the shadow of the firebrand, the tomahawk, and the scalping knife.

CHAPTER XXVIII

THE INDIANS' LAST THRUST

The Indian troubles flaring in the land beyond the Ocmulgee were actually a part of a general Indian crisis now reaching its climax. The federal government was having great difficulty in its efforts to remove the red people from Georgia, Florida, and Alabama to new homes planned for them beyond the Mississippi River. The ancient tribesmen were resisting fiercely the efforts to force them from the scenes of their old homeland. As they found themselves facing bodily eviction from their once-proud Nation, their resentment, born of desperation, mounted dangerously. The Creeks in Alabama and the Seminoles in Florida now moved toward a final effort to unite forces and hurl the remnant of their waning power at their ever-increasing white enemies.

Under the influence of their powerful leader, Osceola, the Seminoles struck at the United States forces attempting to remove them to the west. With the Seminoles in a state of revolt, the Alabama Creeks endeavored to join the Seminoles in Florida for a united thrust against the Americans. In order to reach Florida, the Creeks faced the necessity of breaking through the old land barrier previously established by Andrew Jackson at Fort Jackson to prevent just such a movement. By now, this territory forming the lower part of Georgia was already occupied by white pioneers all the way to the Alabama boundary.

The strategy adopted by the Creek Indians was to cut a corridor leading from Alabama, across South Georgia, and into Florida. The Creeks would strike at the white settlements in their path with such force that the inhabitants would be thrown into a state of panic and flee into the interior of Georgia. With the Southwest Georgia frontier thus abandoned, the Creeks could push on into Florida for a rendezvous with their Seminole allies. [1]

The Indian drive commenced on May 15, 1836, with a night attack upon the town of Roanoke, situated on the Chattahoochee River in Stewart County. Taking the slumbering occupants by surprise, the Indians overwhelmed the settlement and left it in ashes. Having gained a foothold upon Georgia soil, the rampaging Creeks continued their drive southeastward, leaving a trail of destruction behind them. [2]

Now all of Georgia was aroused. Immediate steps were taken to intercept the invaders. Forces of militia were raised in large numbers and rushed to the scene of invasion. Governor Schley, as Commander-in-Chief, took to the field in person and established his headquarters at Columbus, the gateway to the Alabama Indian country. Now strong forces were sent against the red intruders in an effort to halt their destructive march toward Florida. [3]

With the increasing weight of Georgia's military descending upon them, the Indians were forced upon the defensive. From an advanced position in Baker County, they sought to elude their adversaries by lodging themselves upon an island within the fastness of Chickasawhatchee Swamp. An aggressive force of militia went after the redskins. In the action which followed, the Georgians dealt the entrenched Creeks a devastating blow. [4] Other engagements followed swiftly, with victories for the Georgians. Faced with overwhelming opposition, the red men were rapidly going down in defeat.

With the main Creek invasion forces reeling under the blows of the Georgia Militia in the Indians' direct line of march, detached Indian parties attempted to reach Florida adroitly through other avenues. It was now evident that the invaders were outflanking the militia by slipping around them and pushing eastward toward the headwaters of the Alapaha and Suwanee rivers. Then, having eluded the Georgia military barrier, the redskins were attempting to proceed down both streams, far to the rear of the defending white forces, to drive on into the land of the Seminoles. [5]

To prevent such an eventuality, Governor Schley ordered General Mark Willcox to collect a body of men from the Ocmulgee territory and dispatch them to guard the threatened approaches. Crossing over the Ocmulgee again, Willcox stationed his Telfair men in positions designed to intercept any Indians which might elude the main Georgia forces, and at the same time, to provide protection for the neighboring inhabitants. [6]

Following the success of the Creeks in gaining a foothold within Chickasawhatchee Swamp, Governor Schley gave utterance to words through the pages of a Columbus newspaper which General Willcox interpreted as placing the blame on Willcox. The irate General lost no time in letting His Excellency know his sentiments in the matter. In a strongly-worded letter written at Copeland on July 11, 1836, Mark Willcox reminded the Governor that, under his own orders, he had instructed the General to guard the headwaters of the Suwanee and that no Indians had made their escape through that territory. Willcox pointed out that Chickasawhatchee Swamp was fifty miles from the nearest point assigned his guard and that he saw no way that he could be blamed for the situation there. [7]

In spite of the defensive measures put forth, however, parties of Indians were breaking into the territory lying between the Ocmulgee River and the Florida border. Hostiles were penetrating deep into the country and threatening the white settlers along the Alapaha River, the Flint, and at other vulnerable places. [8] Even as General Willcox was penning his heated letter to the Governor, a sharp clash was shaping up not far away.

On July 10, 1836, a large party of Indians was discovered in the upper part of Lowndes (now Berrien) County near the home of A. Maddox and moving eastward. The next day, they were pursued by a force of whites under command of Captain Levi J. Knight, who lived near the scene. Before the pursuit party could overtake them, the Indians raided the homes of William Parker, Willis Peters, and John Gaskins, located on the west side of the Alapaha River near present-day Nashville. At each place, the Indians plundered the premises and carried off valuable objects. At the Parker house, they broke open a trunk and took from it a large sum of money along with a supply of ammunition. Taking the feather beds out into the yard, the audacious intruders cut them open, emptied them of their contents, and appropriated the bed ticks to form packs in which the Indians could carry their stolen goods. As they moved onward, the redskins left a trail of feathers behind.

With the entire countryside now aroused by flying rumors of hostile Indians on the march, men were hurrying from over a wide area to join in the mission of driving out the marauders. Uniting under Captain Knight the party finally numbered eighty men.

Following the trail of the feathers, the whites overtook the Indians on the west bank of the Alapaha on July 13, 1836. As the whites prepared to attack, they divided their forces into three commands led by Jesse Carter, William Knight, and William Peters, respectively. The commands were ordered to encircle the Indians and charge. Caught between the oncoming whites at their backs and the Alapaha River in their front, the red men were in a desperate position. Quickly, they attempted to escape by swimming across the river. Throwing their plunder and guns into the stream, the redskins plunged in after them.

With William Peters leading, his men charged upon the hapless red men. Under the accuracy of the white men's fire, the bullets found their mark. One by one, the swimming Indians were seen to jerk as a bullet struck, leaving a telltale red stain oozing up from the dark water. Only six redskins reached the opposite bank, and three of these were supposed wounded. Peters was badly wounded in the attack. After the action was over, the bodies of twenty to thirty red men were found, along with much of their loot including fifteen packs and ten guns. The Indians had attempted to throw across the river a shot bag containing the stolen money, but the bag was caught within the tangle of a bough overhanging the opposite bank of the stream. The bag was recovered and all the money found safe. [9]

With a wave of alarm sweeping over the countryside once more, General Mark Willcox again attempted to come to the aid of the people. Leading a force of men drawn from the counties of Appling, Irwin, and Telfair, Willcox set out to patrol the headwaters of the Alapaha and Suwanee rivers in search of any redskins gathering there. On July 28, 1836, Willcox reported to the Governor that there was "a great alarm in Irwin County," and that he believed the countryside to be in danger due to Indians skulking about in the swamps at the headwaters of the Alapaha and Suwanee. On several occasions, he had sent out his men to trail and pursue them. His troops had frequently taken the packs and camp utensils of the redskins, but the prowlers had succeeded in eluding the rifles of the Willcox men. [10]

For awhile, sporadic fighting spread out over the South Georgia wiregrass country between parties of marauding Indians and small bodies of whites raised to combat the redskins. Casualties were suffered on both sides of the conflict.

But the Indians were making their last feeble stand. In their futile efforts to avoid capture, parties of red men, women and children attempted to hide within the dense shelter of large swamps, but to no avail. Beaten and destitute, the natives were tracked down and captured. As a final gesture of futility, some of the captive women smothered their children by packing their mouths and nostrils tightly with masses of mud and moss, preferring death to forcible removal from the lost domain of their forefathers. [11] Little by little, the ancient inhabitants were taken from the familiar scenes of their once-powerful Nation, and sent to unknown realms in the distant west.

CHAPTER XXIX

ROLLING WHEELS AND WAYSIDE STOPS

By the late 1820's, the American civilization had overspread most of Georgia, with settlements stretching from the Cherokee country in the north to the Florida border in the south, and from the Atlantic Ocean in the east to the Alabama line in the west. With settlements and clearings scattered well over the state, a network of roadways emerged to provide access to the principal centers of population and to the clearings of the inhabitants.

Situated in the very heart of Georgia, with the capital city of Milledgeville not far away, the Ocmulgee country became a vital part of the state's system of communication and transportation. At this time the stagecoach was the chief means of overland travel, and many routes traversed by the speeding vehicles were interwoven with the Ocmulgee world. During these early stagecoach days, Macon, Hartford, and Jacksonville became hubs from which stage routes radiated out in such numerous directions as to make the river towns key centers of travel.

The principal stagecoach lines usually emerged from pathways used by post riders in the rapid transportation of mail. In the course of time, stagecoaches became the general mode of conveyance for both mail and passengers, and stage routes were largely determined by the location of populous areas needing mail and passenger service.

An early stagecoach line led from Georgia's capital city of Milledgeville in a southwesterly direction through Marion and Shine's Store in Twiggs County to Hartford on the Ocmulgee River. From Hartford, the route of the lumbering vehicle proceeded down the east bank of the river along the Old River Road through Copeland, Temperance, and Jacksonville in Telfair County. At the hub center of Jacksonville, the stagecoach line fanned out in three directions. The river route continued on down the River Road by Ashley's Mills, across the Oconee at Bell's Ferry, through Perry's Mills in Tattnall County, and on to the road's end at Darien on the seacoast. [1]

A second stage path branching out from Jacksonville led southward across the Ocmulgee by ferry, then veered southeastward to follow the old Blackshear Road through today's Broxton,

Douglas, and Waresboro to the end of the line at St. Mary's on the Atlantic Seaboard. [2]

Stagecoaches traveling the third line rolled out of Jacksonville toward the south. Crossing the Ocmulgee River over Swain's Ferry, the speeding vehicles entered the Coffee Road and turned in a southwesterly direction to continue through the heart of the wiregrass country. Passing the site of Alapaha, the stages crossed the Alapaha River over Reuben Marsh's Ferry, then rolled on through today's Nashville and Thomasville to their destination at Tallahassee, the Capital city of Florida. [3]

Travel service on the stage route from Jacksonville to Tallahassee was severely hampered during the dry seasons by a scarcity of water for passengers and horses. During these periods, the stages were shifted to the Hartford-Tallahassee route where water was more plentiful. [4]

The Hartford stage route led from the Hartford hub across the Ocmulgee by ferry and into the Blackshear Road running by Slade's to Fort Early. At Fort Early, the line turned southwestward and proceeded down the Flint River through old Pindertown, Bainbridge, Quincy, and on to Tallahassee. The stages operated a weekly schedule on this line and usually covered the distance in six days. Three days after leaving Milledgeville, the speeding vehicles reached Pindertown; and three days later pulled into Tallahassee. [5]

An early stage route traversing the Ocmulgee territory began at Macon and followed the west side of the river down through Perry and Haynesville in Houston County, and on to Hawkinsville, a flourishing new town rising on the west bank of the Ocmulgee opposite Hartford. From Hawkinsville, the way continued down the west bank of the river through the old Adams settlement just below today's Abbeville, and on to Bowen's Mill at House Creek. From Bowen's Mill, a short mail line led southwestward to Irwinville, the newly-established county seat of Irwin County. [6]

The mail routes following the east and west banks of the Ocmulgee were joined by a short connecting link leading from the Adams settlement to the west bank of the Ocmulgee at Jehu McCall's landing. From McCall's, the route crossed over the river to Boatyard Landing in upper Telfair County. Turning northward at Hopewell Church, the line followed the Old River Road upstream to its terminus at Copeland. [7]

One of the earliest stage lines associated with the Ocmulgee led from Milledgeville in a southwesterly direction along the old Garrison Road, once used as a military way from the environs of the capital city to Fort Hawkins. Striking the Ocmulgee at the foot of the crumbling frontier post, the stage route crossed the river into Macon, the rising metropolis of the Ocmulgee world. Continuing in a southwesterly direction, the route followed the Federal Road to the old Creek Agency on the Flint River. Crossing over the Flint to Fort Lawrence, the way proceeded directly to Columbus on the Chattahoochee River. [8]

In dry weather this was a difficult course to follow, due to deep sands encountered in western Georgia. To avoid this hindrance an alternate route could be used leading from Milledgeville by the way of Clinton in Jones County, across the Ocmulgee at Booth's Ferry, then through Forsyth, Thomaston, Gibson's, and finally to Columbus. [9]

Still another stage line, reflecting the early military days of frontier Georgia, issued from Milledgeville and followed a route running southwestward through Fort Lawrence, Fort Perry, Fort Gaines, and on to Pensacola by the way of Pea River, Conecaugh, and Big Escambia. [10]

While the stagecoach lines provided communication between key centers located along the Ocmulgee River, they rendered a much broader service in the field of travel. At the terminal points reached by the Ocmulgee lines, the stages made connections with other lines leading to the largest cities in the United States. The routes running from Milledgeville to Tallahassee and Pensacola joined other stage lines at these points, and were continued westward to New Orleans on the Mississippi River. At the same time, the routes leading from the Ocmulgee to St. Mary's, Darien, and Augusta made connections with other coach lines traversing the Atlantic Seaboard by the way of Savannah, Charleston, Richmond, Washington, New York, and Boston. A stage coming down from the north was known as the "Northern Stage," while a stagecoach approaching from southern points was designated as the "Southern Stage."

The stagecoach system brought to the country its own unique way of life. The speeding vehicle was ever an object of fascination to spectators as it rushed on its way amid the thundering beat of horses' hoofs, the clatter of whirling wheels, and the intermittent blare of the horn.

A stagecoach could travel up to fifty miles a day, but the horses were run in relays with changes made at shorter distances. For the accommodation of horses and passengers, wayside stations were maintained at convenient intervals where teams could be changed and where passengers were provided with food and overnight lodgings.

The arrival of a stagecoach at a wayside station was an exciting event for most travelers and spectators. While the coach was still some distance away, the driver would give notice of its approach by lustily sounding his horn. Thus notified, the innkeeper could have his hostel made ready for the reception of his expected guests. [11] The vibrant sound of the horn, echoing through the woods and across open fields, aroused roadside dwellers to a state of keen anticipation, and a number would be on hand to see the alluring vehicle come storming into view amid an aura of noise and dust.

The stage travelers were frequently treated with deference by the onlookers, in hopes some bit of news from faraway places would be passed on to them. The welcome prospects of food and rest brought all but the most reticent out of their weary shells so that the wayfarers often became expansive and gossipy. This was not always the case, however, for much of Georgia at this time was still a raw frontier country and at times the way of the stage traveler could be a trying ordeal.

The hospitality provided by wayside taverns varied considerably from place to place. In the older settlements, the inns usually afforded commodious lodgings, along with sumptuous meals and cordial service. But, in the newly-rising sections of western Georgia, accommodations could be meager indeed. On the rawest frontier, a wayside station could provide only a "general" room with a limited number of beds to accommodate ten or twelve guests. It was not unusual for several travelers to sleep together in the same bed, while others sprawled out upon thin pallets on the floor. The food was in keeping with the facilities, being plain and limited in variety. The inconveniences encountered at these bleak wayside stops were often the subject of caustic comment on the part of fastidious travelers from European countries. Some of the earliest observers were inclined to view with disdain the lusty ways of an expanding American frontier as reflected in the outer fringes of the stagecoach system.

The stage driver was in a class of his own as he strutted pompously before his appreciative audience at a wayside stop. This unique character was the symbol of enchanting scenes in faraway places to the home-bound inhabitants who stood in awesome respect for such a sophisticated man-of-the-world.

If the stage driver and passengers had their moments of glory at the wayside stations, they paid dearly for them in the hardships encountered along the way. The weather brought its own problems. When it was dry, water was hard to come by, thus necessitating a complete change of route, or the laborious task of drawing buckets of water for passengers and horses over steep banks from drought-stricken streams.[12] In times of torrential rains, the roads became so boggy and rutted that the clumsy carriage, trying to follow a regular schedule, frequently became embedded in seas of mud from which it was extricated only by the combined labors of driver and passengers. At times of flooding, the streams overflowed their banks and became impassable for the cumbersome stagecoach, leaving passengers stranded at the most inconvenient places.

The smaller streams were crossed without bridge or ferry, and each swirling flood threatened to engulf carriage, horses, and passengers or to sweep them from their perilous course.[13] The large streams were crossed by means of ferries, which presented danger of the flats' breaking from their moorings and being swept downstream, bearing their cargoes to an uncertain fate. Frequently, it was necessary to cross swollen streams at night under the most hazardous conditions. Sometimes, the danger was relieved somewhat by Negro slaves who illuminated the approaches by forming an avenue of light from flaming torches borne aloft by hand.[14] An early traveler found poignant significance in the fact that his friends, in seeing him off on a stagecoach journey, cautiously refrained from wishing him a *happy* journey, but heartily wished him a *safe* journey.[15]

The driver and passengers faced the rigors of the road together. The coachman could plunge the carriage down the most treacherous bank into a furiously swirling stream, with an air of nonchalance that held his passengers in a breathless state of suspense. As the coach bounced along the roughest places in a muddy road, dips were encountered in the ruts at uncomfortably frequent intervals. As the coach approached a dip on either side of the road, the ingenious driver would shout orders to the passengers to lean simultaneously in the opposite direction to keep the carriage in a state of precarious balance. Miraculously, the maneuver worked surprisingly well, as the clumsy vehicle careened along its way.[16]

The open road brought other hazards to the coachman, his cargo, and the passengers. If the stagecoach held a romantic charm for the casual observer along the way, it seemed to have an irresistible appeal for highway robbers. It was not an unusual occurrence for the vehicle to round a curve in the road, only to find its way obstructed by a barricade stretching across its path, and for the occupants to find themselves staring into the barrels of guns brandished by highway robbers. By daring action, the driver was sometimes able to overrun the barrier and escape the robbers, but at other times, he found submissiveness the height of prudence.

But, even as the stagecoaches lumbered complacently along the highways with an important air of permanency, ceaseless change was coming: before long, the era of the clumsy vehicle would fade away, and the familiar wheels would roll no more along the open roads of the Ocmulgee world.

CHAPTER XXX

STEAMBOATS ON THE OCMULGEE

As the old pole boat era faded, a new day dawned for navigation on the Ocmulgee. Even while the use of the cumbersome pole-propelled vessel was at its height, ingenious inventors had created an amazing new craft—the steamboat. The employment of the steamboat as a mode of navigation was revolutionizing transportation on America's waterways, and was on its way to the Ocmulgee.

The steamboat age advanced toward the Ocmulgee by degrees. In Georgia, the new river craft first appeared upon the Savannah River in 1816. [1] Two years later, steamboats were plying the Altamaha waters up to the forks, and some were venturing timidly up the Oconee to Milledgeville. [2] But forward-looking Georgians were anticipating the advent of steamboats up the Ocmulgee as far as Macon, the flourishing new settlement arising upon the opposite bank from Fort Hawkins. In November of 1826, a Macon newspaper writer voiced the opinion that the Ocmulgee was capable of navigation by steamboat to Macon and by pole boat to Cedar Shoals, some distance higher upstream. The optimistic writer urged immediate steps to bring about this desired goal.

The action was not long delayed. Early in 1829, the Ocmulgee world was electrified with excitement when a steamboat made its first voyage all the way from Darien upstream to Macon. This historic vessel was the *North Carolina*, commanded by Captain Salter. Immensely pleased, the writer for the *Macon Telegraph* used the occasion to portray the remarkable feat with these humorous words:

> Many of the people along the river banks were alarmed at the smoke and noise. Some mistook the noise for a roaring lion—others for the sneeze of an elephant. Some protested it was the hissing of a sea serpent, or the groaning of an earthquake. Others thought it was war, pestilence, and famine, but the most general opinion was that it was the Tariff coming in propria personnae to eat up our cotton and corn, and to drink up the river, and that it was an infringement on states rights. There was a climbing of trees and a picking of flints, and had it not made its escape, it would have been hard to tell what the consequences might have been. [3]

If the astonished spectators viewed the steamboat simply as an amusing novelty, this concept was of short duration, for in

196

1833, steamboat navigation became firmly established on the Ocmulgee. During this historic year, a new steamboat, the *Pioneer*, made its first run from Darien to Macon. This appropriately-named vessel was produced by the shipping firm of Day and Butts, who were hailed by the *Macon Telegraph* for their "fearless enterprise in prosecuting an experiment so long pronounced chimerical." The general opinion had prevailed along the Ocmulgee that the river could not be successfully navigated by steam craft. The voyage of the *Pioneer* had dispelled this belief and ushered in a new era of river transportation. The *Pioneer*, under command of Captain Matthias McCormick, had made the voyage from Darien to Macon in the amazingly short time of eight days. It had brought with it two large towboats, *Bonnets O' Blue* and *Lallah Rookh*, with full freights of merchandise. [4]

The *Pioneer* was constructed upon a revolutionary principle new to most river craft: instead of the usual side-wheels, it was propelled by wheels located in the stern of the vessel. This arrangement was especially designed to make possible the boat's safe passage along the narrow, twisting course of the Ocmulgee. Drawing only twenty-four inches of water, the vessel was relatively capable of gliding over hidden obstructions submerged beneath the surface of the water. The main body of the *Pioneer* had been constructed at Macon and drifted down to Darien where it was equipped with its machinery, and subsequently made the successful return voyage. [5]

As predicted by the Macon newspaper writer, the steamboat brought about marked change in the manner of shipping goods on the Ocmulgee waterway. In place of the slow, tedious, and expensive process of shipping by pole boat, the river inhabitants could now avail themselves of the speedy, efficient, and economical service of the steamboat. Instead of three or four weeks previously required for the journey from Darien to Macon, the distance could now be covered within a matter of days. The new mode of travel brought the river country considerably nearer its markets and into closer communication with the outside world. [6]

The use of the steamboat spread rapidly to Georgia's inland waterways. By 1836, seven steamboats were in use on the Ocmulgee and its sister river, the Oconee. These were supplemented by sixty towboats and pole boats. Enormous amounts of cotton were being received at Macon and sent downstream to seaport markets. [7]

The extensive employment of steamboat navigation brought new enterprise and prosperity to the Ocmulgee country. Through this effective medium, the planters could ship great quantities of cotton and other agricultural products from their expanding plantations to Darien and Savannah for trans-shipment to other American or foreign ports. By now, Great Britain and the New England States had become large textile centers and provided an increasing market for Georgia cotton.

The brisk demand for cotton enhanced the plantation system and created the need for greater numbers of Negroes to produce the valuable commodity. During the earliest years of settlement, slaves were few along the Ocmulgee. It was a rarity on the new frontier in 1810 when David McCall, a pioneer settler in Telfair County, indicated ownership of slaves by deeding one to each of two sons. [8] But since this early period, the use of Blacks had become widespread, and now large plantations sprawled where small clearings had once appeared. From the few Blacks of the frontier years, the institution of slavery grew rapidly during the rising steamboat era.

Largely through the impetus of the steamboat, the plantation system was transforming the Ocmulgee world from a raw frontier to the flowering land of the Ante-Bellum Period. As the virgin soil brought forth its abundant fruits, the prospering pioneers advanced from their one-room cabins to more commodious abodes of the double-pen type. These substantial structures contained two large rooms, separated by an open breezeway. As a family increased in size, shed rooms were added to the rear wall of the log house to provide additional sleeping quarters. The kitchen, with its massive fireplace, usually formed a separate building located at a safe distance back of the main structure as a precautionary measure against fire. The kitchen was connected with the "big house" by a covered walkway or "dog trot." The typical plantation house featured a broad piazza extending across its entire front. The low-pitched roof overhung the outer walls a considerable distance to provide welcome shelter against the fierce summer sun and the slashing winter rain.

With continuing prosperity, the Ocmulgee planters built finer houses of wide clapboards, but following the same pattern as the double-pen log structure. As the Greek Revival influence manifested itself in the architecture of the region, many houses featured a row of substantial columns across the front piazza, giving the appearance of stability and attractiveness. The Greek Revival plantation houses varied in appearance, from the one-story structure with short columns, to the imposing two-story edifice with tall, stately columns, gleaming white through a vista of large trees and open fields. During the rising Ante-Bellum

Era, much of the white-columned aristocracy of the Ocmulgee realm was spread along the old tree-lined river roads winding their way on both banks of the Ocmulgee.

Along with the new prosperity, the steamboat age brought adventure and romance to the Ocmulgee world. The low moan of the steamer whistle became a familiar but ever enchanting sound as it echoed over the river banks. To the inhabitants, the plaintive sound brought alluring visions of faraway places. Just as the old pole boat had once been the symbol of the outer world, now the throbbing steamboat brought a restless longing to the people dwelling along the Ocmulgee River.

In addition to cargoes of freight the river vessels transported passengers. The planters made frequent trips down to Darien and Savannah in the interest of their cotton sales and shipments, to purchase supplies for their plantations, and to attend to other affairs of business and pleasure. At times, other members of the family accompanied the planters to the strange land at the end of the rivers. A voyage to Darien, or Savannah, or even to Charleston was a great event in the lives of the isolated Ocmulgee dwellers. To the river people, the journey brought excitement and adventure, as well as prospects for new finery or luxuries to be found in the bountiful shops of the seaport towns.

Just as the old pole boat had once provided zest to the spectators when it pulled up to a river landing, so now the throbbing steamboat played an even greater role. The towns of Macon, Hawkinsville, Abbeville, Jacksonville, and Lumber City were leading river ports; but there were other important landings along the way. Most of the plantations had their own landings where the steamers could pull up to take on a cargo of produce on the way downstream and to unload merchandise on the way back from the seacoast. There were also other common or public landings where supplies could be put ashore to be conveyed to neighboring stores or to plantation commissaries. The river people would haul their produce to the landings by ox cart or wagon to be loaded upon the river vessels for shipment to market. After their incoming merchandise was put ashore, they would convey it in the same manner to its intended destination.

Some steamboat landings were located on the Ocmulgee at places designed to provide supplies for a widely-populated area. One such landing was at Red Bluff, on the Big Bend in Old Irwin County. From Red Bluff Landing, merchandise was hauled to the near-by trading center of Bowen's Mill. Commonly received was an assortment of general merchandise consisting of wearing apparel, cloth, groceries, salt, farm and forest implements, household furnishings, cooking utensils, and a few luxury items. People came to trade at Bowen's Mill from over a wide area stretching upstream toward Hawkinsville, downstream toward Jacksonville, and inland toward the county seat of Irwinville.

Eventually, the river landings dotting both sides of the Ocmulgee emerged into a familiar pattern to the seasoned crews of the steamboats plying the waters of the winding stream. As the steamers proceeded downstream from Macon, the best-known landings encountered on the east side were Durham's Bluff and Buzzard's Roost Bluff in Twiggs County; Bird's Nest Bluff in Pulaski County; and Boatyard, Lampkin's Old Field, Parramore's, Jacksonville, and Lumber City, all in Telfair County. The main landings on the west side of the river along the same route were Macon, Hawkinsville, Poor Robin Landing, Abbeville, Statham's Shoals, Jordon's Bluff, McCall's Landing, Hollingsworth's, Gilder's Bluff, Mobley's Bluff, and Barrow's Bluff.

In addition to the river landings used for handling passengers and freight, the steamboat era produced a special-type of landing designed to provide fuel for the river craft. This was known as the "wood landing." The fire-belching river monster had a voracious appetite and consumed enormous quantities of wood. To supply the wood-burning vessel, numbers of residents operated wood landings at convenient intervals along the course of the river. At each landing, a supply of wood, well-seasoned, cut, and stacked was available. When the steamboat's fuel supply ran low, the puffing vessel would pull up to a convenient wood landing and take on an ample supply. Then, with engines throbbing, bell clanging, smoke belching, and whistle roaring with renewed vigor, the steamboat would go churning along its way.

Although providing romance, adventure, and useful service to the river world, steamboats had their own peculiar troubles. In times of drought, the water level of the river became so low that the vessel was unable to pursue its usual way and remained stranded until the rains came. If the rains were excessive, the swirling waters flooded the river channel and brought hazardous conditions for the harassed captain, the tense pilot, and the uneasy crew and passengers. At all seasons, the twisting river, with its many obstructions, presented to the churning vessel the ever-present danger of being ripped by unseen snags, of crashing into ominous river banks, or running amuck upon treacherous sand bars. But, above all, was the dread of fire or explosion.

Vulnerable as they were to the changing moods of the fickle Ocmulgee, steamboats frequently encountered major catastrophes. In the spring of 1860, the river world was rocked by a terrible steamboat disaster. The *General Manning* was moving upstream with a cargo of merchandise and a large number of passengers. As the steamer passed Manning's Lower Fence Landing just below Jacksonville, the boilers suddenly exploded with a mighty blast. The force of the explosion split the vessel in twain. All on board were blown or thrown from the boat by the violent explosion. Some were hurled into the turbulent waters and drowned. Others were killed outright by the power of the blast. A few unfortunate victims were horribly scalded by live steam spewing from the ruptured boilers. A son of Captain Taylor of Hawkinsville was forcibly ejected from the craft and landed upon the river bank miraculously unharmed. A less-fortunate son met instant death. Among the people losing their lives in the mishap were Joseph Williams, Jacob Parker, and John Harrell, prominent planters from the China Hill settlement in Telfair County. Altogether, seven whites and seven blacks were killed in the tragic accident. The awesome sound of the explosion was heard for miles away and fragments of the steamboat were scattered along the river banks for a distance of more than a hundred yards. [9] Many years would pass before the blast of the *General Manning* would fade from the memories of the people whose lives were entwined with the Ocmulgee domain.

But ceaseless change was continuing along the restless river, and the age of the steamboat too would pass. As the sound of the mournful whistle faded away, the last era of unique river life came to an end along the Ocmulgee.

NOTES

CHAPTER I

1. Variations in the spelling of Indian words are frequently found upon early records. Among these, are journals, government reports, treaties, newspapers, maps, and surveyors' plats. Variations are likewise common among modern writers.

2. For a detailed description of the Ocmulgee River from the Fall Line down to its confluence with the Oconee, see "Survey of Ocmulgee River, Georgia," in *House Ex. Doc. 215,* 51st Cong., 1st Sess., 1890, pp. I-30, with accompanying charts.

CHAPTER II

1. William Bartram, *Travels of William Bartram,* ed. by Mark Van Doren (New York, 1928), pp. 68-69, 307; Verner W. Crane, *The Southern Frontier, 1670-1732* (Ann Arbor, 1929, reissued in 1956), p. 173.

2. John R. Swanton, *Early History of the Creek Indians and Their Neighbors* (Washington, 1922), p. 173.

3. *Ibid.,* p. 176, and Plates 1 and 2.

4. General Milfort, *Memoirs . . .,* trans. and ed. by Ben C. McCary (Kennesaw, 1959), pp. 161-62.

5. Bartram, *Travels,* pp. 68-69, 307.

6. See "Final Report of the United States DeSoto Commission," *House Doc. 71,* 76th Cong., 1st Sess. (Washington, 1939), pp. 166-86.

7. For a noted Flint River crossing place, see Surveyors' Plats for District 15 of Dooly County, and District 1 of Lee County. The Plats are in the Georgia Surveyor-General Department (Hereinafter cited as GSGD), Archives and Records Building, Atlanta, Georgia.

8. The Oswichee Trail may be traced from the Surveyor's Field Notes for Land District Lines of Dooly County, Plat for District 8 of Dooly County, and Surveyor's Plat for Lot 200 in District 1 of Irwin County, GSGD.

9. Surveyor's Plat for District 1, Irwin County, GSGD.

10. *Narratives of the Career of Hernando de Soto,* ed. by Edward Gaylord Bourne (2 vols.; New York), 1922, II, 10.

11. Surveyor's Loose Plat for District 1, Lot 200, Irwin County, GSGD; J. B. Clements, *History of Irwin County* (Atlanta, 1932), p. 34.

12. For evidence of the importance of the Indian landmark at Buzzard's Roost Bluff, see Surveyor's Plat for District 24 in Wilkinson County, and Surveyor's Plat and Field Notes for District 11, Houston County, GSGD.

13. Smith's Trail and Gallimore's Path may be traced from the Surveyors' Plats for Districts 22, 23, and 24, Wilkinson County, GSGD.

14. For the route of the Lower Uchee Path from the Ocmulgee, across the Oconee, and on to the Ogeechee, see the Eleazer Early Map of 1818, GSGD, and Surveyors' Plats for Districts 1, 2, 21, and 22, Wilkinson County, GSGD.

CHAPTER III

1. William Bacon Stevens, *A History of Georgia* . . . (2 vols.; New York, 1847), I, 34-40.

2. Edward Gaylord Bourne, *Spain in America, 1450-1580,* with Introduction by Benjamin Keen (New York, Second Printing, 1962), pp. 177-78.

3. Herbert E. Bolton and Mary Ross, *The Debatable Land* (Berkeley, 1925), pp. 2-3, 19-27.

4. *Ibid.,* pp. 28-44.

5. Crane, *Southern Frontier,* pp. 33-36; Bolton and Ross, *Debatable Land,* pp. 45-53.

6. Crane, *Southern Frontier,* pp. 33-36; Bolton and Ross, *Debatable Land,* pp. 52-54.

7. Crane, *Southern Frontier,* pp. 33-36; Bolton and Ross, *Debatable Land,* pp. 52-54; Bartram, *Travels,* pp. 68-69, 307; Walter A. Harris, *Here the Creeks Sat Down,* (Macon, 1958), pp. 45-52.

8. Crane, *Southern Frontier,* p. 185; Harris, *Creeks,* pp. 45-52.

9. Crane, *Southern Frontier,* pp. 23, 133-36; Harris. *Creeks,* pp. 32-33.

10. Crane, *Southern Frontier,* pp. 23, 35-37, 114-28.

11. Crane, *Southern Frontier,* pp. 44-46, 133; Harris, *Creeks,* pp. 32-33; John H. Goff, "Short Studies of Georgia Place Names," *Georgia Mineral Newsletter,* XIII (Fall 1960), 129-36.

12. Crane, *Southern Frontier,* pp. 71-73.

13. *Ibid.,* pp. 73-74; Bolton and Ross, *Debatable Land,* p. 58.

14. Crane, *Southern Frontier,* p. 74; Bolton and Ross, *Debatable Land,* pp. 58-59; B. R. Carroll, *Historical Collections of South Carolina* . . . (2 vols.; New York, 1836), II, 351. For location of the skirmish, see the Mitchell Map of 1755. A copy of the Mitchell Map is in the Library of the University of Georgia, Athens, Georgia.

15. Carroll, *Historical Collections,* II, 109-10, 351-52.

16. Crane, *Southern Frontier,* pp. 78-79; Bolton and Ross, *Debatable Land,* pp. 60-62.

17. Crane, *Southern Frontier,* pp. 79, 133; Harris, *Creeks,* pp. 12-13.

18. Carroll, *Historical Collections,* II, 351-52, 574-76; Mitchell Map of 1755; Surveyors' Plat of the Public Reserves at Macon, GSGD.

19. Crane, *Southern Frontier,* pp. 165-67; Swanton, *Early History,* pp. 100-01.

20. Crane, *Southern Frontier,* pp. 169-70; Swanton, *Early History,* pp. 225-26; Harris, *Creeks,* pp. 47-52.

21. Crane, *Southern Frontier,* pp. 167-70; Swanton, *Early History,* pp. 100-01, 225-26; Bolton and Ross, *Debatable Land,* pp. 63-65; Harris, *Creeks,* pp. 52-54; Carroll, *Historical Collections,* II, 353-54.

22. James Adair, *History of the American Indians,* ed. by Samuel Cole Williams (Johnson City, Tenn., 1930), pp. 38-39.

CHAPTER IV

1. Benjamin Hawkins, *A Sketch of the Creek Country in the Years 1798 and 1799* (Americus, 1938), pp. 50-56; The Early Map of 1818.

2. Hawkins, *Sketch,* pp. 60-61; Early Map of 1818. The name "Oswichee" has also been spelled Ooseoochee, Ooseuchee, Osochi, Osachee, Oswitchee, etc.

3. Hawkins, *Sketch*, pp. 60-61; Early Map of 1818; *Letters of Benjamin Hawkins, 1796-1806* (Collections of the Georgia Historical Society, Vol. IX. Savannah, 1916), 171-72.

4. Hawkins, *Sketch*, pp. 61-62; Early Map of 1818. The name "Hitchiti" has also been spelled Hitchitee, Hitchetee, etc.

5. Swanton, *Early History*, p. 178; Hawkins, *Letters*, p. 173.

6. Hawkins, *Sketch*, pp. 58-60; Hawkins, *Letters*, pp. 171-72; Swanton, *Early History*, pp. 286-312; Early Map of 1818; Bartram, *Travels*, pp. 312-13. The name "Uchee" has also been spelled Uche, Yuchi, Ewchee, etc.

7. Hawkins, *Sketch*, p. 25; Early Map of 1818.

8. Crane, *Southern Frontier*, pp. 254-57.   9. *Ibid.*, pp. 185, 256-57.

10. Charles C. Jones, Jr., *The History of Georgia* (2 vols.; Boston, 1883), I, 132-35.

11. *Ibid.*, 135-38.   12. *Ibid.*, 139-45.   13. *Ibid.*, 264-66, 315-16.

14. "A Ranger's Report of Travels With General Oglethorpe, 1739-1742," *Travels in the American Colonies*, ed. by Newton D. Mereness (New York, 1916), p. 219.

15. Jones, *History*, I, 316-19.

16. A recent and comprehensive presentation of the treaties of this period may be found in Louis De Vorsey, *The Indian Boundary in the Southern Colonies, 1763-1755* (Chapel Hill, 1966).

CHAPTER V

1. Alexander McGillivray to Thomas Pinckney, Governor of South Carolina, Feb. 26, 1789, in *American State Papers, Indian Affairs* (Washington, 1832), I, 19-20; Governor George Walton to B. Lincoln, C. Griffin, and D. Humphreys, Commissioners, Oct. 4, 1789, *Indian Affairs*, I, 76-77; Absalom H. Chappel, *Miscellanies of Georgia* . . . (Atlanta, 1874), pp. 5-8.

2. *Indian Affairs*, I, 19-29; Chappell, *Miscellanies*, p. 7.

3. "Return of depredations committed by the Creek Indians since the commencement of hostilities in the State of Georgia," Oct. 5, 1789, *Indian Affairs*, I, 77; Chappell, *Miscellanies*, pp. 5-32; James White to McGillivray, April 4, 1787, *Indian Affairs*, I, 21-22.

4. U. S. Commissioners to Charles Thomson, November 17, 1785, *Indian Affairs*, I, 16.

5. *Indian Affairs*, I, 16; John Walton Caughey, *McGillivray of the Creeks* (Norman, 1959), pp. 27-28; Chappell *Miscellanies*, pp. 5-32.

6. Secretary of War Knox to the President of the United States, July 6, 1789, *Indian Affairs*, I, 15; Chappell, *Miscellanies*, pp. 5-8.

7. President Washington to the Senate, Aug. 7, 1790, *Indian Affairs*, I, 81-82; Chappell *Miscellanies*, pp. 5-32.

8. E. Merton Coulter, *Georgia: A Short History* (Chapel Hill, 1947), pp. 182-83; Chappell *Miscellanies*, pp. 5-32.

9. James Seagrove to the President of the United States, July 27, 1792, *Indian Affairs*, I, 305-06; Chappell, *Miscellanies*, pp. 5-32.

10. Treaty of Coleraine, *Indian Affairs*, I, 609-10; Coulter, *Georgia*, pp. 183-84.

11. Hawkins, *Letters*, pp. 196, 296; Early Map of 1818.

1. Hawkins, *Letters,* p. 239.   2. *Ibid.*   3. *Ibid.,* pp. 420-22.

4. Secretary of War Dearborn to U. S. Commissioners, July 17, 1801, *Indian Affairs,* I, 651; U. S. Commissioners to Dearborn, July 15, 1802, *Indian Affairs,* I, 669-70.

5. Treaty of Fort Wilkinson, *Indian Affairs,* I, 669.

6. Talk of James Seagrove to Creek chiefs at Rock Landing, May 18, 1792, *Indian Affairs,* I, 299-300; James Durouzeaux to Seagrove, May 28, 1792, *Indian Affairs,* I, 302; Georgia Executive Minutes (Hereinafter cited as GEM), December 5, 1799; GEM, June 6, 1800.

7. Merritt B. Pound, *Benjamin Hawkins, Indian Agent* (Athens, 1951), pp. 190-95.

8. Hawkins, *Letters,* p. 438.

9. *Ibid.*   10. *Ibid.,* pp. 431-46.

11. Louise Frederick Hays MS, "Letters of Benjamin Hawkins, 1797-1815," in Georgia Department of Archives and History.

12. *Indian Affairs,* I, 691-92.   13. *Ibid.*

14. Hays, "Letters of Hawkins," p. 110.

15. Augustin Smith Clayton, *A Compilation of the Laws of the State of Georgia, . . . 1800 to . . . 1810, Inclusive . . .* (Augusta, 1813), pp. 705-08.

CHAPTER VII

1. Clayton, *Compilation,* pp. 279-81, 357-59.

2. *Ibid.,* pp. 209-10.   3. *Ibid.,* pp. 357 59   4. *Ibid.,* p. 358.

5. Georgia Executive Minutes (Hereinafter cited as GEM), February 19, 1808. The Executive Minutes are in the Georgia Department of Archives and History, Atlanta, Georgia.

6. GEM, April 29, 1809; GEM, Sept. 14, 1809; GEM, Feb. 12, 1810.

7. GEM, April 29, 1809; GEM, June 18, 1810.

8. GEM, April 29, 1809.   9. GEM, Aug. 25, 1811.

10. Superior Court Minutes for Telfair County (Hereinafter cited as SCMTC), April 16, 1810. The records are in the office of the Clerk of Superior Court, McRae, Georgia.

11. SCMTC, April 16, 1810; U. S. Census for Telfair County, 1820. The census records are in the National Archives, Washington, D. C. Microfilm copies are in the Georgia Department of Archives and History (Hereinafter cited as GDAH), Atlanta, Georgia.

12. SCMTC, April 15, 1811.   13. *Ibid.,* Oct. 21, 1811, and April 19, 1813.

14. Clayton, *Compilation,* p. 359.

15. *Ibid.,* p. 492; SCMTC, April 16, 1810.

16. Clayton, *Compilation,* p. 603.

17. Lucius Q. C. Lamar, *A Compilation of the Laws of the State of Georgia . . . since the Year 1810 to the Year 1819, Inclusive . . .* (Augusta, 1821), pp. 180-81.

18. *Ibid.,* p. 196.   19. *Ibid.,* pp. 196, 200.

20. Telfair County Deed Book D., p. 153.

21. Clayton, *Compilation,* pp. 469-70.   22. GEM, May 4, 1809.

23. Clayton, *Compilation,* p. 538.

24. *Ibid.,* p. 606; Surveyor's Plat for District 21, Wilkinson County.

25. *History of Pulaski County, Georgia, 1808-1935* (Compiled by the Hawkinsville Chapter, Daughters of the American Revolution, Atlanta, 1935), pp. 46-47.

26. Superior Court Minutes for Pulaski County (Hereinafter cited as SCMPC), April 23, 1810. The minutes are in the office of the Clerk of Superior Court, Hawkinsville, Georgia.

27. SCMPC, July, 1810; United States Census for Pulaski County, 1850.

28. SCMPC, Oct. 22, 1810.   29. *Ibid.,* April, 1811.

30. *History of Pulaski County,* pp. 230-36; GEM, June 16, 1812.

31. GEM, Nov. 22, 1810.   32. Clayton, *Compilation,* pp. 565-66.

33. *Ibid.,* p. 608.

34. Lanette O'Neal Faulk and Billy Walker Jones, *History of Twiggs County, Georgia* (Columbus, 1960), p. 49.

35. *Georgia Journal* (Milledgeville), June 16, 1835.

36. Lamar, *Compilation,* pp. 8-9.   37. *Ibid.,* pp. 26-27

38. Faulk and Jones, *History of Twiggs County,* pp. 115-16.

39. Clayton, *Compilation,* pp. 357-59.

40. *Ibid.,* p. 484.   41. *Ibid.,* p. 481.

CHAPTER VIII

1. Clayton, *Compilation,* pp. 100-07, 290-96.

2. The early deed books for the Ocmulgee counties show numerous land sales from persons drawing the land to others who actually settled upon the land.

3. See the U. S. Census of 1850 for the origin of many early settlers in the Ocmulgee counties.

4. Clements, *Irwin County,* p. 5.   5. Clayton, *Compilation,* pp. 408-22.

CHAPTER IX

1. Inferior Court Minutes for Pulaski County (Hereinafter cited as ICMPC), 1810-1816, passim. The records are in the office of the Clerk of Superior Court, Hawkinsville, Georgia.

2. ICMPC, 1810-1816, passim; The Early Map of 1818; Stephen F. Miller, *Memoir of General David Blackshear* (Philadelphia, 1858), pp. 448-49.

3. ICMPC, July, 1813.

4. See Chapter XII; *Southern Recorder* (Milledgeville), Sept. 5, 1826.

5. ICMPC, Jan., 1812.

6. Pulaski County Tax Digests for 1809-12, Inclusive. The tax records are in the Office of the Clerk of Superior Court, Hawkinsville, Georgia.

7. *Ibid.;* ICMPC, Jan., 1812.

8. Pulaski County Tax Digests, 1809-12; ICMPC, Jan, 1812.

9. ICMPC, Jan., 1812, and July, 1813.

10. ICMPC, 1810-1816, p. 5; Pulaski Tax Digests, 1809-1812.

11. ICMPC, 1810-1816, p. 5; Pulaski Tax Digests, 1809-1812, *passim.*

12. ICMPC, Jan. 15, 1816; Pulaski Tax Digests, 1809-1812, *passim.*

13. ICMPC, 1810-1816, p. 5; Pulaski Tax Digests, 1809-1812, *passim.*

14. ICMPC, 1810-1816, p. 5; Pulaski Tax Digests, 1809-1812, *passim;* Colton, Map of Georgia, 1861.

15. Telfair County Deed Books, A, D, E, and F (various entries).

16. *Ibid.*   17. *Ibid.*   18. *Ibid.*

19. Miller, *Blackshear,* pp. 448-49; Early Map of 1818.

20. Telfair Deed Books A, D, E, and F (various entries).

21. Miller, *Blackshear,* pp. 449, 461-62.

22. John H. Goff, "Short Studies of Georgia Place Names," *Georgia Mineral Newsletter,* XIII (Fall 1960), 135.

23. ICMPC, p. 5; Clayton, *Compilation,* pp. 644-45.

24. Clayton, *Compilation,* pp. 644-45.

25. ICMPC, August, 1811; Hudgins Map of Pulaski County, GSGD.

26. ICMPC, 1810-1816, *passim.*

27. Hudgins Map of Pulaski County; Early Map of 1818; Surveyors' Plats for Districts 1, 2, 21, 22, Wilkinson County.

28. ICMPC, Feb. 23, 1811, and July, 1813.

29. Hudgins Map of Dodge County, GSGD.   30. ICMPC, July 15, 1816.

31. *Ibid.,* August, 1811.   32. *Ibid.,* Feb. 23, 1811, and July 20, 1812.

CHAPTER X

1. George Gillman Smith, *The Story of Georgia and the Georgia People, 1732 to 1860* (Macon, 1900), pp. 223-25.

2. *Ibid.,* pp. 290-93.   3. *Ibid.,* p. 292.

4. *History of the Baptist Denomination in Georgia* . . . (Atlanta, 1881), p. 88.

5. *Ibid.; Minutes of the Ebenezer Association* (Hereinafter cited as *MEA*), 1814. The printed minutes are in the Mercer University Library, Macon, Ga.

6. Billy Walker Jones, *History of Stone Creek Baptist Church, Twiggs County, Georgia, 1808-1958* (Dry Branch, Ga., 1961), pp. 8-9.

7. *Ibid.,* p. 38.

8. Mount Horeb Church Minutes (Hereinafter cited as MHCM), Oct. 15, 1809. The unpublished minute book is in charge of the church clerk, Hawkinsville, Ga. A copy, typed and bound by this writer, is in GDAH.

9. *Ibid.,* pp. 1-3   10. *Ibid.,* p. 3.

11. John Bennett Boddie, *Births, Deaths . . . Albemarle Parish Register of Surry and Sussex Counties, Virginia* (Redwood City, Calif., 1958), pp. 34-35.

12. Thomas Davis, The Diary of Thomas Davis, 1849. The location of the original of this document is unknown to the writer, but a handwritten copy is in possession of Mrs. Hill Redwine of Fayetteville, Ga. See also Granville County, N. C., Deed Book K, p. 264. The book is in the office of the County Register of Deeds, Oxford, N. C.

13. Davis, Diary; Ruth Blair, *Revolutionary Soldiers' Receipts for Georgia Bounty Grants* (Atlanta, 1928), pp. 47-49.

14. Davis, Diary.

15. *Ibid.,* See Revolutionary War Pension Claim for John Cunningham, Georgia, Ann, W6752, National Archives.

16. Absalom Davis died in Elbert County, Ga. His will is dated Jan. 12, 1807, and recorded in Will Book L-F, 1804-09, p. 30.

17. Headright Book O, p. 32, GSGD.

18. Montgomery County Deed Book F, p. 120. The deed book is in the office of the Clerk of Superior Court, Mt. Vernon, Georgia.

19. Pulaski County Tax Digests, 1809-12; Surveyors' Plat Book for Districts 6-24, Wilkinson County, p. 120.

20. MHCM, p. 22.   21. Pulaski County Deed Book A, p. 7.

22. *Ibid.*   23. MHCM, pp. 3-7.   24. *Ibid., pp. 3-5.*

25. *MEA,* 1814.   26. *MEA,* 1814-20.   27. *Ibid.*

28. MHCM, p. 5.   29. Pulaski County Deed Book C, p. 159.

30. MHCM, p. 2.   31. *Ibid.,* p. 4.   32. *Ibid.,* p. 5.

33. *MEA,* 1814-27.   34. *MEA,* 1814.

35. *Ibid.*   36. *MEA,* 1814-22.

37. Lanette O'Neal Faulk, *Historical Collections of Richland Baptist Church* (Macon, 1950), p. 4.

38. *MEA,* 1814-22.

39. Centennial Edition, *Telfair Enterprise,* (McRae, 1907). This work will hereinafter be cited as CETE.

40. *MEA,* 1814.   41. *MEA,* 1814-26.   42. *MEA,* 1829.

43. *Ibid.*   44. *Ibid.,* 1829-45.   45. James H. McCranie, Eastman, Ga.

46. *Ibid.*

47. George G. Smith, *The History of Georgia Methodism from 1786 to 1866* (Atlanta, 1913), pp. 38, 42-44. Isabella Grant, daughter of Daniel Grant, married Richard Davis, a brother of Chesley Davis. Thus we have the interesting situation wherein two closely-related pioneer families led in bringing Christianity to the Georgia frontier—one through the Baptist order, and the other through the Methodist movement.

CHAPTER XI

1. CETE.   2. *Ibid.*

3. CETE; Thomas Woodward, *Woodward's Reminiscences of the Creek or Muscogee Indians . . .* (Montgomery, 1859, reprinted in Tuscaloosa, 1939), p. 47.

4. Woodward, *Reminiscences,* p. 53; W. R. Bivins MS, Journal, p. 6, GSGD; "Survey of Ocmulgee River, Georgia"; CETE.

5. CETE.   6. CETE.

7. CETE; Warren P. Ward, *History of Coffee County* (Atlanta, 1930), p. 216.

8. *Georgia Journal,* Jan. 2, 1810.   9. *Ibid.,* Dec. 5, 1810.

10. SCMTC, Oct. 17, 1814.   11. *Ibid.,* April, 1818.

12. *Ibid.,* Oct. 19, 1818.   13. *Ibid.,* June 2, 1825.

14. Lamar, *Compilation,* pp. 508-09.

15. *Ibid.,* p. 513; *Georgia Journal,* Aug. 1, 1817.   16. CETE.

17. Adiel Sherwood, *A Gazetteer of the State of Georgia* (3rd ed.; Washington 1837), pp. 191-92; John C. Butler, *Historical Record of Macon and Central Georgia,* with a Foreword by Spencer B. King, Jr. (Macon, 1958 and 1960), p. 73.

18. *Darien Gazette* (Darien), 1820-21. 1824-25.

CHAPTER XII

1. Early Map of 1818; Hawkins, *Letters,* pp. 168-74.

2. Hawkins, *Sketch,* pp. 58-64; Hawkins, *Letters,* pp. 171-73; Early Map of 1818; Surveyors' Plats for District 15, Dooly County; for Lot 5, District 2, Lee County; and for Lot 269, District 14, Lee County, GSGD.

3. Hawkins, *Sketch,* p. 61; Early Map; See Chapter XXI.

4. Hawkins, *Sketch,* pp. 61-62; Hawkins, *Letters,* p. 173; Early Map.

5. Early Map; See Chapter XVIII.   6. Woodward, *Reminiscences,* p. 47.

7. The Indian huts were observed and described to the writer by the late John Land of Rochelle, Georgia.

8. Lieutenant Henry Timberlake, *Memoirs, 1756-1765,* ed. by Samuel Cole Williams (Marietta, 1948), p. 69.

9. Surveyors' Plats for Districts 3, 4, 5, 6, 7, 9, 10, 11, 14, and 15, Dooly County, GSGD; Lamar, *Compilation,* p. 219; *Georgia Journal,* Jan. 16, 1810.

10. Surveyors' Plats for District 3 in Dooly County, and Districts 13, 14, and 15, Houston County, GSGD.

11. Surveyors' Plats for Districts 3, 4, 7, and 9, Dooly County, GSGD.

12. Lamar, *Compilation,* p. 219.

13. Early Map; John H. Goff, Map of Early Indian Trails and Settlements, Georgia and Alabama, n. d., GSGD.

14. MS, "Indian Depredations, 1787-1825," Compiled in 5 vols. by GDAH, Atlanta , Vol. II, Part 3, p. 838.

15. *Southern Recorder,* Sept. 5, 1826.

16. Surveyors' Plats and Field Notes for District 11, Houston County, and District 24, Wilkinson County, GSGD.

17. Surveyor's Plat for Lot 70, District 8, Dooly County.

18. "Indian Depredations," Vol. II, Part 3, p. 838.

19. GEM, March 29, 1814.   20. Lamar, *Compilation,* p. 219.

21. Mary G. Bryan, *Passports Issued by Governors of Georgia, 1785 to 1809* (Washington, 1959), p. 1; *Georgia Journal,* March 25, 1812.

22. Bryan, *Passports,* p. 1.   23. *Ibid.*   24. *Ibid.*

25. *Georgia Journal,* March 25, 1812.   26. *Ibid.,* Sept. 23, 1812.

27. *Argus* (Milledgeville), Nov. 7, 1810.   28. GEM, March 30, 1810.

29. *Ibid.*   30. GEM, Feb. 6, 1812.   31. See Chapter XVI.

32. GEM for the following dates: March 29, 1814; May 5, 1814; May 11, 1814; Aug. 11, 1814.

33. *Georgia Journal,* Sept. 21, 1819.   34. GEM, April 9, 1813.

35. Early Map; Hawkins, *Sketch,* pp. 19-64.

36. Early Map; Hawkins, *Sketch,* pp. 64-65.

37. Early Map; Hawkins, *Sketch,* pp. 64-65.

38. Early Map; See Chapter XVI.   39. Lamar, *Compilation,* pp. 213-14.

40. *Ibid.,* pp. 218-20.   41. *Ibid.*   42. *Ibid.*   43. *Ibid.*

44. *Ibid.*   45. *Ibid.*

CHAPTER XIII

1. *Indian Affairs,* I, 809.
2. James Parton, *Life of Andrew Jackson* (3 vols.; New York, 1860), I, 402-06.
3. *Ibid.*   4. *Ibid.*
5. Parton, *Jackson,* I, 406-09; Big Warrior, Alex. Cornell, and William McIntosh to Hawkins, April 26, 1813, *Indian Affairs,* I, 841.
6. Parton, *Jackson,* I, 409-11; Woodward, *Reminiscences,* pp. 84-85, 95; Albert James Pickett, *History of Alabama . . .* (Tuscaloosa, 1962), pp. 511-14; Hawkins to Creek chiefs, June 16, 1814, *Indian Affairs,* I, 845.
7. Woodward, *Reminiscences,* pp. 35-37; Hawkins to Secretary of War, May 25, 1812, *Indian Affairs,* I, 811 (Hawkins erroneously gave Lott's name as "William").
8. Hawkins to Secretary of War, June 9, 1812, *Indian Affairs,* I, 812; Woodward, *Reminiscences,* pp. 35-36.
9. Hawkins to Creek chiefs, March 29, 1813, *Indian Affairs,* I, 839; John Reid and John Henry Eaton, *The Life of Andrew Jackson . . .* (Philadelphia, 1817), pp. 28-29.
10. Reid and Eaton, *Jackson,* pp. 28-29; Hawkins to Chiefs, March 29, 1813, *Indian Affairs,* I, 839.
11. Reid and Eaton, *Jackson,* pp. 28-29; Hawkins to fanatical chiefs, July 6, 1813, *Indian Affairs,* I, 848; Hawkins to Secretary of War, July 28, 1813; *Indian Affairs,* I, 849-50; GEM, Nov. 6, 1813.
12. Reid and Eaton, *Jackson,* pp. 28-29; Hawkins to Secretary of War, August 10, 1813, *Indian Affairs,* I, 851; GEM, Nov. 6, 1813.

CHAPTER XIV

1. GEM, Nov. 2, 1812.   2. *Ibid.*   3. *Ibid.*
4. "Indian Depredations," Vol. II, Part 3, p. 845.
5. *Ibid., p. 831.   6. Augusta Chronicle,* Sept. 4, 1812.
7. *Georgia Journal,* Sept. 9, 1812.
8. Telfair County Loose Paper File, GDAH.
9. Gov. Mitchell to Lt. Col. Allen Tooke, March 20, 1813, in Georgia Governors' Letter Books (Hereinafter cited as GGLB), Nov. 28, 1809-May 18, 1814, p. 95. The letter books are deposited in GDAH.
10. GEM, May 26, 1813.   11. "Indian Depredations," IV, 264.
12. Hawkins to Mitchell, July 5, 1813, *Indian Affairs,* I, 847.
13. Pulaski County Loose Paper File, GDAH.
14. File II, Allen Tooke, GDAH.
15. GGLB, Aug. 4, 1813; Miller, *Blackshear,* pp. 411-12.
16. Miller, *Blackshear,* pp. 412-13; Georgia Military Records, 1779-1839, pp. 277-78. The Georgia Military Records (Hereinafter cited as GMR) may be found in GDAH.
17. GMR, pp. 277-78.   18. *Ibid.*   19. *Ibid.*   20. *Ibid.*
21. *History of Pulaski County,* pp. 27-32; GMR, pp. 277-78.
22. Miller, *Blackshear,* pp. 412-13.
23. GMR, pp. 277-78; Telfair County Deed Books A, D, E, and F, *passim.*
24. GMR, pp. 277-78; Telfair County Deed Books A, D, E, and F, *passim.*

25. GMR, pp. 277-78; Telfair County Deed Books A, D, E, and F, *passim.*
26. GMR, p. 277.   27. *Ibid.,* GEM, Oct. 1, 1813.
28. Miller, *Blackshear,* pp. 412-13.   29. See Chapter IX.
30. GMR, pp. 278, 290.   31. Parton, *Jackson,* I, 411-21.
32. *Ibid.,* 421-22.   33. GEM, July 30, 1813; GEM, Aug. 18, 1813.
34. Lawton B. Evans, *The Student's History of Georgia* . . . (Macon, 1884), pp. 153-54.
35. *Ibid.;* Coulter, *Georgia,* p. 212.
36. Evans, *Student's History,* pp. 153-54; Coulter, *Georgia,* p. 212; Woodward, *Reminiscences,* pp. 101-02.
37. GEM, Feb. 7, 1814.   38. Parton, *Jackson,* I, 512-23.
39. *Ibid.,* 549-60, 633-36.

CHAPTER XV

1. *Georgia Journal,* Aug. 10, 1814.
2. Allen Tooke to Georgia Governor, *Georgia Journal,* Aug. 10, 1814.
3. *Augusta Chronicle,* Aug. 12, 1814.   4. Miller, *Blackshear,* pp. 418-19.
5. GGLB, 1814-1821, p. 18.
6. Secretary of State to George W. Erving, Nov. 28, 1818, *Annals of Congress* (Washington, 1834), XXXIV, 1926.
7. Miller, *Blackshear,* p. 420.   8. *Ibid.,* p. 421.
9. Hawkins to Ga. Gov., Oct. 30, 1814, Hawkins Papers, GDAH.
10. Early to Pinckney, Sept. 16, 1814, GGLB, 1814-1821, pp. 27-28.
11. Early to Jackson, October 26, 1814, GGLB, 1814-1821, p. 44.
12. Hawkins to Early, Oct. 30, 1814, Hawkins Papers.
13. Hawkins to Early, Nov. 5, 1814, in *Georgia Journal,* Nov. 9, 1814.
14. GEM, Nov. 7, 1814.   15. *Georgia Journal,* Nov. 9, 1814.
16. Early to Tooke, Nov. 10, 1814, GGLB, 1814-1821, p. 52.
17. *Georgia Journal,* Nov. 16, 1814.   18. *Ibid.,* Nov. 23, 1814.
19. *Ibid.*

CHAPTER XVI

1. GGLB, 1814-1821, pp. 56-57.
2. *Ibid.*   3. Miller, *Blackshear,* pp. 426-27.
4. *Ibid.,* p. 428.   5. *Ibid.,* pp. 430-31.   6. *Ibid.*
7. *Ibid.,* pp. 431-32.   8. *Ibid.*   9. *Ibid.,* p. 445.
10. *Ibid.,* pp. 433-35, 439-40.   11. *Ibid.*   12. *Ibid.,* pp. 434-35.
13. *Ibid.,* pp. 435-37.   14. *Ibid.,* pp. 439-40, 445.   15. *Ibid.,* p. 445.
16. *Ibid.,* pp. 439-40.   17. *Ibid.,* p. 426; GGLB, 1814-1821, pp. 56-57.
18. Miller, *Blackshear,* pp. 437-38.   19. *Ibid.,* p. 445.
20. *Ibid.,* pp. 440-42.   21. *Ibid.,* pp. 443-44.   22. *Ibid.,* p. 443.
23. *Ibid.,* pp. 415-17. This letter was erroneously dated January 13, 1814, instead of January 13, 1815.

CHAPTER XVII

1. Miller, *Blackshear,* pp. 448-49.   2. *Ibid.*   3. *Ibid.,* p. 450.
4. *Ibid.,* p. 449.   5. *Ibid.*   6. *Ibid.,* pp. 449-50.
7. *Ibid.,* pp. 450-51.   8. *Ibid.,* pp. 454-56.
9. Lucian Lamar Knight, *Georgia's Landmarks, Memorials, and Legends* (2 vols.; Atlanta, 1913), I, 953-54; CETE.
10. Miller, *Blackshear,* p. 456.   11. *Ibid.,* pp. 456-57.
12. *Ibid.,* pp. 457-58.   13. *Ibid.*   14. *Ibid.,* p. 458.

CHAPTER XVIII

1. Bartram, *Travels,* pp. 306-07.   2. *Ibid.*
3. Secretary of State to George W. Erving, Nov. 28, 1818, *Annals of Congress,* XXXIV, 1923-41.
4. *Ibid.*
5. *Ibid.;* Captain Amelung to Jackson, June 4, 1816, *Annals of Congress,* XXXIV, 1972-73.
6. Gaines to Clinch, May 23, 1816, *Annals of Congress,* XXXIV, 1975-76.
7. Secretary Adams to George W. Erving, Nov. 28, 1818, *Annals of Congress,* XXXIV, 1923-41; J. Loomis to Commodore Patterson, Aug. 13, 1816, *Annals of Congress,* XXXIV, 1978-81.
8. Talk from Little Prince, *Annals of Congress,* XXXIV, 1974; Arbuthnot to Nicholls, Aug. 26, 1817, *Annals of Congress,* XXXIV, 2022-24.
9. Adams to Erving, Nov. 28, 1818, *Annals of Congress,* XXXIV, 1923-41.
10. *Annals of Congress,* XXXIV, 1936, 2271-72.   11. *Ibid.,* 2037-38.
12. Gaines to Secretary of War, Oct. 1, 1817, *Annals of Congress,* XXXIV, 2145-46; Gaines to Jackson, Nov. 21, 1817, *Annals of Congress,* XXXIV, 2149-50.
13. Gaines to Jackson, Nov. 21, 1817, *Annals of Congress,* XXXIV, 2149-50.
14. Adams to Erving, Nov. 28, 1818, *Annals of Congress,* XXXIV, 1923-41; Gaines to Secretary of War, Dec. 2, 1817, *Annals of Congress,* XXXIV, 2151.
15. Calhoun to Gaines, Jan. 16, 1818, *Annals of Congress,* XXXIV, 2163.
16. Calhoun to Jackson, Dec. 26, 1817, *Annals of Congress,* XXXIV, 2158-59.
17. Arbuckle to Jackson, Jan. 12, 1818, *Annals of Congress,* XXXIV, 2172-73; Arbuckle to Glasscock, Jan. 18, 1818, *Annals of Congress,* XXXIV, 2174-75.
18. Gaines to Secretary of War, Jan. 9, 1818, *Annals of Congress,* XXXIV, 2159-60; Glasscock to Gaines, Jan. 10, 1818, *Annals of Congress,* XXXIV, 2166-67; *Georgia Journal,* Jan. 27, 1818; Woodward, *Reminiscences,* p. 155.
19. Woodward, *Reminiscences,* pp. 155-56.   20. *Ibid.*
21. *Ibid.,* p. 156; Report of Major Heard, *Annals of Congress,* XXXIV, 2167.
22. Woodward, *Reminiscences,* p. 156; *Annals of Congress,* XXXIV, 2167.
23. Woodward, *Reminiscences,* p. 156; *Annals of Congress,* XXXIV, 2167.
24. Woodward, *Reminiscences,* p. 156; *Annals of Congress,* XXXIV, 2167.
25. Woodward, *Reminiscences,* pp. 155-56; *Annals of Congress,* XXXIV, 2167.

CHAPTER XIX

1. Jackson to Secretary of War, Feb. 10, 1818, *Annals of Congress,* XXXIV, 2177.

2. Jackson to Secretary of War, Feb. 14, 1818, *Annals of Congress,* XXXIV, 2178-79; Captain Hugh Young, "Itineraries," pp. 117-25. A copy of this document is in GSGD.

3. Young, "Itineraries," pp. 117-25; Jackson to Secretary of War, February 26, 1818, *Annals of Congress,* XXXIV, 2178-79.

4. Young, "Itineraries," pp. 117-25; Jackson to Secretary of War, February 26, 1818, *Annals of Congress,* XXXIV, 2178-79.

5. Jackson to Secretary of War, Feb. 26, 1818, *Annals of Congress,* XXXIV, 2178-79.

6. *Ibid.*   7. *Ibid.*

8. Young, "Itineraries," pp. 125-31; Jackson to Calhoun, March 25, 1818, *Annals of Congress,* XXXIV, 2179-82; Jackson to Chehaw Indians, May 7, 1818, *Annals of Congress,* XXXIV, 2386-87.

9. Young, "Itineraries," pp. 125-31.

10. Jackson to Calhoun, March 25, 1818, *Annals of Congress,* XXXIV, 2179-82.

CHAPTER XX

1. W. W. Paine, "Historical Sketch," in *History of Pulaski County,* p. 33.

2. CETE; John Ben Pate, *History of Turner County* (Atlanta, 1933), p. 13.

3. CETE; Pate, *Turner County,* p. 13.

4. See Chapter XV.   5. GMR, p. 277.

6. Major Josiah D. Cawthon to Gov. Rabun, March 10, 1818, in Cawthon Loose Paper File, GDAH.

7. *Pulaski County,* pp. 33-34.

8. Surveyor's Plat for District 1. Irwin County, GSGD.

9. *Ibid.;* An excellent account of the Indian skirmish was given to the writer by the late John Land, who was born and reared near the site of the conflict. Land's account is generally in accord with the best documentary information this writer has been able to find.

10. Cawthon to Rabun, March 10, 1818, Cawthon File, GDAH.   11. *Ibid.*

12. Surveyor's Plat for District 1, Irwin County; John Land's account.

13. Cawthon to Rabun, March 10, 1818; *Pulaski County,* pp. 33-34; Pate, *Turner County,* pp. 13-14.

14. Land's account; Pate, *Turner County,* p. 14.

15. Cawthon to Rabun, March 10, 1818; CETE; *Pulaski County,* pp. 33-34.

16. *Pulaski County,* pp. 33-34; Land's account; CETE.

17. Clements, *Irwin County,* pp. 34-45; Pate, *Turner County,* pp. 13-14; Land's account.

18. Clements, *Irwin County,* pp. 34-45; CETE; Inscription on monument at Bowen's Mill near Fitzgerald, Georgia.

19. Cawthon to Rabun, March 10, 1818. There are variations in the accounts of the Indian skirmish as given by local historians. In such cases, the writer has given preference to the report of Major Josiah D. Cawthon since this is the only known account of the event by a participant.

20. Pate, *Turner County,* pp. 13-14; Clements, *Irwin County,* p. 34; Land's account.

21. George White, *Historical Collections of Georgia . . . from Its First Settlement to the Present Time* (New York, 1854), p. 647.

22. *Ibid.*

23. "Proceedings of a Brigade Court Martial Held at Dublin, Laurens County . . . May 5, 1819," with a statement by Captain Jacob Robinson attached. These documents are in the Loose Paper File for Laurens County, GDAH.

24. *Ibid.*   25. *Ibid.*   26. *Ibid.*   27. *Ibid.*

CHAPTER XXI

1. Rabun to Jackson, March 21, 1818, *Annals of Congress,* XXXIV, 2382. Rabun erroneously called Joseph Burch "Mr. Bush." Major Cawthon had given the name correctly in his report to Rabun on March 10, 1818.

2. Rabun to Calhoun, June 1, 1818, *Annals of Congress,* XXXIV, 2380-82.

3. Judge C. B. Strong to Rabun, April 27, 1818, in *Georgia Journal,* May 5, 1818; Rabun's orders to Capt. Obed Wright, *Georgia Journal,* May 5, 1818; Rabun to Calhoun, June 1, 1818, *Annals of Congress,* XXXIV, 2380-82; "Indian Depredations," IV, 205.

4. Rabun to Calhoun, June 1, 1818, *Annals of Congress,* XXXIV, 2380-82.

5. Rabun to Wright, April 14, 1818, *Georgia Journal,* May 5, 1818.

6. See Chapter XX, Note 23.

7. Rabun to Wright, April 14, 1818, *Georgia Journal,* May 5, 1818.

8. Rabun to Mitchell, May 20, 1818, *Georgia Journal,* May 26, 1818.

9. *Ibid.*

10. Glasscock to Jackson, April 30, 1818, *Annals of Congress,* XXXIV, 2385-86.

11. Capt. Obed Wright to Gov. Rabun, April 25, 1818, *Georgia Journal,* May 5, 1818.

12. *Ibid.*

13. Glasscock to Jackson, April 30, 1818, *Annals of Congress,* XXXIV, 2385-86.

14. *Ibid.*

15. Jackson to Rabun, May 7, 1818, *Annals of Congress,* XXXIV, 2387-88.

16. Rabun to Jackson, June 1, 1818, *Annals of Congress,* XXXIV, 2382-83.

17. Parton, *Jackson,* II, 495-96.   18. *Ibid.,* 496-97.

19. See Chapter XX, Note 23; GEM, May 25, 1820; Robinson to Grantlands, editors, April 30, 1818, in *Georgia Journal,* May 5, 1818.

CHAPTER XXII

1. Lamar, *Compilation.* pp. 1168-71.

2. Mitchell to Rabun, Jan. 28, 1818, *Georgia Journal,* Feb. 3, 1818; Mitchell to Calhoun, Jan. 28, 1818, *Indian Affairs,* II, 153.

3. Mitchell Treaty, *Indian Affairs,* II, 152.

4. Rabun to John Q. Adams, June 25, 1818, GGLB, 1814-1821, pp. 236-37.

5. Commissioners' Report to Gov. Rabun, in *Georgia Journal,* December 15, 1818.

6. *Ibid.*   7. *Ibid.,* See note at bottom of page.   8. *Ibid.*

9. *Ibid.*   10. *Ibid.*   11. *Ibid.*

12. Treaty of Indian Springs, *Indian Affairs,* II, 248-49.

CHAPTER XXIII

1. Lamar, *Compilation,* pp. 416-17.

2. *Ibid.,* p. 236. 3. *Ibid.,* pp. 236-37.

4. Irwin County Inferior Court Minute Book 1, July 3, 1820.

5. GEM, May 25, 1820.

6. Irwin County Inferior Court Minute Book 1, July 2, 1822.

7. William C. Dawson, *A Compilation of the Laws of the State of Georgia . . . Since the Year 1819 to 1829, Inclusive* (Milledgeville, 1831), p. 126.

8. Clements, *Irwin County,* pp. 431-32. 9. *Ibid.*

10. *Ibid.,* pp. 151-52. 11. *Ibid.,* p. 64.

12. GEM, Oct. 26, 1820, and April 23, 1823. 13. GEM, Feb. 4, 1821.

14. Dawson, *Compilation,* pp. 120, 170; Oliver H. Prince, *A Digest of the Laws of the State of Georgia . . . Previous . . . to Dec. 1837 . . .* (2nd ed.; Athens, 1837), p. 941.

15. Dawson, *Compilation,* pp. 120, 246. 16. *Ibid.,* p. 120.

17. Houston County Minutes of the Inferior Court (Hereinafter cited as HCMIC), May 6, 1822. The minutes are in the office of the Clerk of Superior Court, Perry, Georgia.

18. *Ibid.,* July 7, 1823. 19. *Ibid.,* March 2, 1824.

20. *Southern Recorder,* Aug. 10, 1824. 21. HCMIC, May 21, 1822.

22. *Ibid.,* March 2, 1824. 23. *Southern Recorder,* Aug. 10, 1824.

24. Prince, *Digest,* p. 950. 25. Knight, *Landmarks,* II, p. 797.

26. Dawson, *Compilation,* p. 246. 27. Prince, *Digest,* p. 957.

28. Dawson, *Compilation,* p. 246.

29. *The Messenger* (Fort Hawkins), March 21, 1823; *ibid.,* Dec. 10, 1823.

30. *The Messenger,* March 21, 1823; *ibid.,* Dec. 10, 1823.

31. *The Messenger,* March 21, 1823; *ibid.,* Dec. 10, 1823; Adiel Sherwood, *A Gazetteer of the State of Georgia,* with a Foreword by Spright Dowell (Athens, 1939), pp. 72-73.

32. Sherwood, *Gazetteer,* pp. 72-73.

CHAPTER XXIV

1. Irwin County Inferior Court Minute Book 1, July 2, 1821. The minute book is in the office of the Ordinary, Ocilla, Georgia.

2. *Ibid.;* Irwin County Deed Book 1, passim. The deed book is in the office of the Clerk of the Superior Court, Ocilla, Georgia.

3. Irwin County Deed Book 1, passim; U. S. Census Records for 1820, 1830, and 1840, Irwin County, passim.

4. ICMPC, Jan., 1827. 5. *Ibid.,* Feb., 1822.

6. HCMIC, June 2, 1823. 7. *Ibid.,* Feb., 1824.

8. Houston County Tax Digests for 1829, 1831, 1837, and 1841, passim; Houston County Deed Books A, B, C, and D, passim; U. S. Census Records for Houston County, 1830, 1840, and 1850, passim.

9. ICMPC, Jan. 19, 1829. 10. *Ibid.,* Sept., 1834.

11. *Ibid.,* Jan., 1829.

12. *Ibid.,* Jan., 1830; Surveyors' Plats for Districts 14 and 15, Houston County, and for District 3, Dooly County; Hudgins Map of Pulaski County, GSGD.

13. Hudgins Map of Pulaski County.

14. ICMPC, Jan., 1830; *ibid.,* Jan., 1832.
15. Dawson, *Compilation,* p. 374.

CHAPTER XXV

1. Minutes of the Houston Association (Hereinafter cited as MHA), Oct. 9, 1830. The unpublished minutes are in the office of the Clerk of Superior Court, Cordele, Georgia.
2. *MEA,* 1829.   3. MHA, 1830.   4. MHA, 1830-37.
5. Pulaski County Deed Book H, p. 69.
6. MHA, 1830-38; Pulaski County Loose Paper File, GDAH.
7. MHA, 1830.
8. Letter Collection of Paul Redmond, Birmingham, Alabama.
9. MHA, 1830.   10. *Ibid.*   11. MHA, 1830-38.
12. Minute Book of New Hope Church (Hereinafter cited as MBNHC), July, 1830. The minute book is in charge of the church clerk, Abbeville, Ga.
13. *MEA,* 1830.   14. MHA, 1831.   15. MHA, 1831-38.
16. Minute Book of Ozias Church (Hereinafter cited as MBOC), April 7, 1849. The book is in charge of the clerk of Bethlehem Baptist Church, Fitzgerald, Georgia.
17. *Ibid.; History of the Little River Association of Baptist Churches* (Anon., 1918).
18. MHA, 1838.   19. MHA, 1838-48.   20. MBOC, Sept. 10, 1853.
21. "The One Hundred Anniversary of Mount Zion Baptist Church" (typed pamphlet compiled by Henry Beall of Forest Glen, Ga., 1944), p. 1.
22. *Little River Association.*
23. Clements, *Irwin County,* p. 486.
24. MHA, 1844.   25. MHA, 1844-56.
26. Minute Book of Cedar Creek Church, December 17, 1843. The book is in charge of the church clerk, Abbeville, Georgia.
27. MHA, 1847.   28. MHA, 1847-49.
29. *Baptist Denomination in Georgia,* pp. 93-98.
30. *Ibid.,* pp. 172-73; *MEA,* 1836.   31. MHA, 1839.
32. *Ibid.*   33. *The Messenger,* April 14-28, 1823.

CHAPTER XXVI

1. James C. Bonner, *The Georgia Story* (Oklahoma City, 1960), pp. 201-05.
2. *Ibid.,* pp. 205-06.   3. *Southern Recorder,* Aug. 30, 1836.
4. Pate, *Turner County,* p. 49.   5. CETE.   6. *Ibid.*
7. *Ibid.;* Floris Perkins Mann, *History of Telfair County from 1812 to 1949* (Macon, 1949), p. 16.
8. Surveyor's Plat for District 1, Irwin County, GSGD; Early Map.
9. Letters of the Reverend John Tomberlin, in possession of Miss Martha Wilcox, McRae, Georgia.
10. *Ibid.;* Irwin County Deed Book 1, *passim.*   11. Tomberlin Letters.
12. This incident was related to the writer by the late John Moses Barrentine of Fitzgerald, Georgia. Barrentine was born at Barrentine Ford, near the

scene of the incident, and had a personal acquaintance with many of the participants. His mother, Celete (McCall) Barrentine, a sister of David McCall, was one of the refugees from the Indians.

13. See Chapter XIV.   14. GEM, June 18, 1810.   15. GMR, p. 277.

16. See Executive Minutes for the following dates: Oct. 6, 1820; April 23, 1823; Sept. 17, 1824; Oct. 26, 1829; and Oct. 23, 1833.

17. Tomberlin Letters.   18. *Ibid.*

19. Pate, *Turner County,* pp. 49-50; Irwin County Deed Book 1, p. 193.

20. Clements, *Irwin County,* p. 31; Ward, *Coffee County,* pp. 30-31.

21. Ward, *Coffee County,* pp. 30-31.   22. *Ibid.*

CHAPTER XXVII

1. Dawson, *Compilation,* p. 197; *Southern Recorder,* Jan. 26, 1836.

2. *Southern Recorder,* Aug. 30, 1836.

3. Jonathan Smith to Georgia Governor, Dec. 9, 1833, in Irwin County Loose Paper File, GDAH.

4. *Ibid.*

5. Willcox to Gov. Lumpkin, Jan. 28, 1834, in Telfair County Loose Paper File, GDAH.

6. *Ibid.*

7. Pate, *Turner County,* p. 48; Clements, *Irwin County,* p. 33.

8. "Indian Depredations," IV, 174; Pate, *Turner County,* p. 48.

9. Page, *Turner County,* pp. 47-48; Clements, *Irwin County,* p. 33.

CHAPTER XXVIII

1. Evans, *Student's History,* pp. 225-27; *Southern Recorder,* Jan. 26, 1836.

2. Evans, *Student's History,* p. 226; *Southern Recorder,* May 24, 1836, and July 5, 1836.

3. Evans, *Student's History,* pp. 226-28; *Southern Recorder,* May 31, 1836.

4. Evans, *Student's History,* p. 227; *Southern Recorder,* July 19, 1836.

5. *Southern Recorder,* July 26, 1836.   6. *Ibid.*

7. Willcox to Gov. Schley, July 11, 1836, Telfair County Loose Paper File, GDAH.

8. Letter from Hamilton W. Sharpe, June 24, 1836, in *Southern Recorder,* Aug. 16, 1836.

9. *Southern Recorder,* Aug. 23, 1836.

10. Willcox to Schley, July 28, 1836, Telfair County Loose Paper File, GDAH.

11. *Southern Recorder,* Aug. 23, 1836.

CHAPTER XXIX

1. Adiel Sherwood, *A Gazetteer of the State of Georgia* (3rd ed.; Washington, 1837), p. 56; *Southern Recorder,* July 3, 1823; U.S. Post Office Records: Mail Route Proposal 298, for the year 1824. The Post Office Records are in the National Archives, Washington, D. C.

2. Sherwood, *Gazetteer,* p. 56.   3. *Ibid.*   4. *Ibid.*

5. *Ibid.;* U.S. Post Office Records: Mail Route Proposal 2392 for the years 1830-34.

6. U. S. Post Office Records: Mail Route Proposals 2386 and 2462.

7. *Ibid.,* Proposal 2387.

8. Sherwood, *Gazetteer,* p. 57.

9. *Ibid.*   10. *Ibid.,* p. 58.   11. Pate, *Turner County,* p. 32.

12. Sherwood, *Gazetteer,* p. 56.

13. *Southern Recorder,* Jan. 2, 1821; Charles Lyell, *A Second Visit to the United States of North America* (2 vols.; New York, 1849), II, 34.

14. Lyell, *Second Visit,* II, 34-35.   15. *Ibid.,* p. 34.   16. *Ibid.,* p. 35.

CHAPTER XXX

1. *Augusta Chronicle,* Jan. 26, 1816.

2. *Macon Messenger,* Aug. 4, 1824.

3. Mann, *Telfair County.* p. 21.

4. Sherwood, *Gazetteer,* pp. 192-93.

5. *Ibid.*   6. *Ibid.*   7. *Ibid.,* p. 190

8. Telfair County Deed Book A, p. 72.

9. CETE; U. S. Census Mortality Tables, 1860, for the counties of Telfair and Irwin.

BIBLIOGRAPHY

I. PRIMARY SOURCES
A. *Unpublished*
1. MANUSCRIPTS IN PUBLIC DEPOSITORIES

National Archives, Washington

Bounty Land Applications for Services in the Creek and Seminole Indian Wars.

Bureau of the Census Records, 1800-1880.

Post Office Department Records, 1824-1841.

Revolutionary War Pension Applications.

Georgia Department of Archives and History, Atlanta

Georgia Executive Minutes, 1786-1825.

Georgia Governors' Letter Books, 1800-1840.

Georgia Military Affairs, 1779-1840. 10 vols. Typescript.

Georgia Military Records, 1779-1839. Handwritten volume.

Hays, Louise Frederick. "Unpublished Letters of Timothy Barnard, 1784-1820." Typescript volume.

...... "Unpublished Letters of Benjamin Hawkins, 1797-1815." Typescript volume.

...... "Indian Depredations, 1787-1825." 5 vols. Typescript.

...... "Indian Letters, Talks, and Treaties." 4 parts. Typescript.

Manuscript Collection of Benjamin Hawkins' Letters.

Manuscript Collection of Allen Tooke's Letters.

Manuscript Collection. Loose Paper Files for the following Georgia Counties: Appling, Baldwin, Bullock, Dooly, Effingham, Elbert, Houston, Irwin, Jasper, Jones, Laurens, Monroe, Montgomery, Pulaski, Telfair, Twiggs, Warren, Washington, Wilcox, Wilkes, Wilkinson.

Georgia Surveyor-General Department, Atlanta.

Bivins, W. R. Journal, 1837. A description of the Oconee River.

Goff, John H. Manuscript Collection. A wide assortment of maps and notes pertaining to Indian trails, pioneer pathways, and early Georgia settlements.

Headright Land Grant and Surveyors' Plat Books. Various dates.

Land Grant Record Books, Surveyors' Plat Books, and Surveyors' Field Notes for the following Georgia Land Lotteries:
Lottery of 1805.
Lottery of 1807.
Lottery of 1820.
Lottery of 1821.
Lottery of 1827.
Lottery of 1832.   The Cherokee Lottery.

Young, Hugh. Itineraries. A record of the route followed by General Andrew Jackson's army from Hartford to Fort Scott during the Seminole War of 1818.

County Courthouse Records

Deeds, Inferior and Superior Court Records, Tax Digests, and other miscellaneous records in the counties and county seats listed below:

Alabama Counties:

Chambers, LaFayette
Randolph, Wedowee
Tallapoosa, Dadeville

Georgia Counties:

Appling, Baxley
Baldwin, Milledgeville
Berrien, Nashville
Bibb, Macon
Bullock, Statesboro
Carroll, Carrollton
Cherokee, Canton
Columbia, Appling
Coweta, Newnan
Crawford, Knoxville
Crisp, Cordele
Decatur, Bainbridge
Dooly, Vienna
Effingham, Springfield
Elbert, Elberton
Fayette, Fayetteville
Floyd, Rome
Forsyth, Cumming
Glascock, Gibson
Hall, Gainesville
Hancock, Sparta
Henry, McDonough
Houston, Perry
Irwin, Ocilla
Jasper, Monticello
Jefferson, Louisville
Jones, Gray
Laurens, Dublin
Lincoln, Lincolnton
Macon, Oglethorpe
Marion, Buena Vista
Meriwether, Greenville
Monroe, Forsyth
Montgomery, Mount Vernon
Newton, Covington
Pulaski, Hawkinsville
Richmond, Augusta
Screven, Sylvania
Tattnall, Reidsville
Telfair, McRae
Troup, LaGrange
Twiggs, Jeffersonville
Warren, Warrenton
Washington, Sandersville
Wilcox, Abbeville
Wilkes, Washington

Wilkinson, Irwinton
Worth, Sylvester

North Carolina Counties:

Anson, Wadesboro
Bertie, Windsor
Edgecombe, Tarboro
Granville, Oxford
Mecklenburg, Charlotte
Northampton, Jackson
Richmond, Rockingham

South Carolina Counties:

Abbeville, Abbeville
Anderson, Anderson
Charleston, Charleston
Darlington, Darlington
Edgefield, Edgefield
Kershaw, Camden
Laurens, Laurens
Marlboro, Bennettsville
Sumter, Sumter

Virginia Counties:

Brunswick, Lawrenceville
Caroline, Bowling Green
Halifax, Halifax
Isle of Wight, Isle of Wight
Lunenburg, Lunenburg
Prince George, Prince George
Southampton, Courtland
Surry, Surry

2. UNPUBLISHED CHURCH RECORDS

Bethlehem (Ozias) Baptist Church. Minutes, 1849-1872. Fitzgerald, Georgia.

Cashua (Cashaway) Baptist Church. Minutes, 1759, 1767. Microfilm, Furman University, Greenville, South Carolina.

Cedar Creek Baptist Church. Minutes, 1850-1887. Abbeville, Georgia.

Houston Association (Baptist). Minutes, 1830-1856. Cordele, Georgia.

Houston Factory Baptist Church. Minutes, 1836-1850. Perry, Georgia. Microfilm, GDAH.

Methodist Episcopal Church, South. Minutes, Georgia Conferences, 1845-1850. Candler School of Theology Library, Emory University, Atlanta, Georgia.

Mount Horeb Baptist Church. Minutes, 1809-1894. Cochran, Georgia.

Mount Zion (Spectacle) Baptist Church. Minutes, 1870-1898. Forest Glen, Ga.

Nevil's Creek Baptist Church. Minutes, 1810-1855. Statesboro, Georgia. Microfilm, GDAH.

New Hope Baptist Church. Minutes, 1842-1902. Abbeville, Georgia.

Perry Baptist Church. Minutes, 1838-1850. Perry, Georgia. Microfilm, GDAH.

Powelton Baptist Church. Minutes, 1786-1800. Powelton, Georgia. Microfilm, GDAH.

Richland Baptist Church. Minutes, 1811-1820. Jeffersonville, Georgia.

Welsh Neck Baptist Church. Minutes, 1759-1775. Society Hill, South Carolina.

3. MANUSCRIPTS IN PRIVATE COLLECTIONS

Martha Wilcox, McRae, Georgia

Letter Collection of the Reverend John Tomberlin, 1916-1918. A series of letters describing pioneer life along the Ocmulgee River.

Paul Redmond, Birmingham, Alabama

Letter Collection, 1953-1954. A series of letters giving historical and genealogical information concerning the family of the Reverend James Gouldwire Davis.

Mrs. Hill Redwine, Fayetteville, Georgia.

The Diary of Thomas Davis, 1849. A handwritten copy of the original.

The Beall Family, Forest Glen, Georgia

"The One Hundred Anniversary of Mount Zion Baptist Church, 1944." Typed pamphlet compiled by Henry Beall.

Kate Stephens Shingler, St. Petersburg, Florida

Letter. Collection of Isaac Woodard, 1890-1895. A series of letters concerning the Davis, Pollock, Singleton, Woodard, and related pioneer families of Houston County, Georgia.

Mrs. R. L. Stone, Fitzgerald, Georgia

Account Book of Abner and Samuel Brown. An Ante-Bellum and Civil War account book kept by Abner and Samuel Brown, merchants living at Browning, Georgia.

B. Published

1. NEWSPAPERS

Emory University Library, Atlanta, Georgia.

Georgia Journal (Milledgeville), 1820-1821, 1834-1835.

Macon Telegraph, 1826-1832.

Niles Weekly Register (Baltimore), 1817-1819.

Georgia College at Milledgeville Library, Milledgeville, Georgia.

Georgia Argus (Milledgeville), 1810.

Georgia Department of Archives and History, Atlanta (Microfilm).

Augusta Chronicle, 1786-1820.

Columbian Museum and Savannah Gazette (Savannah), 1818.

Fort Hawkins (Macon) Messenger (Fort Hawkins and Macon), 1823-1825.

Southern Recorder (Milledgeville), 1820-1824.

Georgia State Library, Atlanta.

Augusta Chronicle, 1811-1816.

Darien Gazette, 1820-1821, 1824-1825.

Southern Recorder (Milledgeville), 1826, 1829-1850.

University of Georgia Library, Athens.

Georgia Journal (Milledgeville), 1810-1819.

Louisville Gazette, 1801-1803.

2. OFFICIAL RECORDS
a. United States

"Altamaha, Oconee, and Ocmulgee Rivers, Ga." *House Ex. Doc. 443,* 62nd Cong., 2nd Sess., *Statutes at Large of the United States of America.* Washington: Govt. Printing Office, 1912. Serial Set 6207.

American State Papers. 38 vols. Washington: Gales and Seaton, 1832-1861.

Annals of Congress, 1789-1824. 42 vols. Washington: Gales and Seaton, 1834-1856.

Final Report of the United States DeSoto Expedition. Washington: Govt. Printing Office, 1939.

"Survey of Ocmulgee River, Georgia." *House Ex. Doc. 215,* 51st Cong., 1st Sess. Washington: Govt. Printing Office, 1890. Serial Set 2747.

b. Georgia

Blair, Ruth, ed. *Georgia's Official Register.* Atlanta: Department of Archives and History, 1927, 1929, 1931.

. . . . . . *Revolutionary Soldiers' Receipts for Georgia Bounty Grants.* Atlanta: Georgia Department of Archives and History, 1928.

. . . . . . *Some Early Tax Digests of Georgia.* Atlanta: The Georgia Department of Archives and History, 1926.

Bryan, Mary Givens. *Georgia's Official Register, 1957-1958.* Hapeville: Longino & Porter, n. d.

Candler, Allen D., ed. *Colonial Records of the State of Georgia.* 25 vols. Atlanta: Various printers, 1904-1916.

. . . . . . *Revolutionary Records of the State of Georgia.* 3 vols. Atlanta: The Franklin Turner Co., 1908.

Clayton, Augustin Smith. *A Compilation of the Laws of the State of Georgia, Passed by the Legislature Since the Political Year 1800, to the Year 1810, Inclusive.* Augusta: Adams & Duyckinck, 1813.

Cobb, Thomas R. R. *A Digest of the Statute Laws of the State of Georgia, in Force Prior to the Session of the General Assembly of 1851.* Athens: Christy, Kelsea, & Burke, 1851.

Dawson, William C. *A Compilation of the Laws of the State of Georgia, Passed by the General Assembly, Since the Year 1819 to the Year 1829, Inclusive.* Milledgeville: Grantland and Orme, 1831.

Henderson, Lillian, ed. *Roster of the Confederate Soldiers of Georgia, 1861-1865.* 6 vols. Hapeville: (Vols. I and II, n. d.; Vols. III, IV, and V, 1960; Vol. VI, 1964.)

Knight, Lucian Lamar, ed. *Georgia's Roster of the Revolution.* Atlanta: Index Printing Co., 1920.

Lamar, Lucius Q. C. *A Compilation of the Laws of the State of Georgia, Passed by the Legislature Since the Year 1810 to the Year 1819, Inclusive.* Augusta: T. S. Hannon, 1821.

Marbury, Horatio, and Crawford, William H. *Digest of the Laws of the State of Georgia.* Savannah: Seymour, Woolhopter, and Stebbins, 1802.

Prince, Oliver H. *A Digest of the Laws of the State of Georgia . . . Passed . . . Previous to . . . Dec., 1837.* 2nd ed. Athens: By the Author, 1837.

3. UNOFFICIAL PUBLICATIONS

Adair, James. *The History of the North American Indians.* Edited by Samuel Cole Williams. Johnson City, Tennessee: The Watauga Press, 1930.

Anthony, Bascom. *Fifty Years in the Ministry.* Macon: The J. W. Burke Co., 1937.

Anthony, J. D. *Life and Times of J. D. Anthony.* Atlanta: C. P. Byrd, 1896.

Bartram, William. *Travels of William Bartram.* Edited by Mark Van Doren. New York: Macy-Masius, 1928.

Boddie, John Bennett. *Births, Deaths, and Sponsors, 1717-1778, From the Albemarle Parish Register of Surry and Sussex Counties, Virginia.* Redwood City, California: Pacific Coast Publishers, 1958.

Bourne, Edward Gaylord, ed. *Narrative of the Career of Hernando de Soto . . .* 2 vols. New York: Allerton Book Co., 1922.

Bryan, Mary G. "Passports Issued by Governors of Georgia, 1785 to 1809." Reprinted from *National Genealogical Society Quarterly.* Washington: The Society, 1959.

Carroll, B. R., ed. *Historical Collections of South Carolina.* 2 vols. New York: Harper & Brothers, 1836.

Davidson, Grace Gillam, ed. *Records of Elbert County, Georgia.* (Historical Collections of the Georgia Chapters, Daughters of the American Revolution, Vol. III). Atlanta: Stein Printing Company, 1930.

. . . . . . *Records of Richmond County, Georgia: Formerly Saint Paul's Parish.* (Historical Collections of the Georgia Chapters, Daughters of the American Revolution, Vol. II). Athens: The McGregor Co., 1929.

. . . . . . *Early Records of Georgia: Wilkes County.* 2 vols. Macon: The J. W. Burke Company, 1932.

Dow, Lorenzo. *History of Cosmopolite . . . His Experiences and Travels . . . to Which is Added* "The Journey of Life," by Peggy Dow. 6th ed. Cincinnati: H. M. Rulison, Queen City Publishing House, 1857.

Ebenezer Baptist Association, Minutes, 1814-1850. Mercer University Library, Macon, Georgia.

Hall, Basil. *Travels in North America in the Years 1827 and 1828.* 2 vols. Philadelphia: Carey, Lea, and Carey, 1829.

Hall, Mrs. Basil. *The Aristocratic Journey: Being the Outspoken Letters of Mrs. Basil Hall Written During a Fourteen Months' Sojourn in America, 1827-1828.* Edited by Una Pope-Hennessy. New York: G. P. Putnam's Sons, 1931.

Hawes, Lilla M., ed. *The Papers of James Jackson, 1781-1798.* (Collections of the Georgia Historical Society, Vol. XI). Savannah: The Society, 1955.

Hawkins, Benjamin. *Letters of Benjamin Hawkins, 1796-1806.* (Collections of the Georgia Historical Society, Vol. IX). Savannah: The Society, 1916.

. . . . . . *A Sketch of the Creek Country in the Years 1798 and 1799.* Americus: Americus Book Company, 1938.

Houston, Martha Lou. *Reprint of Official Register of Land Lottery of Georgia, 1827.* Columbus: Walton-Forbes Co., 1928.

Knight, Lucian Lamar. *Georgia's Landmarks, Memorials, and Legends.* 2 vols. The Byrd Printing Co., 1913.

Lyell, Sir Charles. *A Second Visit to the United States of North America.* New York: Harper and Brothers; London: John Murray, 1849.

Mereness, Newton D., ed. *Travels in the American Colonies.* New York: The MacMillan Company, 1916.

Milfort, General (LeClerc). *Memoirs, or a Quick Glance at My Various Travels and My Soujourn in the Creek Nation.* Translated and edited by Ben C. McCary. Kennesaw: Continental Book Company, 1959.

Miller, Stephen F. *The Bench and Bar of Georgia: Memoirs and Sketches.* 2 vols. Philadelphia: J. B. Lippincott & Co., 1858.

. . . . . . *Memoir of Gen. David Blackshear . . .* Philadelphia: J. B. Lippincott & Co., 1858.

Motte, Jacob Rhett. *Journey into Wilderness: An Army Surgeon's Account of Life and Field during the Creek and Seminole Wars, 1836-1838.* Edited by James F. Sanderman. Gainesville: University of Florida Press, 1963.

Richardson, Simon Peter. *The Lights and Shadows of Itinerant Life.* Nashville: Publishing House of the Methodist Episcopal Church, South, 1900.

Salley, Harriet Milledge, ed. *Correspondence of John Milledge, Governor of Georgia, 1802-1806.* Columbia: The State Printing Company, 1949.

Sherwood, Adiel. *A Gazetteer of the State of Georgia.* (A facsimile reprint of the original 1827 publication). Athens: The University of Georgia Press, 1939.

. . . . . . *A Gazetteer of the State of Georgia.* 3rd ed. Washington: P. Force. 1837.

. . . . . . A *Gazetteer* of Georgia. 4th ed. Macon: S. Boykin, 1860.

Smith, James F. *The Cherokee Land Lottery.* New York: Harper & Brothers, 1838.

Stuart, James. *Three Years in North America.* 2 vols. Edinburgh: R. Cadell, 1833. (From the 2nd London ed., and J. Harper, New York, 1833.)

Timberlake, Lieut. Henry. *Lieut. Henry Timberlake's Memoirs, 1756-1765.* With Introduction by Samuel Cole Williams. Marietta: Continental Book Company, 1948.

Townsend, Leah. *South Carolina Baptists, 1670-1805.* Florence: The Florence Printing Company, 1935.

White, George. *Historical Collections of Georgia.* New York: Pudney and Russell, 1854.

. . . . . . *Statistics of the State of Georgia.* Savannah: W. Thorne Williams, 1849.

Williams, Carolyn White. *History of Jones County, Georgia, for One Hundred Years, Specifically 1808-1907.* Macon: The J. W. Burke Company, 1957.

Wood, Virginia S., and Ralph V., eds. *1805 Georgia Land Lottery.* Cambridge: The Greenewood Press, 1964.

Woodmason, Charles. *The Carolina Backcountry on the Eve of the Revolution.* Edited by Richard J. Hooker. Chapel Hill: University of North Carolina Press, 1953.

Woodward, Thomas S. *Woodward's Reminiscences of the Creek, or Muscogee Indians, Contained in Letters to Friends in Georgia and Alabama.* Montgomery: Barrett and Wimbish, 1859. Reprinted in Tuscaloosa, Alabama Book Store; and in Birmingham, Birmingham Book Exchange, 1939.

4. MAPS

A wide assortment of maps was employed in the preparation of this work. The most useful were maps produced by early American, English, French, and Spanish cartographers, covering the southeastern part of North America, and particularly the area comprising present-day Georgia and neighboring territory. Originals or reproductions of the maps consulted are in the map collections of the following depositories:

Emory University Library, Atlanta, Georgia.

Georgia State Library, Atlanta, Georgia.

Georgia Surveyor-General Department, Atlanta, Georgia.

South Carolina Archives Department, Columbia, South Carolina.

University of Georgia Library, Athens, Georgia.

II. SECONDARY SOURCES
A. Articles in Periodicals

Bolton, Herbert E. "Spanish Resistance to the Carolina Traders in Western Georgia, 1680-1704." *Georgia Historical Quarterly,* IX (June, 1925), 115-130.

Bonner, James C. "The Open Range Livestock Industry in Colonial Georgia." *Georgia Review,* XVII (Spring, 1963), 85-92.

Brannon, Peter A., ed. "Journal of James A. Tait for the Year 1813." *GHQ,* VIII (September, 1924), 229-239.

Coulter, E. Merton. "The Chehaw Affair." *GHQ,* XLIX (December, 1965), 369-395.

...... "When John Wesley Preached in Georgia." *GHQ,* IX (December, 1925), 317-351.

...... "The Creek Troubles of 1793." *GHQ,* XI (September, 1927), 274-280.

Goff, John H. "Cow Punching in Old Georgia." *Georgia Review,* III (Fall, 1949), 341-348.

...... "Some Major Indian Trading Paths Across the Georgia Piedmont." *Georgia Mineral Newsletter,* VI (Winter, 1953), 122-131.

...... "The Devil's Half Acre." *GMN,* XII (Spring-Summer, 1959), 27-29.

...... "Short Studies of Georgia Place Names." *GMN,* XIII (Fall, 1960), 129-138.

"Letters from General John Twiggs's Letter Book." *GHQ,* XI (December, 1927), 334-341.

Murdoch, Richard K. "The Seagrove-White Stolen Property Agreement of 1797." *GHQ,* XLII (September, 1958), 258-276.

O'Donnell, J. H. "Alexander McGillivray: Training for Leadership, 1777-1783." *GHQ,* XLIX (June, 1965), 172-186.

Phillips, Ulrich Bonnell. "New Light Upon the Founding of Georgia." *GHQ,* VII (December, 1922), 276-284.

Saye, Albert B. "The Genesis of Georgia Reviewed." *GHQ,* L (June, 1966), 153-161.

Smith, Daniel M. "James Seagrove and the Mission to Tuckaubatchee, 1793." *GHQ,* XLIV (March, 1960), 41-55.

Thomson, M. T. "The Grist Mill in Georgia." *Georgia Review,* VII (Fall, 1953), 332-346.

Wright, J. Leitch, Jr. "Creek-American Treaty of 1790: Alexander McGillivray and the Diplomacy of the Old Southwest." *GHQ,* LI (December, 1967), 379-400.

B. BOOKS

Benedict, David. *A General History of the Baptist Denomination in America, and Other Parts of the World.* 2 vols. Boston: Lincoln & Edmands, 1813.

Bolton, Herbert E., and Ross, Mary. *The Debatable Land.* Berkeley: University of California Press, 1925.

Bonner, James C. *The Georgia Story.* Oklahoma City: Harlow Publishing Corporation, 1960.

Bourne, Edward Gaylord. *Spain in America, 1450-1580.* New York: Barnes and Noble, Inc., 1962.

Brooks, Robert Preston. *History of Georgia.* Boston: Atkinson, Mentzer & Co., 1913.

Butler, John C. *Historical Record of Macon and Central Georgia.* Macon: J. W. Burke and Co., 1879. Reissued with a Foreword by Spencer B. King, Jr., Macon: J. W. Burke Co., 1958, 1960.

Campbell, J. H. *Georgia Baptists: Historical and Biographical.* Macon: J. W. Burke & Co., 1874.

Caughey, John Walton. *McGillivray of the Creeks.* Norman: University of Oklahoma Press, 1938, 1959.

Chappel, Absalom H. *Miscellanies of Georgia, Historical, Biographical, Descriptive, Etc.* Atlanta: James F. Meegan, 1874.

Clements, J. B. *History of Irwin County.* Atlanta: Foote & Davies Co., 1932.

Cobb, Mrs. Wilton Philip. *History of Dodge County.* Atlanta: Foote & Davies, 1932.

Coleman, Kenneth. *The American Revolution in Georgia, 1763-1789.* Athens: University of Georgia Press, 1958.

Cook, Mrs. Anna Maria Green. *History of Baldwin County.* Anderson, S. C.: Keys-Hearn Printing Co., 1925.

Cook, Harvey Toliver. *The Life and Legacy of David Rogerson Williams.* New York: N. p., 1916.

Corkran, David H. *The Creek Frontier, 1540-1783.* Norman: University of Oklahoma Press, 1967.

Cotterill, R. S. *The Southern Indians: The Story of the Civilized Tribes Before Removal.* Norman: University of Oklahoma Press, 1954.

Coulter, E. Merton. *Georgia: A Short History.* Chapel Hill: The University of North Carolina Press, 1933 (Revised ed., 1947).

Covington, W. A. *History of Colquitt County.* Atlanta: Foote and Davies Company, 1937.

Crane, Verner W. *The Southern Frontier, 1670-1732.* Ann Arbor: University of Michigan Press, 1929 (First reissued in 1956).

Davidson, Victor. *History of Wilkinson County.* Macon: Published by the John Ball Chapter, Daughters of the American Revolution, 1930.

Debo, Angie. *The Road to Disappearance.* Norman: University of Oklahoma Press, 1941.

De Vorsey, Louis, Jr. *The Indian Boundary in the Southern Colonies, 1763-1775.* Chapel Hill: The University of North Carolina Press, 1961.

Dunbar, Seymour. *History of Travel in America.* New York: Tudor Publishing Company, 1937.

Eaton, John Henry and Reid, John. *The Life of Andrew Jackson.* Philadelphia: M. Carey and Son, 1817.

Evans, Lawton B. *The Student's History of Georgia.* Macon: John W. Burke & Co., 1884.

Faulk, Lanette O'Neal, ed. *Historical Collections of Richland Baptist Church.* Macon: The J. W. Burke Company, 1950.

Faulk, Lanette O'Neal, and Jones, Billy Walker, eds. *History of Twiggs County, Georgia.* Jeffersonville: Major General John Twiggs Chapter, Daughters of the American Revolution, 1960.

Flanigan, James C. *History of Gwinnett County, 1818-1943.* Hapeville: Tyler & Company, 1943.

Gifford, John C. *Billy Bowlegs and the Seminole War.* Coconut Grove, Florida: The Triangle Company, 1925.

Gregg, Alexander, *History of the Old Cheraws.* New York: Richardson and Company, 1867.

Grice, Warren. *The Georgia Bench and Bar.* Macon: The J. W. Burke Company, 1931.

Harris, Walter A. *Here the Creeks Sat Down.* Macon: The J. W. Burke Company, 1958.

Harris, Mrs. Wallace Leigh, ed. *History of Pulaski and Bleckley Counties, Georgia, 1808-1956.* Macon: The J. W. Burke Company, 1957.

Hart, Bertha Sheppard. *The Official History of Laurens County, Georgia, 1807-1941.* Dublin: John Laurens Chapter, Daughters of the American Revolution, 1941.

History of the Baptist Denomination in Georgia. Compiled for the *Christian Index.* Atlanta: Jas. P. Harrison & Co., 1881.

History of Pulaski County, Georgia. Edited by the Hawkinsville Chapter, Daughters of the American Revolution. Atlanta: Walter W. Brown Publishing Company, 1935.

Howell, Robert Boyle C. *The Early Baptists of Virginia.* Philadelphia: The Bible and Publication Society, 1857.

Huxford, Folks. *Pioneers of Wiregrass Georgia.* 5 vols. Homerville: By the Author, 1951-1967.

Jones, Billy Walker. *History of Stone Creek Baptist Church, Twiggs County, Georgia, 1808-1958.* Dry Branch: Published by the Church and B. W. Jones, 1961.

Jones, Charles C., Jr. *The History of Georgia.* 2 vols. Boston: Houghton, Mifflin, and Company, 1883.

Kilpatrick, W. L. *The Hephzibah Baptist Association Centennial, 1794-1894.* Augusta: Richard and Shaver, 1894.

King, Spencer B., Jr. *Georgia Voices: A Documentary History to 1872.* Athens: University of Georgia Press, 1966.

Knight, Lucian Lamar. *A Standard History of Georgia and Georgians.* 6 vols. Chicago: New York: The Lewis Publishing Company, 1917.

McCall, Ettie Tidwell. *McCall-Tidwell and Allied Families.* Atlanta: By the Author, 1931.

McCall, Mrs. Howard H. *Roster of Revolutionary Soldiers in Georgia.* Atlanta: John T. Hancock, 1941.

McCall, Hugh. *The History of Georgia.* 2 vols. Savannah: Seymour and Williams, 1811-1816.

McLendon, S. G. *History of the Public Domain of Georgia.* Atlanta: Foote & Davies Co., 1924.

McReynolds, Edwin C. *The Seminoles.* Norman: University of Oklahoma Press, 1957.

Malone, Henry Thompson. *Cherokees of the Old South: A People in Transition.* Athens: University of Georgia Press, 1956.

Mann, Floris Perkins, ed. *History of Telfair County from 1812 to 1949.* Macon: The J. W. Burke Company, 1949.

Martin, John H., ed. *Columbus, Georgia, 1827-1865, Part 1, 1827-1846.* Columbus: Thomas Gilbert, 1874.

Meyer, Duane. *The Highland Scots of North Carolina, 1732-1776.* Chapel Hill: The University of North Carolina Press, 1957.

Owen, Thomas McAdory, ed. *Report of the Alabama History Commission to the Governor of Alabama, December 1, 1900.* Montgomery: Publications of the Alabama Historical Society, 1901.

Parton, James. *Life of Andrew Jackson.* 3 vols. New York: Mason Brothers, 1860.

Pate, John Ben. *History of Turner County.* Atlanta: Stein Printing Company, 1933.

Patrick, Rembert W. *Florida Fiasco: Rampant Rebels on the Georgia-Florida Border, 1810-1815.* Athens: University of Georgia Press, 1954.

Phillips, Ulrich Bonnell. *A History of Transportation in the Eastern Cotton Belt to 1860.* New York: Octagon Books, Inc., 1968. A reprint of the 1908 edition by the Columbia University Press.

Pickett, Albert James. *History of Alabama and Incidentally of Georgia and Mississippi, from the Earliest Period.* Tuscaloosa, Alabama: Republished by Willo Publishing Co., 1962.

Pound, Merritt B. *Benjamin Hawkins: Indian Agent.* Athens: The University of Georgia Press, 1951.

Read, William A. *Indian Place-Names in Alabama.* University Studies Number 29. Baton Rouge: Louisiana State University Press, 1937.

Robinson, R. L. *History of the Georgia Baptist Association.* Union Point: By the Author, 1928.

Silver, James W. *Edmund Pendleton Gaines, Frontier General.* Baton Rouge: Louisiana State University Press, 1949.

Smith, George Gillman. *The Story of Georgia and the Georgia People, 1732 to 1860.* Macon: By the Author, 1900.

. . . . . . *The History of Georgia Methodism from 1786 to 1866.* Atlanta: A. B. Caldwell, Publishers, 1913.

Stacy, James. *A History of the Presbyterian Church in Georgia.* Elberton: Privately printed, 1912.

Stevens, William Bacon. *A History of Georgia from its First Discovery by Europeans to the Adoption of the Present Constitution.* 2 vols. New York: D. Appleton and Co., 1847.

Suddeth, Ruth Elgin; Osterhout, Isa Lloyd; and Hutcheson, George Lewis. *Empire Builders of Georgia.* Austin, Texas: The Steck Company, 1951.

Swanton, John R. *Early History of the Creek Indians and Their Neighbors.* Smithsonian Institution, Bureau of American Ethnology Bulletin 73. Washington: Government Printing Office, 1922.

Wade, John Donald. *John Wesley.* New York: Coward-McCann, Inc., 1930.

Wallace, David Duncan. *South Carolina: A Short History, 1520-1948.* Chapel Hill: The University of North Carolina Press, 1951.

Ward, Warren P. *History of Coffee County.* Atlanta: Foote and Davies Co., 1930.

Willson, Minnie Moore. *The Seminoles of Florida.* New York: Moffat, Yard and Company, 1911.

INDEX

Abbeville, Georgia, 2, 5, 6, 78, 149, 167, 176, 191, 199, 200
Abbeville District, S. C., 59
Adams, Colson, Pulaski County pioneer, 51, 62
Adams, Miles, 167, 176
Adams Settlement, 191
Agent for Indian Affairs, 30
Alabama boundary, 181, 186
Alabama Creeks, 101, 173, 186
Alabama Indian country, 187
Alabama line, 173, 190
Alabama River, 10, 15, 25, 75, 88
Alabama, state of, 164, 173, 174, 181, 186
Alabama territory, 15, 31, 75, 79, 99, 102, 104, 128
Alapaha River, 164, 181, 187, 188, 189, 191
Albany, Georgia, 16, 148
Albemarle Parish, Va., 59
Alcovy River, 1
Aldersgate, Wesley's experience at, 64
Al-ka-sac-ki-li-ki Creek, 2, 148, 150, 151
Allen, Bouser, Irwin County official, 156
Allen, James, 62, 154
Allen, J. W., 169
Altamaha-Ocmulgee line, 147, 148
Altamaha River, formation of, 2; mentioned, 18, 19, 21, 50, 53, 70, 78, 117, 120, 196
Ambrister, Robert, 124
Amelia Island, 125
America, 11, 64, 92
American colonies, 18, 56
American immigrants, 41
American Indian problem, 25
American pioneers, reach Ocmulgee River, 32; establish new ways along Ocmulgee, 40
Americans, 21, 27, 28, 41, 123, 124, 153, 156, 186

Anglican Church, 56
Anglicans, 56
Anglo-American Christians, 62
Anglo-Americans, 79
Ante-Bellum Period, 158, 166, 168, 198, 199
Apalachee country, invasion of by Carolinians and Creeks, 13; towns attacked, 13
Apalachee Indians, won to Spanish cause, 8; harass Carolina traders, 11; invade Creek country, 12
Apalachicola River, 103, 112, 113, 114, 123, 125, 130
Apalachicolas, 8
Appling County, 153, 189
Arbuckle, Lt. Col., commandant at Fort Scott, 126
Arbuthnot, Alexander, espouses Seminole cause, 124
Articles of Confederation, 22, 23
Asbell, John, 62
Asbury, Francis, Methodist bishop, 65
Ashley, William, Telfair County pioneer, 51
Ashley's Mills, 190
Associations (Baptist), 57
Atlanta, Georgia, 1, 15
Atlantic Coast, 10, 50, 70, 116
Atlantic Ocean, 2, 3, 11, 20, 190
Atlantic Seaboard, 191, 192
Atkinson, Shadrack, Pulaski County pioneer, 50
Auchenhatchee, 2
Augusta, Georgia, 7, 17, 22, 45, 52, 55, 103, 192
Augusta, Treaty of, 22, 23, 24
Au-muc-cul-le, Chehaw Indian town on Muckalee Creek, 5, 16, 75, 113, 130, 139, 140, 144
Auttossee, attach upon, 100
Ayaville, Apalachee town taken by Carolinians, 13

231

Back country, 71
Baggett, Barton, Pulaski County pioneer, 51
Baggett family, 51
Baggett, John, Pulaski County pioneer, 51
Baggett, Nicholas, Pulaski County pioneer, 51
Baggett, Thomas, Pulaski County pioneer, 51
Baggett's Creek, 51
Bainbridge, Georgia, 5, 191
Baker County, invasion of, 187
Baker, Jordan, 167
Baldwin County, creation of, 32; boundaries of, 32; division of, 33, 40
Ball, Archibald, 63
Ball, Caswell, Telfair County pioneer, 51
Baptists, 56, 57, 58, 64
Barbaree, Stansell, 166
Barden, Celie, 60
Barden, Simon, Pulaski County pioneer, 50, 60
Barnard, Timothy, interpreter at Treaty of Washington, 31; keeper of trading post on Flint River, 31; mentioned, 75, 77, 84, 110
Barnard Road, 163
Barnard's Trading Path, 25, 77, 78, 84, 163
Barnard's Trading Post, 31, 75, 77, 78, 82, 84, 110, 113, 156, 163
Barrentine, Elizabeth, 168
Barrentine, Jacob (Captain), Irwin County pioneer, 161; Irwin County official, 178; mentioned, 167, 168, 176, 178
Barrentine, James, Irwin County pioneer, 176
Barrentine, Rocelia, 167
Barrentine, William, Irwin County pioneer, 161, 176
Barrett, James, 159
Barrow's Bluff, 200
Barton, Allen, 162
Barton, Henry, 162
Barton, John, Twiggs County pioneer, 39; plantation of, 39
Barton's Springs, 39

Beard's Bluff, 25, 78
Beaverdam Creek, 50, 60, 97
Bell, Joseph, Telfair County official, 34
Bell, Reddick, 162
Bell's Ferry, 52, 54, 117, 119, 190
Bennett, John, 53
Berrien County, 156, 188
Berryhill Bluff, 33, 54
Bethlehem Baptist Church, 167, 168
Beulah Church, Houston Association formed at, 165
Big Bend of the Ocmulgee, description of, 2, 34; mentioned, 5, 36, 78, 82, 85, 92, 93, 106, 117, 131, 132, 135, 136, 137, 138, 140, 149, 153, 155, 161, 163, 164, 175, 176, 181, 199
Big Creek, location of, 2; Jackson's encampment at, 129
Big Escambia, 192
Big House Creek, location of, 2; mentioned, 5, 30, 133, 149, 150, 151, 161, 175, 191
Big Indian Creek, 2
Big Sandy Creek, 53
Big Warrior, 83, 90
Bird, Jesse, Telfair courts held at house of, 36
Bird's Nest Bluff Landing, 200
Blackshear, David (General), carves out Blackshear Road, 82; designs frontier forts, 96; appraisal of forts, 98; leads expedition into Creek country, 108-15; marches to invaded seacoast, 116-20; mentioned, 104, 108, 109, 110, 111, 112, 113, 114, 115, 156, 163
Blackshear, Elijah (Major), 82, 117
Blackshear Ford, 153
Blackshear roads, establishment of, 82, 112, 115; mentioned, 85, 126, 127, 129, 139, 150, 151, 156, 179, 190, 191
Bleckley County, 2, 54, 58
Bluff Creek, 2, 169
Boatyard Landing, 191, 200
Bolling, John, 102
Booth's Ferry, 192
Bothwell, Captain, Commandant of Fort Early, 139
Bowen, Enoch, 63
Bowen, Stephen, 168

Bowen, William, Irwin County pioneer, 161

Bowles, William Augustus, American-born British agent, 28; goes into Spanish Florida on clandestine mission among Seminoles, 28; gains title, "Director General of Muscogee," 28; opposed by Hawkins, 28; supports England against the United States, 28; diverts Indians from Fort Wilkinson, 28; capture of, 29; mentioned, 29

Bowles party, 28, 29

Boyd, Samuel, 154

Bozeman, John, 164

Bracken, William, 37, 54

Bradshaw, Clayton, 163

Bradshaw, John, 53

Breakfast Branch, description of, 133-34; battle of, 134-35; mentioned, 137, 144, 149, 155, 178, 182

Brewer, Solomon, 60, 61

Bridges, John, 127

Brim, Emperor, leads Muscogees from Chattahoochee to Ocmulgee, 10; supports English expedition against Spaniards and Apalachees, 12; plans revolt against English, 14

British agents, 89, 92, 100, 101, 103

British forces, 92, 103, 105, 108, 113; designs of, 103, 105, 116, 120; mentioned, 122, 123, 124

British fort, 123

British government, 123, 124

British Isles, 56

Brown, Benjamin, Pulaski County pioneer, 5; pilot, 94

Brown, Frederick, 63

Brown, "Indian Jim," 183

Brown, Isaac, coronet, 127

Brown, James, Irwin County pioneer, 161, 167

Brown, Jemima, 167, 168

Brown, Lucretia, 60

Brown, Philip, Telfair County pioneer, 51, 63; raid upon premises of, 93, 94, 118, 119, 177; Irwin County pioneer, 161; mentioned, 167, 176, 177

Brown, Richard, Irwin County pioneer, 161

Brown, Samuel, 178

Broxton, Georgia, 190

Brunson, Daniel, Houston County pioneer, 162

Bryan, Ezekiel, 166

Bryant, Edward, captain of Pulaski militia, 38

Bryant, Jemima, 60

Bryant, Needham, 62

Bryant, William, 62

Buchanan, Georgia, 15

Buck Creek, 166

Bunn, Henry, trustee of Ocmulgee Academy, 39

Burch, Allen, 164

Burch attack, 178

Burch, Charles, Telfair County pioneer, 63

Burch, Joseph, massacre of, 131, 132, 134, 149, 155

Burch, Littleton, attack upon, 131, 132, 133, 149, 155

Burch, Michael, killed in battle, 134, 144

Burke, Edward, Telfair County pioneer, 51

Burkhalter, Isaac, 60

Burkhalter, Sarah, 60

Burnham, William, 50

Burton, Joseph, 168

Bush, James, 60, 61

Bush, Levi, pioneer minister, 58

Butler, Jesse, 51

Buzzard's Roost Bluff, Indian landmark, 6; trading post, 50, 78, 157; steamboat landing, 200; mentioned, 152, 158

Callaway, David, Telfair County pioneer, 51, 63; Irwin County pioneer, 153

Calfrey, Lewis, 73

Callibee, attack upon, 100

Camden County, 99

Camp Blakeley, Blackshear's troops at, 109

Camp Hope, 99

Camp Thirty-six Mile Creek, 111

Camp Twelve Miles East of Flint River, 111

Camp Twenty-six Mile Creek, 111

Canada, 11
Capital of United States, 31
Caravans, of immigrants, 42; to trading centers, 45; to Southwest, 80
Carnes, Thomas, presides over Telfair Superior Court, 35; presides over Pulaski Superior Court, 157
Carolina, 13
Carolina frontier, 14
Carolina trading centers, 10
Carolina traders, open trade with Muscogees, 9; mentioned, 11, 13
Carolinas, 21, 37, 39, 41, 42, 146, 155
Carolinians, 13, 14, 17, 41
Carroll, William, Telfair County official, 34
Captain Salter, 196
Carr's Shoals, 6, 52, 53
Carr's Ned, 105
Carter, Farish, 117
Carter, Jesse, leads charge against Indians, 188
Carver, James, Telfair County official, 34
Carver, Jesse, Telfair County official, 34
Cashua (Cashaway) Baptist Church, 57
Cathledge, Elijah, 60
Cattle raising, 45
Cawthon, Ashley, 63
Cawthon, Josiah D. (Major), Telfair County official, 35, 51, 97; erects forts on Telfair frontier, 97; leads in Battle of Breakfast Branch, 133-35; mentioned, 103, 149, 150
Cawthon, William, Telfair County pioneer, 51
Cedar Creek (Wilcox County), 2, 78
Cedar Creek (Crisp County), ambush at, 127, 128, 129
Cedar Creek Baptist Church, 169
Cedar Shoals, 196
Chalker, James, Houston County pioneer, 162
Chancey, Amos, Houston County official, 158
Chancey, Nathan, 166
Charleston, S. C., founding of, 8; mentioned, 45, 70, 192
Chattahoochee Indians, 182

Chattahoochee River, dwelling place of Hitchiti Indians, 3; dwelling place of Muscogee Indians, 3, 9; mentioned, 10, 15, 16, 17, 19, 28, 75, 76, 77, 83, 84, 85, 91, 99, 100, 108, 112, 113, 123, 131, 147, 174, 186, 192
Chehaw Indians, 16, 75, 83, 92, 113, 114, 130
Chehaw Town, 75, 94, 126, 130, 139, 140, 141, 144
Chehaw villages, 111, 138, 139
Chenubby, chief of Fowltown Tribe, 126
Cherokee boundary line, 15, 85
Cherokee country, 15, 178, 190
Cherokee Indians, dwelling place of, 15
Cherry, George, 163
Chickasawhatchee Swamp, battle of, 187; mentioned, 21, 59
Chickasaws, 11
China Hill, 97, 133, 201
Choctaws, 11
Christianity, brought to the Ocmulgee, 56-66
Christian faith, 56
Clarke, Elijah, Georgia commissioner, 23; troops of, 59; mentioned, 72
Clarke, Gibson, Telfair County pioneer, 51, 72
Clarke, John, 162
Clark's Ferry, 162
Clements, Abraham P., Irwin County official, 155
Clements, Jacob, 52
Clinton, county seat of Jones County, 40, 192
Coalson, Sanders, Pulaski County pioneer, 37, 50
Cobb, Howell, Houston County official, 158
Cochran, Georgia, 53
Coffee County, 179
Coffee, John (General), Telfair County pioneer, 51; road commissioner, 164
Coffee Road, 164, 191
Cofitacheque, 7
Cole, Daniel, 50
Colerain, Treaty of, 25, 83
Collier, Probert, 166

Collins, Wilson, 158
Colonial Period, 56
Colson, John, 166
Columbus, Georgia, 187, 192
Conecaugh, 192
Conley, Michael, 63
Conner, Wilson, frontier missionary, 64, 167
Cook, Phillip, 73
Cool Springs, 58
Cooper, George W., 159
Cooper, John T., 159
Coosa River, 10, 15, 17, 21, 75, 83, 88, 101
Copeland settlement, 6, 35, 51, 97, 132, 133, 176, 182, 183, 187, 190, 191
Cordele, Georgia, 129
Corn shuckings, 44
Cornwall, Daniel, Houston County official, 157
Coweta, 11, 16
Cowetas, establish settlement on Ocmulgee River, 9
Coweta Town, 12, 13, 14, 20, 82, 91, 113
Cowpens, battle of, 59
Cray, Benjamin G., Telfair County pioneer, 52; Telfair official, 73
Cray, Scott, Darien merchant, 71
Creek Agency, establishment of, 25; mentioned, 31, 83, 84, 99, 129, 157, 163, 192
Creek Confederacy, formation of, 3-4; mentioned, 9, 10, 11
Creek country, 92, 95, 99
Creek frontier, defense of, 13
Creek Indians, 15, 17, 21, 22, 24, 26, 30, 31, 40, 41, 86, 87, 94, 121, 146, 149, 152, 156, 159, 175, 186, 187, 189
Creek Nation, 14, 15, 25, 26, 29, 31, 36, 38, 52, 59, 60, 76, 77, 78, 79, 80, 81, 82, 83, 84, 87, 89, 90, 93, 98, 106, 109, 110, 128, 129, 152, 156, 157, 163, 173, 174
Creeks, 9, 10, 12, 13, 14, 18, 21, 26, 87, 88, 93, 149, 173, 174
Crocker, William, Twiggs County official, 39
Crooked Creek, 2
Crum, James, 154

Cuba, 144
Cumberland Island, 116, 120
Cumming, Robert, Twiggs County official, 39
Cunningham Ford, 164
Cunningham, John (Colonel), at Battle of Cowpens, 59
Curl, Kinchen, Houston County official, 157
Curry, Duncan, Telfair County official, 34
Cypress Creek, 2

Dakota, Georgia, 184
Daniel, Charles, 50
Daniel, John, Pulaski County pioneer, 51
Darien, trading place, 44, 55, 67, 70, 71; mentioned, 45, 50, 53, 117, 120, 190, 192, 196, 197, 198, 199
Davis, Absalom, family of, 58
Davis, Anne, 58
Davis, Chesley, Pulaski County pioneer, 50; early church official, 58; family of, 59; life of, 59; contributions of, 59; mentioned, 60, 62, 158
Davis, Elisha, trustee of Stone Creek Academy, 39
Davis, Gidion, Revolutionary Soldier, 59
Davis, James, 162
Davis, James Gouldwire, captain of Pulaski County militia, 38, 170; Houston County pioneer, 162; Baptist minister, 59, 166, 170; death of, 166
Davis, John, 63
Davis, Joseph, 167
Davis, Lewis, Revolutionary Soldier, 59
Davis, Lydia, 58
Davis, Ozias, 62
Davis, Richard, 59
Davis, Richard H., Houston County official, 158; mentioned, 60, 162
Davis, Wiley, Revolutionary Soldier, 59
Davis, William, Twiggs County official, 39
Davis, Zion, Pulaski County pioneer, 54, 62

Dawson, Kinchen, Pulaski County pioneer, 54
Dean, Lieutenant, 109
Decatur County, Georgia, 5
Dees, Drury, Pulaski County pioneer, 58, 62
Dees, John, 50
Dees, Sarah,
Dennard, Hugh L., 158
Denson, John, 62
Denson, Sarah, 62
DeShazo, Robert, 50
DeShazo, William, 50
DeSoto, Hernando, expedition of, 4-7, 17, 121
Devil's Elbow, 70
Devil's Trash Pile, 70
Dewert, Robert, Pulaski County pioneer, 50
Dicks, Samuel, Twiggs County official, 39
Dickson, Elizabeth, 60
Dillard, Phillip, 62
Dissenters, 56
Dixon, John B. F., 161
Dixon, Lucy, 167
Dixon, Robert, 167
Dixon, Robert H., Telfair County pioneer, 51; Irwin County official, 154, 155; mentioned, 161
Dodge County, Georgia, 2, 6, 54
Dodsworth, Anthony, intercepts invasion, 12
Dooly County, Georgia, creation of, 156; location of, 156; public site for, 156; mentioned, 159, 162, 163, 183
Dorminey, John B., Irwin County pioneer, 161
Douglas, Georgia, 179, 191
Drawdy, Daniel, 134
Drawdy, Thomas, Irwin County official, 155
Drayton, 156, 163
Dublin, Georgia 6, 27, 52, 53, 54
DuPree, Benjamin, trustee for Ocmulgee Academy, 39
DuPree, Daniel, Houston County official, 157
DuPree, Edmund, trustee for Ocmulgee Academy, 39

DuPree, Jeremiah, Houston County pioneer, 162
Durham's Bluff, 50, 78, 200
Durham's Ford, 53
Dykes, Abigail, 60
Dykes, Daniel, Pulaski County pioneer, 54
Dykes, Fatha, 60, 61
Dykes, Henry, 62
Dykes, Mary, 60
Dykes, Susannah, 61

Early, Eleazer, investigates affray at Fort Hawkins, 82
Early, Peter, presides over Telfair Superior Court, 35; presides over Pulaski Superior Court, 38; governor of Georgia, 82, 103, 104, 105, 106, 108, 113, 114, 116, 118, 119
Eastman, Georgia, 54
Ebenezer Association (Baptist), formation of, 58; mentioned, 60, 62, 64, 165, 166, 167, 170
Ebenezer settlement, 17, 20
Echeconnee Creek, 2, 130, 162
Edwards, Christopher, 72
Edwards, Cullen, Telfair County official, 34
Elbert County, Georgia, 15, 59
Ellis, Ebenezer, Pulaski county pioneer, 54
Ellis, Edwin, 166
England, at war with France, 11; mentioned, 18, 89, 92, 93, 122, 123
England, Church of, 56, 64
English, establish settlement in lower Carolina, 9; pierce Indian trade barrier, 9; establish Georgia colony, 18-19; mentioned, 10, 11, 13, 14, 17, 18, 28, 56
English traders, 9, 10, 11, 12, 13, 14
Europe, 18
Evans, Elisha, Pulaski County pioneer, 51
Everett, James A., Houston County pioneer, 157
Everett, Jehu, Telfair County pioneer, 51
Everett, Josiah, Pulaski County official, 37; mentioned, 50

Everett, Martin B., 169
Everett, Turner, Houston County official, 157
Everglades, 178
Evergreen Church, 53
Evergreen Creek, 53

Factory system of trade, establishment of, 25
Fain, Matthew, Telfair County pioneer, 51
Fain, Thomas, Telfair County pioneer, 51
Fall Line, 1, 70
Falling Creek, 1
Fayetteville, Tennessee, 128
Federal authorities, 26
Federal factory system, 25
Federal government, agrees to extinguish Indian title to Georgia territory, 28; mentioned, 23, 24, 26, 79
Federal land reserves, 25
Federal Road, creation of, 79; uses of, 80-81, 129; mentioned, 81, 82, 99, 192
Federal trading houses, 25
Felder, Samuel, 158
Fish traps, 76, 77
Fitzgerald, John, Irwin County pioneer, 161, 176
Fitzgerald, Miles, 176
Fitzgerald Road, 154
Flat Creek, 1, 39
Fletcher, Griffin, 132
Fletcher, John, 132, 51
Fletcher, Joseph, 132
Fletcher, William, Telfair County pioneer, 51
Fletcher, Ziba, Telfair County official, 36; mentioned, 97
Flint Academy, 158
Flint River, dwelling place of Muscogee Indians, 3; crossed by DeSoto expedition, 5; seat of Oswichee Indian settlement, 16; mentioned, 5, 10, 12, 16, 17, 31, 75, 76, 77, 78, 82, 83, 84, 85, 92, 99, 100, 108, 109, 110, 111, 112, 113, 115, 123, 125, 126, 129, 130, 131, 133, 138, 139, 151, 156, 157, 159, 162, 163, 164, 165, 185, 187, 188, 191, 192

Florida, 17, 75, 92, 102, 121, 122, 163, 164, 178, 186, 187
Florida border, 23, 25, 153, 188
Florida Indians, 103
Florida province, 121
Florida Spanish government, 122, 123
Floyd, John (General), Georgia forces under command of, 99; establishes line of defense, 99; launches attacks against hostile Creeks, 100; mentioned 100, 108, 120, 173
Folsom, Lawrence, Pulaski County pioneer, 51
Folsom, William, Irwin County official, 154
Ford, Jemima, 60
Forney, Daniel M., commissioner, 151
Forsyth, county seat of Monroe County, 159, 171, 192
Forsyth Female Academy, 159
Fort Adams, erection of, 97; location of, 97, 118, 119, 132; mentioned, 132, 155, 177, 178
Fort Barrington, 117, 119, 120
Fort Clarke, erection of, 97; location of, 97, 118, 119
Fort Early, erection of, 82, 112, 113; Glasscock's troops encamped at, 126, 127; mentioned, 82, 85, 129, 130, 138, 139, 140, 142, 143, 156, 163, 191
Fort Gaines, 101, 147, 192
Fort Green, erection of, 97, location of, 97, 118
Fort Hawkins, frontier stronghold, 40; establishment of, 40, 53, 77; trading center, 80; gateway to Creek Nation, 81; rendezvous for Georgia troops, 99, mentioned, 50, 58, 70, 71, 77, 79, 82, 96, 98, 105, 107, 108, 111, 128, 129, 157, 159, 160, 163, 192, 196
Fort Jackson (Alabama), Treaty of, 85, 101, 106, 121, 122, 123, 147, 148, 153, 186; mentioned, 125, 128, 181
Fort Jackson (Georgia), erection of, 97
Fort James, 25
Fort Laurens, erection of, 97; location of, 97, 118
Fort Lawrence, 83, 99, 107, 192
Fort McIntosh, 97, 98, 118, 119
Fort Mims, massacre at, 99

Fort Mitchell (at Hartford), erection of, 97; location of, 97, 118
Fort Mitchell (on the Chattahoochee), 85, 99, 100, 104, 112
Fort Perry, 99, 192
Fort Pike, erection of, 97; location of, 97, 118
Fort Scott, 123, 124, 125, 128, 129, 130, 137, 139
Fort Stoddart, 79
Fort Telfair, erection of, 97
Fort Toulouse, erected by the French, 17
Fort Twiggs, erection of, 97
Fort Wilkinson, Treaty of, 27, 28, 30; mentioned, 28, 31, 33
Fowltown, destruction of, 125
France, at war with England, 11, 87; mentioned, 89
Franklin County, Georgia, creation of, 22
Frederica, 64
French, establish colony on Atlantic, 8; gain control of Mississippi territory, 10; harass English traders, 11; erect Fort Toulouse, 17; mentioned, 10, 12, 19
Friendship Church, 129
Frokock, John, 102
Fulemmy's Town, 126
Fulghum, Hardy, 62
Fulghum, Henry, Pulaski County official, 38; mentioned, 53, 60
Fullwood, Thomas, Telfair County pioneer, 51
Furlow's store, affray at, 81
Fussell, William, Irwin County pioneer, 161

Gaines, Edmund Pendleton (General), 123, 125, 128, 129, 130
Gaines, George G., Pulaski County pioneer, 38, 53, 60
Gallimore's Path, 6
Galphin's Old Town, 7
Galphinton, Treaty of, 23
Garrison Road, creation of, 52; mentioned, 192
Gaskin, John, 188
Gatlin, Furney, Pulaski County pioneer, 50, 135
Gatlin, Stephen, Pulaski County pioneer, 50
General Assembly, 22, 23, 34, 36, 37, 53, 82, 85, 154, 164
General Manning, the, destruction of, 201
Georgia, dwelling place of Creek Indians, 4; founding of, 18-19; western boundary proposed, 26; cedes western territory to United States, 28; military organization of, 46; mentioned, 15, 16, 17, 18, 19, 22, 24, 25, 30, 41, 42, 57, 64, 65, 72, 84, 91, 92, 99, 173, 186, 187, 190, 193
Georgia, colony of, 20
Georgia frontier, 22, 23, 30, 52, 83, 87, 91, 94, 104, 105, 113, 147, 181
Georgia, government of, 21
Georgia, governor of, 80, 82, 83, 84, 98, 105, 106, 116, 117, 121, 141, 143, 187, 189
Georgia Militia, 100, 178, 182, 187
Georgians, 21, 23, 24, 26, 27, 28, 31, 41, 92, 99, 146, 147, 196
Georgia seacoast, invasion of, 116, 117
Georgia trustees, 19
Georgia, unlocated territory of, 85
Ghent, Treaty of, 120, 121
Gibbs, John, 176
Gibson's, 192
Gilder, John S., Irwin County official, 156; mentioned, 161, 175
Gilder's Bluff, 2, 200
Glasscock, Thomas (General), encamped at Fort Early, 126; attack upon pack train of, 127, 129; mentioned, 140, 141
Glenn, Robert, trustee for Ocmulgee Academy, 39
Glenn, Sarah, 62
Goff, Eliza, 167
Goff, Penelope, 167
Goff, Samuel, 167
Goff, Steely, 167
Goff, William, 167
Goodson, William, Pulaski County pioneer, 51; pilot, 94; raid upon premises of, 94-95
Goose Creek, 148

Graham, Green G., 167, 169

Graham, James, 51

Grant, Daniel, 65

Grant, Thomas, 65

Grant's Meetinghouse, 65

Graves, marking of, 48

Great Britain, 123, 198

Great Lakes, 88

Greek-Revival Architecture, 62, 198, 199

Green, William, surveyor, 150

Griffin, Benjamin Mitchell, Telfair County official, 34, 51; death of, 134

Griffin, Joshua, Irwin County official, 154

Griffin, Lewis, Telfair County pioneer, 52

Griffin, William, Telfair County official, 34, 51, 132

Griffin's Creek, 2

Grinsted, John, Pulaski County pioneer, 53

Grist mill, importance of, 46

Groce, Captain, 110

Gross, William H., Pulaski County official, 53, 73

Gulf of Mexico, 8, 10, 11, 15, 83

Gwinnett County, 1, 15

Hall, William, Irwin County official, 156

Hall, William, Pulaski County pioneer, 51

Hammock, Anna, 62

Hancock County, Georgia, 57

Harden, James, 162

Harden, John, Twiggs County official, 39

Harrell, Ethelredge, 62

Harrell, John, death of, 201

Harris, William, Telfair County pioneer, 51, 63

Harrison, Benjamin, Pulaski County pioneer, 54, 60, 61, 62

Harrison, Elizabeth, 60, 61

Harrison, James, captain of Twiggs County militia, 135

Hart, Barnabas, Pulaski County pioneer, 50, 60

Hart, Edward, 62

Hart, Keziah, 60

Hart, Samuel, 60, 62

Hartford, county seat of Pulaski County, 37; creation of, 37; management of, 37; commissioners for, 37; mentioned, 6, 52, 53, 54, 75, 77, 82, 85, 94, 95, 96, 97, 102, 104, 105, 106, 108, 110, 111, 115, 116, 117, 119, 120, 126, 127, 128, 138, 140, 149, 151, 153, 156, 162, 163, 190, 191

Hartford Road, 53

Hartford's Counting House, 71

Hartford's Wharf at Darien, 71

Harvey, Thomas, Houston County official, 157

Hatten, Abb L., Telfair County official, 51

Hatten, William, Telfair County pioneer, 51

Hawkins, Benjamin, seeks treaty with Creek Indians, 23; U. S. commissioner for Treaty of Colerain, 25; appointed Indian Agent, 25; establishes Indian Agency on Flint River, 25; reports to Secretary of War, 26; places plan of civilization into effect, 26; U. S. commissioner for Treaty of Fort Wilkinson, 27; offsets influence of Bowles, 28; participates in plan to capture Bowles, 29; rejected in council at Oswichee, 29; attends General Council at Tuckabatchee, 29; writes Governor Milledge of Georgia, 29; makes treaty with Creeks at Agency, 29-30; reports treaty to Secretary of War, 30; leads Creek delegation to Washington for treaty, 31; mentioned, 26, 27, 30, 82, 83, 87, 89, 90, 91, 103, 104, 108, 112, 113, 114, 148, 157

Hawkinsville, Georgia, 2, 6, 17, 162, 163, 164, 171, 191, 199, 200

Hawthorne, William, 62

Haynesville, Georgia, 191

Heard, Franklin (Major), at Cedar Creek ambuscade, 127

Henly, Milly, 64

Henly, William, Telfair County pioneer, 51, 64, 93

Henry County, Georgia, creation of,

159; location of, 159; mentioned, 162
Hephzibah Association (Baptist), 57, 58, 60, 62
Higgs, Elisha, Pulaski County pioneer, 50
Highland Scots, immigration of, 57; mentioned, 155
Hightower Trail, 85
High Shoals of the Apalachee, 27, 30, 85
Hilliard, William, 50
Hitchiti Indians, 3, 16, 75, 92, 113
Hobbs, Berry, 63, 169
Hobbs, L., 166
Hobby, Jesse, 182
Hodges, Chloe, 62
Hogan, Edmund, Pulaski County official, 37
Holland, Lewis, Pulaski County pioneer, 37, 50, 54
Hollingsworth's Landing, 200
Holt, James, 158
Hooking, 70
Hopaunee, Indian chief, 138, 139, 144
Hopewell Baptist Church, formation of, 63; location of, 63; delegates from, 63; mentioned, 64
Horne, Joab, Pulaski County pioneer, 50
Horne, Michael, Pulaski County pioneer, 78
Horne's Trading Path, 78
Horne's Trading Post, 178
Horse Creek, 2, 36, 97
Horseshoe Bend, battle of, 100, 102, 122, 128, 181
Houston Association (Baptist), formation of, 165; mentioned, 166, 167, 168, 169, 170
Houston County, creation of, 156-57; boundaries of, 156-57; county seat of, 157; officials for, 157; courts of, 157-58; communication lines for, 158; education in, 158-59; mentioned, 162, 166, 191
Houston County Ocmulgee Academy, 158
Howard, Major, death of, 140
Howell, McKinna, 166
Howell, Thomas, Pulaski County pioneer, 50
Howell, Wright, 165
Hudson, Nathaniel, Telfair County official, 34
Hunter, Amos, 72
Hunter, David, Telfair County pioneer, 51; Irwin County official, 154
Hunter, Elijah, 72, 167
Hunter, Eliza, 167
Hunter, Hardy, 167
Hunter, Mary, 167
Hunter, Penelope, 167
Hunter, Redding, 72, 134, 155, 167
Hunter, Thomas, 161

Indian Agency, 107
Indian Agent, 79, 80, 83, 84, 85, 86, 87, 106, 113
Indian camps, 76, 131, 133, 134
Indian settlements on Ocmulgee River, 11
Indian Springs, landmark of, 11; Treaty of, (1821), 152, 156, 162; Reserve of, 159; Treaty of, (1825), 173, 174
Indian troubles, *passim*
Inferior Courts, description of, 155
Irwin County, creation of, 153; location of, 153; courts of, 153-55; officials of, 154; Justices of Inferior Court of, 154; county seat of, 154; militia districts of, 155-56; mentioned, 156, 161, 162, 175, 178
Irwinville, county seat of Irwin County, 154, 191, 200
Isabella, Georgia, 148
Isler, John, Pulaski County pioneer, 50
Isler, William, Pulaski County pioneer, 50

Jackson, Andrew (General), Jacksonville named for, 38; commands Tennessee forces, 99; victory at Horseshoe Bend, 100, 102; gains Treaty of Fort Jackson, 101; faces British on Gulf of Mexico, 105, 108, 113, 114; victory at New Orleans, 120; appointed commander of Georgia frontier troops, 125; marches to Hartford, 128; marches from Hartford to Fort Early, 128-29; marches from Fort

Early to Fort Scott, 129-30; victory over Seminoles, 140; feuds with Governor Raburn of Georgia, 137-45; President of the United States, 181; Indian policies of, 181; mentioned, 101, 102, 106, 119, 122, 123, 126, 131, 137, 138, 139, 140, 141, 142, 143, 144 145, 146, 148, 156, 186

Jackson, Frederick, Telfair County official, 34

Jacksonville, Georgia, county seat of Telfair County, 2, 36, 51, 63, 78, 85, 117, 119, 150, 153, 163, 164, 175, 179, 190, 191, 199, 200, 201

Jamming, a river expression, 70

Jasper County, Georgia, naming of, 40; immigrants to, 40; plantation system of, 40; path to, 83; jurisdiction of, 85; mentioned, 128

Jasper, Sergeant, hero of the Revolutionary War, 40

Jefferson County, Georgia, 7, 60

Jefferson, Thomas, President of the United States, 27

Jelks, Dixon, Pulaski County pioneer, 50

Jelks, William, Pulaski County pioneer, 50

Jenkins, John S., 182

Jernigan, Ezekiel, Irwin County official, 155

Jerreson, John, 81

Jesup, Georgia, 101, 148

Joiner, Meredith, Houston County official, 158

Jones County, creation of, 33; boundaries of, 40; seat of government, 40; growth of, 40; jurisdiction of, 85.

Jones, Isaac, Dooly County pioneer, 156

Jones, James, Pulaski County pioneer, 54

Jones, Samuel, Pulaski County pioneer, 50

Jordan, Isham, 135

Jordan, Willoughby, Houston County official, 162

Jordan's Bluff, 2, 5, 6, 133, 134, 176, 178, 200

Jordan's Creek, 6, 50, 53

Joyner's Spring, 39

Keener, John, Houston County official, 157

Kellam, Gideon, Pulaski County official, 38, 50

Kelly, John, 62

Kenhagee, Seminole chieftain, 125

Kent, Laban, Pulaski County pioneer, 50

Kersey, Rachel, 168

Kettle Creek, 30

Kialigee, destruction of, 91

Killen, John, 158

Killen, Samuel, 158

Kinchafoonee Creek, 16, 84, 130

King Henry VIII, 56

Kinnard, Jack, 84, 113

Kinnard's Trading Path, 84, 130

Kinnard's Trading Post

Knight, Levi J. (Captain), leads expedition against Indians, 188

Knight, William (Captain), leads charge against Indians, 188

Lake Blackshear, 75, 77, 92

Lake Jackson, 1

Lake Miccosukee, 17

Lampkin, Samuel, Telfair County pioneer, 51

Lampkin's Old Field, 200

Lancaster, William S., Pulaski County official, 37, 38, 50

Land, Frederick, Irwin County pioneer, 161, 176

Land, Henry, Irwin County pioneer, 161, 176

Land, Seaborn, 182

Land Lottery System, 41

Lanier, Benjamin, Pulaski County official, 38, 135

Lanier, Clement, raises volunteer force, 94

Lasseter, Archibald, Pulaski County official, 38, 50

Laurens County, creation of, 33, 36; division of, 36, 37, 53; mentioned, 61

Lawson, John, wounded in battle, 134

Lee, Jesse, 60, 61

Lee, Joshua, 60, 61

Lee, Lewis, Pulaski County official, 38
Lee, Sarah, 61
Lee, Susannah, 60
Leesburg, Georgia, 5, 16
Leigh, Thomas (Captain), ambush of, 127
Lester, John, 51
Limebaugh, Assistant Indian Agent, 104, 105
Limestone Creek, 2, 6, 50, 94
Little Brier Creek Baptist Church, 57
Little Ocmulgee River, 2, 52, 53, 119
Little, William, 54
Little's Trail, 78
Livingston, Peter L., 162
Loftis, Samuel, massacre of, 127
Log rollings, 44
Longino, Bartholomew, 50
Longstreet, 53
Lott, Arthur, murder of, 91
Lott, William, Telfair County official, 34
Lott, William, Jr., Telfair County official, 34
Louisiana, 79, 91, 99
Louisiana Territory, 79
Louisville, capital of Georgia, 7, 32
Loveless, Jemima, 60
Loveless, William, 60, 62
Lower Creeks, 15, 16, 17, 19, 75, 83, 87, 88, 89, 90, 91, 92, 100, 113, 173
Lower Trading Path, course of, 11; mentioned, 13, 25, 75
Lower Uchee Trail, 6, 7, 53
Lowndes County, 12
Luke, Daniel, Irwin County pioneer, 154, 161, 167, 176
Luke, Jasper, 168, 178
Luke, Joshua, 178
Luke, Nancy, 178, 179

McAnnally, John, Telfair County pioneer, 51, 132; family of, 176
McCall, Abraham Loftin, Irwin County pioneer, 161, 176, 178
McCall, Catherine, constituting member of Ozias Baptist Church.
McCall, David, Telfair County pioneer, 51, 198
McCall, David, son of Jehu McCall, 176, 177
McCall, David L., 168
McCall, Jehu, Telfair pioneer, 51, 132; lieutenant of Telfair militia, 34; Irwin County official, 155; mentioned, 161, 176, 177, 178, 191
McCall, Nathaniel, Houston County official, 157
McCall, Roger, 74
McCall, Sellaway, Irwin County official, 154, 155; mentioned, 161
McCall's Landing, 191, 200
McCormick, James, 162
McCormick, Matthias (Captain), 166, 197
McCormick, William, Twiggs County official, 39
McCranie, Daniel, Telfair County official, 34
McDaniel, Daniel, Telfair County pioneer, 51
McDonald, Alexander, 110, 111, 118, 154
McDonald, Eliza, 167
McDonald, John, 167
McDonald, Mary, 167
McDonald, Randall, 167
McDonough, county seat of Henry County, 159, 171
McDuffie, George M. B., 168
McDuffie, Mr., identifies stolen cattle, 139
McDuffie, Murdock, Telfair County official, 34, 51; Irwin County pioneer, 154, 161
McGillivray, Alexander, rises to power among Creeks, 21; opposes cession of land, 22; incites Creeks to depredations, 22; rejects Treaty of Galphinton, 23, 24; agrees to Treaty of New York, 24; in alliance with Spaniards, 24
McGriff, John, Pulaski County pioneer, 54
McGriff, Thomas, Pulaski County pioneer, 53
McInnis, Archibald, Telfair County pioneer, 51
McIntosh, John (General), 108, 110, 112, 113, 114, 116, 117

McIntosh, William, rises to prominent position among Lower Creeks, 31; renders aid to Georgia forces, 100; participates in Treaty of Indian Springs, 173; murder of, 173; mentioned, 100, 152

McIntyre, Archibald, Twiggs County official, 39

McKenzie, John, pioneer Baptist minister, 166

McKinnon, Charles, Telfair County official, 36, 51

McLenan, Daniel, Pulaski County pioneer, 54

McLeod, Murdock, 54

McLeod, Norman, Telfair County official, 34, 51

McQueen, Peter, leader of hostile Creeks, 122

Macon County, 75

Macon, Georgia, site of Ocmulgee Old Fields, 3; establishment of, 159; strategic location of, 160; rapid growth of, 160; churches of, 172; mentioned, 162, 171, 172, 190, 191, 192, 196, 197, 199, 200

Macon Telegraph, the, 196, 197

Maddox, A., 188

Magnan, Mr., assistant factor at Fort Hawkins, 81, 82

Mail, transportation of, 190, 191

Mann, David, Houston County official, 157

Manning, Lawrence, Telfair County pioneer, 51

Manning's Lower Fence Landing, 201

Marion, county seat of Twiggs County, 39, establishment of, 39; location of, 39; mentioned, 62, 190

Marion Academy, creation of, 39

Marsh, Reuben, Irwin County official, 154; ferry of, 191

Marshall, John, 167

Mashburn, David, 163

Mashburn, James, 168

Mashburn, Nicholas, 158

Mason, Mark, Pulaski County pioneer, 58, early church official, 59, 60, 61, 62

Massias, A. A., Captain

Mathis, John, Houston County official, 157

Matthews, Jeremiah, 168

May, Drury. 54

Mayo, Charles, Pulaski County pioneer, 53

Mayo, Gideon, Pulaski County pioneer, 53

Mayo, William, Pulaski County official, 38

Medical practices, 46

Meriwether, David, U. S. commissioner in General Council at Tuckabatchee, 29; commissioner at Indian Springs, 151

Methodist camp meetings, 65, 66, 170

Methodist Church, 64-66

Methodist Movement, 56-57, 64-66, 170, 171

Methodists, 57, 64-65, 170

Metts, Redding, family of, 180

Mewborn, Captain, 95

Middle Trail, 78

Military musters, 46

Military organization, 46

Military system, provision for, 33

Milledge, Governor, 29, 30

Milledgeville, chosen as state capital, 33; location of, 33; mentioned, 52, 53, 71, 103, 147, 182, 190, 191, 192, 196

Milledgeville Road, construction of, 53; route of, 53

Miller, Anderson W., 169

Mississippi River, 7, 28, 181, 186, 192

Mississippi Valley, 12

Mitchell, David Brydie, Governor of Georgia, 34, 94; appointed Indian Agent, 148; gains treaty with Creek Indians, 148, 150-51

Mitchell, Thomas, Telfair County pioneer, 52

Mitchell, Stephen, Sr., Pulaski County pioneer, 51, 78

Mitchell's Ferry, 78

Mitchell's Treaty, 148, 151, 153

Mixon, Edward B., 63

Mixon, James, 168

Mixon, Jesse, Telfair County pio-

neer, 51
Mixon, Mary, 108
Mixon, Matthew, 168
Mixon, Samuel, 182
Mizell, Griffin, Telfair County pioneer, 51
Mizell's Creek, 2
Mobile, 105
Mobile River, 10; pathway to, 31, 79
Mobley, Lemuel, Telfair County official, 34
Mobley, Ludd, Irwin County official, 153; mentioned, 161, 175
Mobley's Bluff, 2, 200
Mock, Harmon, 163
Monroe County, creation of, 159; boundaries of, 159; landmarks of, 159; county seat of, 159; education in, 159; mentioned, 156, 162
Montgomery County, 36, 50, 57, 59, 85
Monticello, county seat of Jasper County, 40, 128
Mooney, William, killed in battle, 134
Moore, James (Governor of South Carolina), leads assault against St. Augustine, 12
Moore, James (Colonel), leads invasion into Apalachee country, 13
Moravians, 64
Morgan County, creation of, 33
Morgan Stokely, 73
Morrison, William, killed in battle, 134
Mosquito Creek, 2, 6, 50, 51
Mossy Creek, 2, 158
Mounted spies, duties of, 98
Mount Horeb Baptist Church, formation of, 58; location of, 58; membership of, 58, 60; mentioned 59-62, 97
Mount Moriah Meetinghouse, 63
Mount Zion (Spectacle) Baptist Church, formation of, 167; location of, 168; membership of. 168
Muckalee Creek, site of Chehaw Indian town, 5, 16, 75
Mulkey, Owen, 168
Mulkey, Susan, 168
Muscogee Indians, gain control of Ocmulgee domain, 3; occupants of

Ocmulgee Old Fields, 4; enter into trade with English, 9; migrate from Chattahoochee to Ocmulgee, 9; mentioned, 9, 16
Musslewhite, Recy, 184
Musslewhite settlement, 183-184
Musslewhite, Thomas, 184

Nashville, Georgia, 164, 188, 191
Nashville, Tennessee, 128
Negro Fort, 123, 124
Newberry, Penelope, 167
Newberry, Robert, 167
New Hope Baptist Church, formation of, 166-67; membership of, 167
New Orleans, 113, 114, 120, 123, 128, 192
Newtown, 159
New York, Treaty of, 24; mentioned, 70, 192
Nicholls, Edward (Colonel), British agent, 122, 123, 124
Nix, Edward, 62
Nonconformists, 56
North Carolina, 57
North Carolina, The, voyage of, 196
Northern stage, 192
Norwood, William, 62
Nunn, Eli, Houston County official, 157

Ochese Creek, 9
Ocilla, Georgia, 101, 122, 147, 148
Ocmulgee Academy, creation of, 39; trustees of, 39
Ocmulgee Association (Baptist), 62
Ocmulgee Baptist Church, formation of, 63; location of, 63; representatives from, 63
Ocmulgee, churches of, 56-66
Ocmulgee Fork, description of, 26; coveted by Georgians, 26; partially gained by treaty, 27; sought at Oswichee, 29; gained by treaties, 27, 28, 29, 30, 31; divided into counties, 32; settlement of, 32; site of new capital, 33; gains in prestige, 33; survey of, 41; mentioned, 28, 29, 30
Ocmulgee frontier, 35, 36, 39, 40, 53,

54, 94, 100, 121, 128, 131, 163

Ocmulgee Old Fields, site of ancient mounds, 3; dwelling place of Hitchiti Indians, 3; seat of government for Muscogee Indians, 4; site of Coweta Town, 9; desolation at, 14; reserve at, 30; mentioned, 11, 13, 16, 32, 40

Ocmulgee pioneers, immigration of, 42; life of, 41-48; origin of, 56; religion of, 56-66; mentioned, 70

Ocmulgee River, origin of, 1; course of, 1-2; dwelling place of Creek Indians, 3; dwelling place of Hitchiti Indians, 3; crossed by DeSoto's expedition, 5; becomes western boundary of Georgia, 31; fishing rights in, 31; scene of Indian civilization, 32; becomes scene of white man's civilization, 32; artery of communication, 66-74; mentioned, 1, 2, 3, 4, 5, 6, 7, 8, 10, 11, 12, 13, 14, 15, 18, 20, 26, 32, 33, 35, 36, 38, 39, 40, 41, 44, 45, 46, 47, 48, 49, 50, 55, 56, 57, 58, 59, 60, 61, 63, 65, 75, 76, 77, 78, 79, 80, 81, 82, 85, 86, 87, 93, 102, 103, 104, 105, 108, 115, 117, 118, 119, 122, 128, 131, 132, 133, 135, 137, 138, 146, 148, 149, 150, 151, 152, 153, 156, 158, 159, 160, 161, 162, 163, 164, 165, 166, 167, 169, 173, 174, 175, 177, 178, 179, 181, 182, 183, 184, 185, 186, 190, 191, 192, 195, 196, 197, 198, 199, 200, 201

Ocmulgee Town, a Hitchiti Indian settlement, 16

Ocmulgee Tribe, 75, 92, 113

Oconee boundary dispute, 26

Oconee frontier, 24

Oconee Indians, 121

Oconee River, a tributary of the Altamaha, 2; dwelling place of the Hitchiti Indians, 3; dwelling place of the Oconee Indians, 121; mentioned, 6, 21, 22, 23, 24, 25, 26, 30, 32, 33, 40, 52, 53, 54, 58, 70, 96, 117, 119, 121, 149, 190, 196, 197

Oconee War, 22, 24, 25

Ocute, 6

Ogeechee River, 7, 11, 17, 20, 21, 23, 24

Oglethorpe, a Flint River town, 17, 164

Oglethorpe, James Edward (General), advocates founding of Georgia Colony, 18; establishes Savannah, 19; makes treaty with Indians, 19; camps on bank of Ocmulgee, 20; attends Indian council at Coweta Town, 20; returns to England, 20; mentioned, 21

Ohio River, 91

Okefenokee, 30

Old Daniels Church, 97

Old Hickory, 128, 130, 137, 140, 141, 142, 143, 181

Oliver, P., Houston County official, 157

Osceola, leader of Seminole revolt, 186

Oscewichee Springs, 131-32

Oswichee Bend, 16

Oswichee Indians, form Oswichee Trail, 5; establish settlements, 16; resist white man's civilization 29; mentioned, 16, 75, 83, 118

Oswichee Town, a Lower Creek Indian town favorable to Bowles party, 29

Oswichee Trail, formation of, 5; course of, 5; mentioned 6, 33, 78, 85, 93, 184

Ouweekachumpa, leader of Oconee Indians, 19

Overland communication, 45

Ozias Baptist Church, creation of, 167; membership of, 167; mentioned, 167, 168

Pace, William, Pulaski County official, 38

Packer, John B., 50

Palmetto Creek, 27

Panton-Leslie and Company, 24, 28

Parker, William, 188

Parkerson's Church, 54

Parramore, James, Telfair County pioneer, 51

Parramore, John, deeds land for Telfair County seat of government, 36; mentioned, 51, 72

Parramore, Noah, 51

Parramore's Landing, 72, 200

Parrott, Sally, 62

Pasmore's, 53

Passports, 80

Patillo, Charles, F., 158

Pearre, James, 73
Pea River, 192
Pee Dee River, 57
Pensacola, 8, 24, 83, 192
Perry, Commodore, naval hero in War of 1812, 157
Perry, County seat of Houston County, 157, 158, 171
Perryman's, concentration of hostiles at, 101, 104
Perry's Mills, 190
Peters, William (Captain), leads charge against Indians, 188; wounded, 189
Peterson, home of, 35; family of, 179-80
Phillemmee, Indian town near Flint River, 138, 139, 140, 144
Phillips, Zachariah, Sr., 85
Pickens, Andrew (General), seeks Indian treaty, 23; U. S. commissioner at Treaty of Fort Wilkinson, 27
Pindertown, 5, 185, 191
Pine Landing, 158
Pioneer pathways, formation of, 49-55, 161-64
Pioneer, The, voyage of, 197
Plantation houses, description of, 198-99
Plantation system, 197, 198, 199
Point Petre, 120
Pole Boat Era, 68-74
Pole boatmen, 68-74
Pole boats, 68-74
Polk's Trail, 78
Pollock, John, Houston County official, 158; mentioned, 162
Pollock, Jesse, Houston County pioneer, 162
Poor Robin Bluff, 6, 200
Pope, Collin, 83
Pope's Ferry, 83
Posey, Andrew, Telfair County pioneer, 93
Posey, John, 132
Posey, Lain, 132
Posey, Nehemiah, 51
Posey, William, 51
Powell, Abraham, Telfair County pioneer, 34, 51
Powell, Jesse, Pulaski County pioneer, 50, 53

Powell, Nancy, 62
Powelton Baptist Church, 57
Presbyterian influence, 57
Presbyterians, 56
Prophet Francis, 122
Prophet, the, 88
Pulaski County, Georgia, creation of, 37; public officials of, 37; seat of government for, 37; courts of, 37-38, 54; military officials for, 38; county academy for, 38; mentioned, 50, 52, 53, 58, 59, 60, 61, 73, 74, 85, 93, 96, 97, 103, 117, 118, 156, 158, 162, 164, 166, 169, 200
Pulaski frontier, 95, 104

Quilting parties, 44
Quincy, Florida, 191

Rabun, John, attack upon, 102
Rabun, William, Governor of Georgia, 135, 137; feud with General Andrew Jackson, 137-45; mentioned, 131, 135, 137, 138, 141, 142, 143, 144, 145, 149
Rafting, 67
Rainey, John, Pulaski County official, 37
Randolph County, creation of, 33; name changed to Jasper, 40
Randolph, John, 40
Reaves, Drury, Telfair County pioneer, 51, 63, 64
Reaves, John, 63
Red Bluff, 2
Red Clubs, 91, 99
Red Sticks, 91, 100, 101, 108, 122, 128, 156
Reeves, John, 169
Reid, George R., Irwin County pioneer, 161, 167, 176
Revolutionary War, 21, 22, 59, 64
Revolutionary War Period, 56
Richland Creek, 62
Richland Creek Baptist Church, formation of, 62; membership of, 62; mentioned, 62
Richmond, Virginia, 192
Ricks, Jacob, Twiggs County official, 39, 62

Ricks, Susannah, 62

Rivermen, expressions of, 69-70

River Road (East), creation of, 49-52, 98; course of 49-52; residents of, 49-52; mentioned, 50, 51, 52, 53, 54, 60, 63, 71, 93, 94, 117, 118, 132, 191

River Road (West), creation of, 161-63; mentioned, 154, 158, 166, 167, 168, 169, 190, 191

River Trail (East), 68, 98

River Trail (West), 133, 161

Roach, James, Pulaski County pioneer, 50, 60

Roanoke settlement, destruction of, 186

Robinson, Jacob, captain of Laurens militia, 135, 136, 138, 144

Rochelle, Georgia, 5

Rock Landing, 11, 25, 52, 121

Rogers, James, 72

Rountree, Moses, Telfair County pioneer, 51, 132; wounded in battle, 134

Rountree, William, Telfair County pioneer, 51, 132

Rouse, James, Telfair County pioneer, 51

Ryals, David, 63, 168, 169

Ryals, William, Revolutionary Soldier, 64

St. Andrew's Sound, 116

St. Augustine, English attack upon, 12; mentioned, 13, 84

St. Marks, 28, 140

St. Mary's, Georgia, pillaged, 120; mentioned, 191, 192

St. Mary's River, 20, 23, 25, 82, 84, 85, 120, 148, 163, 179

St. Simons Island, 64

Santa Fe Mission, destroyed by Carolinians, 12

Savage Creek, 2, 39

Savannah River, 3, 7, 15, 17, 18, 19, 20, 52, 92, 196

Savannah Road, construction of, 54; route of, 54

Savannah, settlement of, 19

Savannah Town, English trading reservoir, 11

Seagrove, James, appointed Agent for Indian Affairs, 25

Schley, Governor of Georgia, 187

Scotch-Irish, 155, 171

Scotland, 57

Scots, 57, 171

Secretary of War, 30, 31

Segrest, Laban, 159

Seminole country, 108, 112, 137

Seminoles, description of, 17, 121; influenced by Bowles, 28; joined by Red Stick refugees, 102; threaten Ocmulgee frontier, 105; mentioned, 75, 77, 83, 89, 92, 93, 100, 121, 122, 123, 124, 125, 128, 156, 173, 175, 181, 186

Seminole troubles, 38, 121-45, 156, 173

Senate of the United States, rejects Hawkins' treaty, 30

Senterfeit, Barbara, 60

Senterfeit, Henry, Pulaski County pioneer, 38, 50

Separatists, 56

Seven Islands, 30, 159

Seventeen Mile Creek, 180

Shalem Baptist Church, 165, 166

Shawnees, 91

Shellstone Creek, 2, 6, 50, 59, 60, 158

Shiloh Baptist Church, 166

Shine's Store, 190

Shoulderbone Creek, Treaty of, 23, 24

Sikes, Solomon, 63, 72

Simpson, Solomon, Houston County official, 157

Singleton, Biguas, Houston County pioneer, 162

Singleton, George W., Houston County educator, 158; mentioned, 162

Singleton, Richard A., Houston County pioneer, 162

Slone, William, 161

Slosheye Road, 163

Slosheye Trail, 163

Smith, David, 182

Smith Harrison, 74

Smith, Jobe E. W., 165

Smith, John, Telfair County official, 34

Smith, Jonathan, 182

Smith, Lovett B., Twiggs County official, 39

Smith, Richard, trading establishment of, 50, 78; mentioned, 162
Smith's Trail, 6
Snell, Jacob, Pulaski County pioneer, 37, 53
Snelling, Jacob, 53
Snelling, John, 50
South Carolina, 12, 13, 14, 17, 18, 121
Southern stage, 192
South Georgia, 186, 189
South Georgia frontier, 181
South River, 1
South Seas, 18
Southwest, 79
Southwest Georgia frontier, 186
Spaniards, establish St. Augustine, 8; win alliances of Apalachee Indians, 8; seek to gain dominion over Muscogees, 8; hold mouth of Apalachicola River, 10; lead incursions into Creek Country, 11; mentioned, 12, 17, 19, 121
Spanish, 12
Spanish authorities, 29
Spanish Florida, 28, 121, 140
Spanish Government, 124
Spanish missions, establishment of, 8; mentioned, 10
Spectacle Baptist Church, 168
Spivey, Solomon C., 167
Steagall, Benjamin, 162
Stagecoach, 190-195
Stagecoach lines, 190-192
Stagecoach travels, 192-93
Stagecoach wayside stops, 192-93
Stand, description of, 179
Standing Peachtree, settlement of, 15, 85
Stanley, Sands, 51
Statenville, Georgia, 12
Statham, Thompson, Nathaniel, Telfair soldier, 134, 155; Irwin County official, 155; mentioned, 178
Statham's Shoals, 2, 200
Steamboat Age, 196-201
Steamboat landings, 199-200
Stephens, James, 166
Stephens, Needham, Pulaski County pioneer, 50
Stephens, Thomas B., 166

Stewart County, Georgia, 186
Stone, Leah, 167, 168, 186
Stone, Leonard, Irwin County pioneer, 161, 176
Stone, Samuel, Irwin County pioneer, 161, 167, 168, 176
Stone, Samuel B., 167
Stone Creek, 58
Stone Creek Academy, 39-40
Stone Creek Baptist Church, formation of, 58; location of, 58
Storey, Samuel, Sr., 182, 183, 184
Storey, Samuel, Junior, 182
Studstill, William, Telfair County pioneer, 51, 132
Sugar Creek, 54
Sugar Creek Baptist Church, formation of, 62; location of, 62
Summerford, William, 159
Sussex County, Virginia, 54
Sutton, David, Telfair County pioneer, 51
Sutton, John, 153, 155
Suwanee River, 187
Suwanee Town, 15
Swain, Thomas S., Telfair County official, 36, 51; commissioner for Coffee Road, 164
Swain's Ferry, 164, 191
Sylvester, John, Pulaski County pioneer, 51

Tallahassee, Florida, 4, 17, 164, 191, 192
Tallapoosa River, 15, 17, 21, 75, 83, 88, 100, 101
Tallassee, attack upon, 100
Tallassee County, Indian territory, 23, 24, 101, 122, 147
Tallassee King, death of, 100
Tarver's, 39
Tattnall County, 190
Taylor, Captain, son of, killed in steamboat explosion, 201
Taylor, Dempsey, 178
Taylor, Elizabeth, 167
Taylor, Ezekiel, Pulaski County pioneer, 50, 53, 60; early church official, 60
Taylor, James M. (Major), 73, 97

Taylor Lemuel, 178
Taylor, Seaborn, 182
Taylor, William, Pulaski County pioneer, 51
Tecumseh, Shawnee Indian leader, 88, 89, 90, 122
Telfair County, Georgia, creation of, 33; location of, 33-34; county functions of, 34; officials chosen for, 34; military system established for, 34-35; courts of, 35; county seat of, 35-36; division of, 36; forts of, 97-98, 100; mentioned, 2, 36, 50, 51, 63, 72, 73, 74, 78, 85, 93, 117, 118, 119, 131, 122, 135, 137, 138, 149, 150, 152, 176, 177, 178, 182, 184, 187, 189, 198, 200, 201
Telfair frontier, 136
Temperance settlement, 51, 97, 119, 132, 135, 176, 191
Tennessee, 99, 128
Tharpe, Benjamin F., 158
Tharpe, Jeremiah, trustee for Stone Creek Academy, 40
Tharpe, Vincent Allen, pioneer Baptist minister, 40, 58
Tharpe, William, trustee for Stone Creek Academy, 39
Thomas, James T., Pulaski County pioneer, 50
Thomas, Richard H. (Captain), Pulaski County official, 37, 94, 95, 104, 109; mentioned, 105-06, 135
Thomaston, Georgia, 192
Thomasville, Georgia, 164, 191
Thompson, Robert, Pulaski County pioneer, 54, 162
Timucuan Indians, attack upon, 12
Tomberlin, John, Irwin County pioneer, 161, 176
Tomberlin, Wright, 178
Tombigbee River, 15
Tomochichi, 19
Tooke, Allen, Pulaski County official, 37; commander of Pulaski militia, 38; sends warning to Georgia governor, 95-96; erects frontier forts, 97; defends Pulaski frontier, 104, 105, 106
Towaliga Creek, 190

Trader's Hill, 55, 82, 85, 150, 163, 179
Trail Branch Baptist Church, 53, 61
Truluck, Elizabeth, 62
Truluck, Sutton, Pulaski County pioneer, 51
Tuckabatchee, Great Council at, 89, 90; destruction of, 91
Tucksawhatchee Creek, 2
Turkey Creek, 53
Turner, Melinda, 167
Twiggs, Colonel, commandant of Fort Scott, 125; attacks Fowltown, 125
Twiggs County, creation of, 37; seat of government chosen, 39; commissioners for, 39; public buildings erected, 39; growth of, 39; academies established, 39; courts of, 39; frontier forts of, 96-97, 118; mentioned, 2, 6, 50, 53, 58, 62, 63, 78, 85, 106, 110, 158, 190, 200
Twiggs, John (General), 23, 24

Uchee Creek, 17
Uchee Indians, element of Creek Confederacy, 16; settlements of, 17, 75, 92; mentioned, 6, 83, 84
Uchee Road, formation of, 53; route of, 53; mentioned, 53
Uchee Shoals, crossing place for Uchee Indians, 2; site of Indian town, 17, site of Hartford settlement, 37; hub for network of Indian trails, 37; mentioned, 53, 77, 110, 162, 163
Uchee Town, 20
Uchee Trail, 85, 110
Ulcofauhatchee River, 1, 30
United States, 21, 24, 28, 30, 77, 89, 92, 93, 105, 141, 148
United States Army, 116
United States Commissioners, convene council at Fort Wilkinson, 27; convene council at Oswichee Town, 29
United States Constitution, 23
United States Government, 87, 99, 123
Upper Creek country, French push into, 17
Upper Creeks, a division of the Creek Confederacy, 15; location of, 75, 83;

uprising of, 88-91; join Seminoles, 102; mentioned, 92, 95, 99, 102, 173
Upper Trading Path, 11
Upper Uchee Path, 53
Uriza, Captain, leads expedition against English outposts, 12

Vickers, Hardy, Pulaski County pioneer, 51, 62
Vickers, James M., 162
Vinton, Stephen, 72
Virginia, 21, 37, 39, 41, 72, 146, 155
Virginians, 41
Vivian-Dunham and Company, Darien merchants, 71

Walker, George, Pulaski County official, 37, 38, 53
Wallace, James, Telfair County pioneer, 52
War of 1812, 89, 121
Waresboro, Georgia, 191
Warren County, 39, 40, 57, 58
Warren, Hinchey, Pulaski County pioneer, 50
Washington, city of, 31, 144, 192
Washington County, creation of, 22; mentioned, 59, 60
Washington, George, 24, 25
Washington, Treaty of, 31, 32, 40, 52, 77, 79, 146, 177
Watson, Frederick, Houston County official, 162
Watson, Laban, Pulaski County pioneer, 51
Watson, Michael, Houston County official, 158; mentioned, 162
Watson, Orandates, Pulaski County pioneer, 50
Watts, Thomas, Telfair County official, 34
Wattsville, first county seat of Houston County, 157
Wayne-Camden line, 94
Wayne Country, 122, 147
Welsh, 56, 155
Welsh Neck Baptist Church, 57
Wesley, Charles, 64
Wesley, John, 64
Westlake, 6, 78

Whiddon, Lott, 182
Whitehurst, Simon, Telfair County pioneer, 52
Whitney, Josiah, murder of, 183-84
Wiggins, Jesse, Jr., 36
Wilcox County, Georgia, crossed by DeSoto expedition, 5; mentioned, 167, 168
Wilkes County, Georgia, 59
Wilkinson County, creation of, 32; boundaries of, 32; division of, 33, 39; mentioned, 36, 40, 57
Wilkinson, James, (General), U. S. Commissioner at Treaty of Fort Wilkinson, 27
Willcox, Elizabeth, 168
Willcox, James Lea, Telfair County soldier, 134; Irwin County official, 155; mentioned, 161, 167, 168, 176, 178
Willcox, John, Pulaski County pioneer, 5; commissioner to improve navigation on the Ocmulgee, 73; erects boatyard in Telfair County, 135; produces river craft, 74, 118; mentioned, 132, 134
Willcox, Mark, rescue of at Battle of Breakfast Branch, 134, 178; made general in Georgia Militia, 182; leads expedition against Indians, 182, 183
Willcox, Thomas, Telfair County official, 34
Williams, David, Irwin County pioneer, 153, 154, 155, 161
Williams, John A., Pulaski County official, 38
Williams, Joseph, death of in steamboat explosion, 201
Williams, Wiley, 162
Williamson, James, 63
Williamson, William W., trustee for Ocmulgee Academy, 39
Willis, Benjamin, 182, 184, 185
Willis family, massacre of, 184-85
Wimberly, Abner, commissioner for improvement of navigation on the Ocmulgee, 73
Wimberly, Ezekiel (Colonel), erects forts in Twiggs County, 96-97; mentioned, 106, 108, 109

Winderweedle, William, 168, 178

Winter Jack, Creek Indian marauder, 93

Withington, Baptist mission in Creek Nation, 169

Wolf pits, description of, 45-46

Woodard, Isaac, Houston County pioneer, 162

Woodard, Thomas, Houston County pioneer, 162

Wood landings, description of, 200

Woodward, Henry, opens trade with Muscogee Indians, 8

Woodward, Thomas (Major), 126

Wooten, Joel, Telfair County official, 34

Worth County, Georgia, 5

Yamacraw Bluff, 19

Yamacraws, 19

Yamassee Indians, turn upon Carolinians, 14

Yamassee War, 14, 15, 17, 121

Yellow River, 1

Young, Jacob, Irwin County official, 154

Young, Jane, 168

Young, Richard, 168, 178

Zuniga, Governor of Spanish Florida, sends expedition into Creek country, 12